# BUSH ON THE COUCH

# BUSH ON THE COUCH

## INSIDE THE MIND OF THE PRESIDENT

## JUSTIN A. FRANK, M.D.

**1⊙ ReganBooks**
Celebrating Ten Bestselling Years
*An Imprint of* HarperCollins*Publishers*

HarperCollins books may be purchased for educational, business, or sales promotional use. For information please write: Special Markets Department, HarperCollins Publishers Inc., 10 East 53rd Street, New York, NY 10022.

FIRST EDITION

Printed on acid-free paper.

Library of Congress Cataloging-in-Publication Data has been applied for.

ISBN 0-06-073670-4

04 05 06 07 08 PDC/RRD 10 9 8 7 6 5 4 3 2 1

This book is dedicated with love to the memory of my parents,
Dorothy and Justin Frank,
whose social conscience continues to be an inspiration;

To my sister, Ellen,
who courageously carries on their tradition;

And to our children Joey, Abe, Ginevra, and Nyssa,
who hold the future.

# CONTENTS

Introduction: Curious about George      xi

**1**   The First Family      1

**2**   Affability and Disability      19

**3**   Message in the Bottle      37

**4**   In God I Trust      53

**5**   Outlaw      77

**6**   The Smirk      101

**7**   Twisted Tongues      121

**8**   Oedipus Wrecks      141

**9**   He's Our Man      163

**10**   I Am the Chief      179

Epilogue      211

Source Notes      221

Acknowledgments      239

Index      243

# BUSH ON THE COUCH

# INTRODUCTION

## CURIOUS ABOUT GEORGE

IF ONE OF my patients frequently said one thing and did another, I would want to know why. If I found that he often used words that hid their true meaning and affected a persona that obscured the nature of his actions, I would grow more concerned. If he presented an inflexible worldview characterized by an oversimplified distinction between right and wrong, good and evil, allies and enemies, I would question his ability to grasp reality. And if his actions revealed an unacknowledged—even sadistic—indifference to human suffering, wrapped in pious claims of compassion, I would worry about the safety of the people whose lives he touched.

For the past three years, I have observed with increasing alarm the inconsistencies and denials of such an individual. But he is not one of my patients. He is our president.

George W. Bush is a case study in contradiction. All of us have witnessed the affable good humor with which he charms both supporters and detractors; even those of us who disagree with his policies may find him personally likeable. As time goes on, however, the gulf between his personality and those policies—and the style with which they are executed—grows ever wider, raising serious questions about his behavior:

- How can someone so friendly and playful be the same person who cuts funds from government programs aiding the poor and hungry?
- How is it that our deeply religious president feels free to bomb Iraq—and then celebrate the results with open expressions of joy?
- How can a president send American soldiers into combat under false pretenses and then proceed to joke about the deception, finding humor in the absence of weapons of mass destruction under his Oval Office desk?
- How can someone promise to protect the environment on the one hand and allow increased arsenic in the public water supply on the other? And why does he feel he can call his plan to lift logging restrictions in national forests the "Healthy" Forest Initiative?
- If the president's interpersonal skills are strong enough to earn him the reputation of being a "people person," why is he so unwilling and even unable to talk to world leaders, such as Jacques Chirac or Gerhard Schroeder, who disagree with him?
- How can the president sound so confused and yet act so decisively? And given the regularity with which he confuses fact with fantasy, how can he justify decisions based largely on his own personal suspicions with such unwavering certainty?

As a citizen, I worry about what these contradictions and inconsistencies say about the president's ability to govern; as a psychoanalyst, I'm troubled by their implications for the president's current and long-term mental health, particularly in light of certain information we know about his past. Naturally, the occasional misstatement or discrepancy between word and deed may be dismissed as politics as usual. But when the most powerful man on the planet consistently exhibits an array of multiple, serious, and untreated symptoms—any one of which I've seen patients need years to work through—it's certainly cause for further investigation, if not for outright alarm.

President Bush is not my patient, of course, but the discipline of applied psychoanalysis gives us a way to make as much sense of his psyche as he is likely ever to allow. At its simplest level, applied psychoanalysis means the application of psychoanalytic principles to anybody outside one's own consulting room. The tradition of psychoanalyzing public figures dates back almost as far as psychoanalysis itself; Freud based some of his most important theories on his observations of individuals he could never get onto his couch, Moses and Leonardo da Vinci most notable among them.

Indeed, if Freud were alive in the second half of the twentieth century, he might well have been recruited to offer his genius in the service of the U.S. intelligence effort. Somewhere in the bowels of the George H. W. Bush Center for Central Intelligence in Langley, Virginia, psychoanalysts are currently reviewing audio recordings, videotapes, and biographical information on dozens of contemporary world leaders, using the principles of applied psychoanalysis to develop detailed profiles for use by the CIA and the U.S. government and military. According to political psychiatrist Jerrold M. Post, M.D., who has chronicled the history of "at-a-distance leader personality assessment in support of policy," the marriage of psychoanalysis and U.S. intelligence dates back to the early 1940s, when the Office of Strategic Services commissioned two studies of Adolf Hitler. The effort was regarded as enough of a success that it was institutionalized in the 1960s, Post writes, first under the aegis of the Psychiatric Staff of the CIA's Office of Medical Services, which "led to the establishment of the Center for the Analysis of Personality and Political Behavior" (CAPPB), which Post founded within the Directorate of Intelligence.

As Post reveals, CIA psychological profiles of Anwar Sadat and Menachem Begin played an important role in Jimmy Carter's handling of the 1978 Camp David negotiations. And applied psychoanalysis continues to enjoy a privileged place in the intelligence universe. "At the time of his confirmation hearings, Secretary of the Defense

Donald Rumsfeld identified as his nightmare [the possibility of] not understanding the intentions of dangerous adversaries," Post writes. "Accentuated by some of the recent intelligence 'surprises,' the need to have a robust applied political psychology capability has been highlighted and increased resources are currently being applied to human intelligence and to the study of the personality and political behavior of foreign leaders, both national leaders and terrorists."

A vote of confidence from today's CIA, of course, might be described as a mixed blessing. Nevertheless, applied psychoanalysis remains a vital tool for understanding political leaders. And since one can scarcely imagine Bush Center resources being committed to a Bush son's psychological profile, this must be an independent inquiry, albeit one that is informed by the CAPPB goal as articulated by its founder, Jerrold M. Post: "to understand shaping events that influenced core attitudes, political personality, leadership and political behavior."

Still, the task of embarking upon a rigorous, independent psychoanalytical study of a sitting president as he faces reelection is without precedent—in importance as well as form. Its urgency cannot be overstated; as Post points out, "the leader who cannot adapt to external realities because he rigidly adheres to an internally programmed life script has . . . displaced his private needs upon the state and has rationalized it in the public good."

Because Bush and I have not sat in session, this investigation won't have the benefit of the powerful tools of transference and countertransference. But I will have some advantages I never have within my own practice. Like the rest of us, I get to see his behavior outside the consulting room—to hear his speeches and press conferences, watch how he relates to people and issues, and witness the discrepancies between what he says and what he does. I can study the messages that—despite his best efforts at controlling and suppressing them—run beneath the surface of the president's public appearances, embedded in his nonverbal presentation, his repetitive speech patterns, and his famously idiosyncratic use of the English language. And I can refer to the historical record for information about his past and his family.

The advantages of having access to such a detailed biographical record are many. Unlike in standard psychoanalysis, from the outset we already know a lot about George W. Bush and the sequence of events that shaped his personality. As a psychoanalyst, I am typically at the mercy of a patient's willingness to reveal biographical data, which is rarely presented in a standard chronological fashion. I may not learn something very important about a patient until years into treatment. For example, it was years before I learned that one patient had a dead brother; he never mentioned it, but simply assumed that I knew. Psychoanalysis is not linear; rather, it is a circular process of discovery, akin to unraveling knots by loosening them rather than by violent tugging. We look for slips of the tongue; we examine pieces of forgotten memories, and the links between them, before deciding whether and when they can be used to lead us toward a previously hidden or unrecognized truth.

Our exploration of Bush's psyche will thus follow what may at times seem like a circular pattern, deviating from a standard narrative chronology in favor of the more free-associative, fluid approach to time that is a critical part of the psychoanalytic discipline.

Other elements of the process by which I diagnose and treat patients in my clinical work can be used in applied psychoanalysis as well. As I listen to a patient, I pay attention simultaneously to what I see, think, and feel; Bush never needs to grace my couch for me to respond to him in ways that yield many useful insights. I can also draw on over thirty years of experience treating many people who have similar character styles. Finally, my theoretical approach informs all of my analytic thinking, providing psychological frames of reference that help me understand and make new connections between all that I observe.

The theoretical approach I have adopted and developed is particularly well suited to a study of President Bush. In its simplest terms, it takes as a starting point the assumption that the original anxieties that accompany and follow the trauma of birth not only shape our early emotional development, but can also remain influential for the rest of our lives. At the core of these first anxieties is the infant's early awareness that the idyllic world he knew before birth has been suddenly shattered, and that he somehow played a role in its destruction—perhaps from his kicking and efforts to get out of the womb. In other words, the child greets the world with a primitive awareness of his destructive capacities, an insight that comes into play in his first relationships with the outside world. As the child's grasp of these capabilities evolves over time and into adulthood, so do the anxieties that accompany it; the degree to which he successfully manages those anxieties, whether they be expressed as fear, guilt, denial, or delusions of omnipotence, is central to an individual's overall mental health.

These theories, derived from the groundbreaking work of child psychoanalyst Melanie Klein and others, have informed my practice for more than three decades, guiding my efforts to bring countless patients to deeper levels of self-awareness. Klein's work has lately come into dramatically wider acceptance in a variety of therapeutic circles, from psychoanalysts to pastoral counselors; her ideas provide ever greater influence in the twenty-first century. Beyond its resurgence in fashion, however, Klein's emphasis on destruction and its attendant anxieties provides a natural analytical tool with which to decode the psyche of George W. Bush.

For whom could a healthy resolution of his capacity for destruction be more important than the most powerful man on the planet? Who else has been more vocal in his view that the world has already been somewhat destroyed—by previous administrations, foreign evil-doers, and anyone whose morality differs from his own? And who has already shown his willingness and ability to exert his destructive power on the world as we know it, on everything from distant nations and international organizations to our own civil rights, economy, environment, even the electoral process itself?

Explicit examples of Bush's aggression are but a small part of a psychoanalytic investigation in the Kleinian model, which I have thus far presented only in simple, deliberately reductive terms. This study is far more ambitious and vital than a litany of the considerable ruin already left in the president's wake; the particulars of the damage done in the past are often less instructive than the clues he unwittingly offers us regarding how he does—or doesn't—manage the life-long anxieties that stem from the destructive impulse. These clues are the focus of *Bush on the Couch,* a psychoanalytic investigation in which we search for glimpses of these and other anxieties resonating throughout his life.

My search will take us into every aspect of the way the president relates to the world, public and private, present and past. Nothing will be regarded as off limits or inconsequential—from his adolescent clowning to his presidential smirk, from his earlier struggles with learning disabilities and alcoholism to his current dependence on fundamentalist religion and rigid routine. Some events will be revisited more than once; as anyone familiar with psychoanalysis well knows, a single event from an individual's past can yield a variety of trenchant insights when considered from different perspectives. Interpretation is the essence of the psychoanalytic task—there is no proof to offer, only evidence to consider and theoretical constructs to guide us. Nevertheless, when seen through the powerful lens of applied psychoanalysis, the familiar elements of Bush's history and character begin to form a new and troubling portrait of an individual whose psychological challenges are profound, pervasive, and deeply ingrained.

*Bush on the Couch* explores how the president's unending effort to cope with his anxieties threads its way through his familiar life story, including:

- The privileged, secretive family into which he was born, and its impact on his view of the world;
- The lasting influence early fantasies and feelings had on his perception;
- The role played by aggression, and the sometimes sadistic ways it is expressed in his behavior;
- His attempts to seek escape through substances, exercise, and religion;
- His relationships with authority figures, both individual and institutional;
- His impaired abilities to mourn, to admit responsibility, and to know himself, all of which are necessary for psychological growth;
- His unwillingness to be wrong or to consider divergent perspectives, indicators of the clarity and quality of his thought processes;
- The inconsistencies between his words and his actions—and between his words and the truth.

To accomplish this, we will draw and expand upon the vital work that has been done by recent chroniclers of the Bush life and presidency. While the first several years of his term were characterized by an almost willfully uncritical perspective on Bush's words and actions—perhaps due to a residual shock over the events of November 2000 and September 2001—the end of 2003 and start of 2004 brought a variety of insightful new voices to the national conversation. The widespread attention paid to such critical observers as former Bush advisors Paul O'Neill and Richard Clarke, as well as Bob Woodward, Kevin Phillips, David Corn, Molly Ivins and Lou Dubose, Al Franken, Michael Moore, and others, demonstrates that the nation was ready and eager to find out more about what Bush has been doing while the nation was perhaps distracted (or even misled). In addition to providing much-needed energy to a once-muted debate, their invaluable efforts have shed light on Bush's actions that heightens our ability to begin to assess his motives.

Of course, a good doctor is not unduly influenced by his preconceptions. I have certainly treated many patients with whom I have differed philosophically, and I have tried to preserve a distinction between my personal questions about President Bush's politics and my psychoanalytic evaluation of his character. Most of the behaviors to be examined here have far less to do with the substance of his governance than its style: The president's propensity for denial would seem unhealthy whatever the nature of the unspoken truth; the grandiosity of the stage-managed heroics of his landing a jet on an aircraft carrier would be apparent regardless of the legitimacy of the war celebrated by the gesture.

But as we explore the origins and elements of Bush's personality in the following chapters, it is impossible to ignore the political ramifications. His defensive measures not only reflect conflicts within his character, they can also cause serious problems that can have a severe impact on the quality of his leadership—and on the quality of our lives. When, after considering the evidence, theory, and precedents from my own years of practice, I offer a final assessment of Bush's mental condition, keep this in mind: The diagnosis may be his, but the prognosis pertains to all of us as long as he is our president.

# ONE

# THE FIRST FAMILY

*November 1953: Intake session with the wealthy, powerful B. family. Father, GHWB, is indifferent and absent—literally: arrived late, left early; mother, BPB, is cold and unresponsive. The couple is mourning daughter PRB, age 3, who died last month. Two sons survive. Infant JEB was not present for the session. First-born GWB, age 7, is affable, energetic, eager to please; indications of possible hyperactivity, learning disabilities. Parents seem unwilling to communicate openly with the boy, who learned of his sister's illness only after her death. He seems to have been left to fend for himself, and the appearance of social skills may mask developmental difficulties that will trouble him in later years. Indications for future therapy are pronounced, but parents display little comfort with therapeutic process or interest in pursuing.*

OF COURSE, THIS session never happened. The concept of Bush family therapy defies everything we know about the Bush clan and its famous aversion to introspection. As Jeb Bush recently said of his family, "It's not natural for us . . . to turn on this reflective mode and somehow spill our guts." His father has been vocal about his disdain for "the couch," which George W. Bush would grow up to inherit, deriding as "psychobabble" any attempt to assess the Bush character.

1

Had one been consulted, however, a family therapist would have seen that by the age of seven young George W. was already facing challenges to his psychological development that would resonate for the rest of his life. Though it is impossible to pinpoint every long-term effect that Bush's family has had on his development and on his current behavior as president, the influences of his early childhood yield many defining insights. The story of George W. Bush's early years, up through his first vivid memories, contain the roots of several fundamental elements of what we have come to know as his character. As we'll see, while the family's response to his young sister Robin's illness and death certainly revealed underlying tensions and made some matters worse, Bush's family history—emotional even more than factual—was deeply seated in his heart and mind, even before his little sister was born.

By now, the basic outline of George W.'s early years is familiar to us from several published biographies. The first child of a well-connected war hero and his young social-register bride, George W. was born in July 1946 while his father was still at Yale, where his demanding social, athletic, and academic schedules must have left little time for assisting his wife in the parenting duties. The day after he graduated in 1948, the elder Bush set out to pursue his fortunes in the West Texas oil boom, landing in Odessa, the working-class sister town to Midland. The family's two-room apartment was a long way from Barbara's privileged suburban New York upbringing—"as different from Rye, New York as any place imaginable," according to her memoir, in which she describes a family of prostitutes with whom their apartment shared a bathroom. Isolated from her family, Mrs. Bush was again left to fend for herself during the seven-day work weeks and frequent travels her husband's new business venture required. Within a year, they moved to the first of a series of four California residences where they lived during Mrs. Bush's pregnancy with their daughter, Robin, who was born in December 1949. The child was named after Mrs. Bush's mother, Pauline Robinson Pierce, who had been killed in an automobile accident that fall; though she had traveled east for a family wedding just a few weeks earlier, Mrs. Bush did not attend her mother's funeral.

The next year, the young family returned to Texas, this time to Midland, where they were living when their second son, Jeb, was born in early 1953. Mrs. Bush handled much of the parenting on her own as her husband traveled. "I had moments where I was jealous of attractive young women out in a man's world," she explained in Pamela Kilian's biography, *Matriarch of a Dynasty*. "I would think, well, George is off on a trip doing all these exciting things and I'm sitting home with these absolutely brilliant children who say one thing a week of interest."

George W. was six years old at the beginning of the tragic episode that he has said yielded his first vivid childhood memories—the illness and death of his sister. In the spring of 1953, young Robin was diagnosed with leukemia, which set into motion a series of extended East Coast trips by parents and child in the ultimately fruitless pursuit of treatment. Critically, however, young George W. was never informed of the reason for the sudden absences; unaware that his sister was ill, he was simply told not to play with the girl, to whom he had grown quite close, on her occasional visits home. Robin died in New York in October 1953; her parents spent the next day golfing in Rye, attending a small memorial service the following day before flying back to Texas. George learned of his sister's illness only after her death, when his parents returned to Texas, where the family remained while the child's body was buried in a Connecticut family plot. There was no funeral.

No parent is ever prepared for the devastation of losing a child, and Mrs. Bush would later express doubts over how she handled the matter with her son, who was certainly old enough to be affected by the loss of the sister. When families have come to me seeking therapy in the wake of such an overwhelming event, I listen to both parents and children for insight into the family's response to the loss. I also look for any evidence of preexisting developmental trends that had already begun to take shape in the child's infancy. The surviving child's psychological development is well underway before tragedy strikes, and the trauma often only compounds whatever problems were already there.

As a therapist working in the tradition of Melanie Klein, who traced the formation of personality from birth, I am particularly interested in the relationship between mother and infant, which has an enormous and lasting influence on how the child grows up to see the world. Given a mother's selective memory and a child's cognitive limitations, we can never know exactly what transpired between a mother and her baby. Nevertheless, we can explore the mother's history and behavior for clues to the exact nature of the initial mother/child dynamic to deduce the formative impact it had on the child's development. In the case of Barbara Bush, who has written revealingly about her experiences as both a mother and a child, one needn't look far.

Referred to by her children as "The Enforcer," Barbara Bush has by her own admission always been the family disciplinarian. She was, from most accounts, a cold disciplinarian, and she spanked the children readily. Called "the one who instills fear" by a close family friend, she would boldly break up fights between her sons, "bust them up and slap them around," according to a brother-in-law. Decades later, she still embraces her role as an arbiter of punishment, as when she describes her son's famous near-fatal pretzel-choking incident as a "heaven-sent message that he should stop knocking his mother's cooking." Like her own mother, Mrs. Bush did not leave much of a cooking legacy for her children to knock. "My mother never cooked," Ron Suskind reports President Bush telling Nancy O'Neill in *The Price of Loyalty,* "The woman had frostbite on her fingers. Everything right out of the freezer." And she remains quite vocally willing to step into certain frays, telling Larry King's viewers that "you can criticize me, but don't criticize my children and don't criticize my daughters-in-law and don't criticize my husband, or you're dead."

Beyond her reputation for strength, if not hostility, Mrs. Bush has shed little direct light on her approach to mothering her first baby. Her memoir is noticeably silent on the topic, focusing instead on the many times she had to move during W.'s early years, and the frequency of his father's absences. Her most candid discussions of motherhood involve her own mother, in which she provides telling glimpses of her relationship with the woman from whom she was most likely to learn about being a mother. What she reveals are two deep strains running through her mother's family into her own: a continuous undervaluing of the self and a need for detached discipline. And throughout, she is the mother who leaves feelings behind, whose attitude ends discussion or curtails emotional engagement. On the morning after her husband lost his reelection effort to Bill Clinton, according to her son George's memoir, Barbara Bush uttered a single telling sentence: "Well, now, that's behind us. It's time to move on." Here is a woman bent on protecting herself and her family from feelings of pain or anger.

Barbara became a stern enforcer naturally. As a child, she "would determine who [among her circle of friends] was speaking to whom when we got on the bus together," explained June Beidler, a member of the young Barbara's circle, to Bush biographer Pamela Kilian. "She was sort of the leader bully. We were all pretty afraid of her because she could be sarcastic and mean. She was clever, never at a loss for what to say—or what not to say." At home, Barbara's mother, Pauline Robinson Pierce, "did most of the scolding" and frequently spanked Barbara and her siblings with a hairbrush or wooden clothes hanger. Her mother's authoritarian ways evidently made a lasting impression on young Barbara: The first two memories Bush shares of her mother in her memoir involve a "humiliating incident" in which the mother confronted a ten-year-old Barbara for overeating in public, and an "outrageous" request, made when the Bushes visited a decade later, that Barbara's new husband not use the toilet at night (which Mrs. Pierce claimed disturbed her sleep). She clearly remembers that her mother's spankings were harder than the ones she administered to her own children, but struggles to justify her behavior nonetheless, claiming with certainty that she was naughtier than her own children, and that her spankings were deserved—while acknowledging that she can't remember anything she did to deserve them. (Such convenient forgetfulness seems to have been passed on to her son, who has shown similar problems recalling mistakes he may have made in his past.)

Equally vivid in Mrs. Bush's memoir is the impression that her "striking beauty" of a mother paid little attention to aspects of maternal life associated with traditional nurturing. Mrs. Bush may recall Mrs. Pierce publicly chastising her at the table for overeating, but she doesn't "remember that mother cooked." Mrs. Bush's regret that her mother never taught her "things like how to cook, clean and wash clothes" is evident, as is the sense of remorse that her mother assumed her daughter "should be able to pick [them] up reading." Pauline Pierce's inability to provide maternal nurturing led young Barbara to gravitate to a neighborhood family, a common childhood attraction Freud described as the "family romance." Freud observed that some unhappy children imagine they belong to a different family; for Barbara it was the Southern, openly warm and affectionate Schoolfield family, whose matriarch was "like a second mother" to Barbara.

What is noticeable in the jibes about overeating, and the assumed reason for punishment, is that Barbara Bush quite clearly learned from her mother how to put herself down. Self-esteem problems were rampant for the little girl, who describes herself as "the biggest pain in the world." This is perhaps most touchingly clear in her descriptions of Miss Covington's Dancing School, where the self-conscious young Barbara "always raised [her] hand to play the part of a boy" when the boys and girls paired up in dancing partners to avoid "being the last girl chosen, or rejected altogether," while her mother was "by far the prettiest" mother watching the lesson from the balcony. Even so, Barbara was again "humiliated" by the fact that hers was the only mother in the balcony not wearing a hat.

Mrs. Bush gives some indication of the source of this maternal distance when she discusses the most important lesson her mother did impart to her, which "was an inadvertent one: You can like what you do, or you can dislike it. I have chosen to like it." Her mother clearly chose otherwise, wistfully referring to her future happiness with phrases like "when my ship comes in." Decades later, Mrs. Bush was able to observe that her mother's "ship had come in—she just didn't know it. That is so sad." But young Barbara was left to make excuses for a mother who was chronically depressed, too preoccupied by her own pain to engage her daughter with maternal nurturing or teach the child its basic elements.

When a young girl is not adequately nurtured physically or emotionally by her mother, she often grows up to pass this deficiency on to her children. The impact this deficiency would have on a child has been illuminated by the work of Melanie Klein. According to Klein's theories, our psychological life begins at birth, characterized by a primitive ability to differentiate between the nurturing environment of the womb and the chaotic, terrifying terrain into which we are born. Our internal world is shaped by our struggle to manage the overwhelming anxieties of infancy; these anxieties, along with our initial coping strategies, can be reactivated throughout adulthood, thus influencing our emotional health and development for the rest of our lives.

Klein traces these anxieties to our attempts to understand the sudden wreckage of our idyllic prenatal world. With no one to blame but ourselves, we conclude that we must possess the powers to wreak such devastation; our sense of loss is tainted by responsibility and guilt, our anxieties fueled by the rudimentary awareness of the destructive powers we assume are our own. The awareness of our destructive capacities likewise remains in play over the course of our emotional development, as we attempt to manage anxiety that arises from our knowing we possess the power to destroy again.

As we progress through infancy, a myriad of challenging experiences—hunger, colic, discomfort—fuels our fear of destruction. This is complicated by a natural desire to return to the plentiful, mindless paradise we experienced in the womb—Freud's so-called "death instinct," which counters our equally natural instinct to survive. The first method to cope with the death instinct is to protect the self by converting that instinct into aggression. By this point, however, we are also enjoying positive experiences that we must distinguish from the negative. From this need we develop the first mental attitude for dealing with the fear of destruction: We split our world into the good and the bad, separating experiences into the safe and the dangerous. Further, to defend ourselves against fear and insulate ourselves from the destructive forces within, we split our sense of self along the same lines; projecting the negative outward onto the environment, we ally ourselves with the good self while we try to deny and get rid of the aspects of the self we experience as threatening and undesirable. This unconscious mental process, called "projection," leaves us without any feelings of actually being destructive.

This is where the mother/child dynamic begins to make itself felt—and where the kind of maternal reserve shown by a Barbara Bush can have a devastating impact. The first focus of the infant's consciousness is his mother, whom he experiences as a loving extension of himself when he is contentedly being fed by her. The baby's positive experiences at the breast of an attentive, nourishing mother—for whom we use the breast as a metaphor, whether the baby is actually fed by breast or bottle—forms the core of self-esteem, of identification with a beneficial source of nourishment and love.

If the baby is deprived or uncomfortable, he might spit up or act frustrated during the feeding, subjectively visualizing the breast as the source of its discomfort. The infant, however, is not yet mature enough to perceive its frustration and satisfaction as coming from the same breast. Thus, there are two early relationships the baby has—one with the good breast/good mother, the other with the bad breast/bad mother. The mother's state of mind during nursing—whether she is paying attention to the baby or letting her mind wander elsewhere— can cause dramatic differences in the baby's experience, as every mother can attest. Mothers know that their babies can tell when they are and are not emotionally in touch with their baby. When the mother is preoccupied with something else, the baby has difficulty taking in nourishment and experiencing the positive relationship that can help him manage his frustrations. The baby experiences his mother at these moments as the source of his discomfort: She becomes the mother of frustration. This is of vital importance, because the mother/baby relationship eventually becomes the inner model of the world that affects all of the child's future relationships.

At this stage of development, the baby needs to identify with the ideal mother, to see himself as sharing her essential goodness, as he projects onto the bad mother the negative attributes that his split ego is still too fragile to internalize. But as he grows and develops new capacities, he must move beyond this oversimplified way of ordering the universe—of splitting and projecting—or else run the risk of distorting his perceptions of it. This next stage of development depends on the relationship with the mother, who helps the baby transform his despair and anxiety into something more manageable. Through an ineffable process of unconscious interaction with her baby, the mother senses what the baby is experiencing and reacts accordingly—using facial and verbal responses as well as active care-giving. If the baby cries, for example, the mother takes in and processes the baby's experience and then makes enough sense of it to take appropriate action, such as feeding, changing, or soothing. Sensing the truth of the baby's feelings of discomfort, the mother returns them to the child in a tolerable form. This helps the baby develop his own sense of his emotions to feel connected to (and contained by) his mother; over time, he internalizes the maternal function and can transform the bad feelings independently.

At some point, the infant recognizes that his good and bad mothers are one person, able both to comfort and protect him and to anger and disappoint him. The baby comes to understand that he can love and hate the same person; it is from this coexistence of love and hate that the vital notion of ambivalence is introduced. He is also able to internalize the destructiveness he had previously projected, resulting in despair over the knowledge that his rage could hurt the very person he loves.

Because the mother has helped the baby develop the ability to regulate his emotions, his feelings are rendered less threatening. The baby is able to cope with his contradictory feelings and to recognize his own destructiveness. He creates an internal mental representation of himself and others that helps him understand and respond to the mental states of the people in his life. The better nurtured a child is, the more closely his perceptions will reflect material reality. His overall psychic reality strengthened, he is able to avoid being overwhelmed by anxiety when something goes wrong and to feel challenging emotions such as guilt and concern when appropriate.

When the mother is unable to feel her child's discomfort or recognize his needs—due to her own depression, distraction, or emotional distance, or simply because the baby himself is too fussy or hyperactive for the mother to make sense of his needs—this vital exchange between mother and infant does not take place. The effect on the child's psychological development is profound. His fear persists, and the split between good and bad remains unhealed. Dependent on his original crude tools to manage his anxiety, the emotionally uncontained baby continues to project his negative feelings on his surroundings, desperate to rid himself of his bad feelings without learning to manage them as his own. Relying on such unevolved mechanisms to protect his idealized image of himself and his inner world, he is unable to integrate his conflicting emotions. His world remains simplified, peopled with unreal figures, uncomplicated by ambiguity.

⟶

The cries unheard by an ineffective mother can reverberate through the lifetime of the child. As Melanie Klein has said, throughout life we return to varying degrees to variations upon our infantile mental positions, traces of which remain in all of our interactions. The child who fails to progress significantly beyond his split world view into the process of integration will, in adulthood, fall back on primitive mental mechanisms, with devastating results. The infant's unintegrated split between good and bad will reappear in similarly divided adult perspectives, such as a reliance on black-and-white thinking, a tendency to view other people as either allies or enemies, or the cultivation of a fantasy world dominated by the struggle between good and evil. All children go through this process; for George W. it was probably expressed in games of cowboys and Indians.

The oversimplified fantasy world of such an individual can be filled only with equally oversimplified and fragmented figures that mirror his own state of mind. The people he seeks to attack and destroy are experienced as evil and one-dimensional, rather than integrated in his mind as whole people. Because he experiences them this way, he feels free to harm them without pity or loss. He may not even recognize his role in the attack; rather, he feels constantly under attack himself, a feeling that further helps him evade responsibility. And with nothing to threaten his idealized self-image, he has no cause to feel vulnerable or to acknowledge the possibility that he can be wrong. These are clues to arrested psychological development that I look for in patients I treat both as children and adults. I see them all too clearly in the actions and attitudes of George W. Bush.

It's not hard to see how Mrs. Bush, through no fault of her own, would be unprepared as an undernurtured young mother to provide vital early nurturing to her own newborn child. Her memoir offers a subtle but unmistakable portrait of a self-blaming daughter who consistently doubted herself and her lovability, and who evolved into a stern and distant mother. She split her worldview into good and bad—all the good lived outside of her, while the bad remained locked within. As a memoirist, Mrs. Bush makes light of her reliance on the word "wonderful" to describe the people she met in adulthood, but the joke points out her reflexive need to see every person she writes about as uniquely wonderful. At first glance, it may seem that she is just putting on a public face for her readership, yet this habit suggests not just false humility but genuine insecurity and recrimination. The more she lionizes others, the worse she feels about herself.

Being turned so profoundly inward herself, Mrs. Bush would have had trouble soothing her infant son; in turn that would have hampered her son's ability to heal his original psychic split and manage his anxieties. These anxieties would be magnified rather than modified, forcing him to resort to his own means to modify them. An anxious baby has limited resources to dissipate his discomfort: He can kick and scream—physical means to discharge anxiety or tension, but he may soon learn that such behavior doesn't always invite further nurturing. Fixed in the internal world of his infancy, he must continue to project his unintegrated destructive impulses, resulting in the primitive worldview that divides people and experiences into good and bad, ideal and persecutory.

George W. Bush's public, adult behavior bears distinct hallmarks of this lack of integration, coupled with an inability to perceive the complex nuances of reality. One result is the black-and-white posturing that is so prevalent in his rhetoric—the worldview of a man who declares, "There are no shades of gray in this fight for civilization. . . . Either you're with the United States of America, or you're against the United States of America." Bush's decisions and actions are clearly informed by a need to order his world into good and bad. He shows a rigid inability to consider the idea that anything in his own behavior might qualify as destructive; instead he projects such impulses onto his many perceived persecutors, to maintain his sense of self. He denies his fallibility, vulnerability, and responsibility because on a fundamental unconscious level he feels he must do so to survive.

But this primitive mechanism, as in infancy, is doomed to fail. Ultimately, the only way for an individual burdened by such a perspective to be safe—to protect against the delusion of external persecution—is to annihilate the persecutors. But this process, set in motion to quash anxiety and guilt, also compromises his perceptive abilities and nullifies his intellectual understanding of the problem at hand.

There is every reason, then, to consider George W. Bush's drive to rid the world of dangerous people as not simply the policy judgment of a president—but as the drive of an undernurtured and emotionally hobbled infant, terrified of confronting the dangers within his own psyche.

hroughout this book, I'll discuss how this basic dynamic resonates through so many of the choices Bush has made in adulthood and continues to make as president. While he was still a child, however, Bush experienced a watershed event that further shaped his worldview. The death of a young sibling is inevitably a defining moment in the life of a child. In the case of young George W., the tragic blow to the family was perhaps matched in its impact on the boy's development by the family's response to it, which was fuel to the psychological fire that raged unnoticed in the child's underdeveloped psyche.

It has been said that the nursery rhyme "Humpty Dumpty" was written with the first-born child in mind. It seems to capture perfectly the irrevocable trauma felt when the second child is born: Nothing can put the first-born back together again. But first-born offspring find different ways to manage this insult. Some can be overly nice to mask their fury; others can be suspicious of being taken advantage of; still others are overcome with the fear of losing what they have. But if that next sibling dies, then an entirely new and complex dynamic is set in motion. The first-born often has to disown his destructive fantasies, splitting them off from his consciousness. He then projects them outward with even greater vigor, exacerbating his simplified internal world.

A child who is already relying too heavily on a split worldview developed in infancy is thus especially vulnerable to the lasting impact of a sibling's death. As the Bushes' first-born child, young George would inevitably have harbored resentment toward Robin for taking his mother away from him; when the child's illness led to absences that took his mother further away, the resentment would have grown stronger—and stronger still in the face of his mother's grief after Robin's death. If George's feelings were never addressed, his natural animosity toward his sister would have remained unresolved; he would have been left with a host of forbidden feelings that were too threatening to acknowledge, only furthering the process of splitting and projecting unwanted aspects of the self.

Such experiences, of course, can be an opportunity for healing; sorrow has been called the vitamin for growth, and there is certainly ample reason to feel sorrow when a child suffers a terminal illness. In Bush's household, however, sorrow was evidently suppressed. The elder Bushes' silence on the topic around young George deprived him of the ability to prepare for the child's death, to say goodbye, to deal with the unavoidable sadness of such a loss. The sorrow that could have challenged George's split worldview, by forcing him to integrate the negative feelings and to view his world in less simplistic terms, was denied.

And the historical record confirms that within the restrained environment of the Bush family young George was wrestling with powerful and troubling feelings. Biographer Bill Minutaglio recounts the story of George W.'s first sleepover after the family's loss, "not long after Robin's death," when the "usually insouciant" boy went to the home of a friend to spend the night. "Throughout the night," Minutaglio writes, George "was engulfed in constant nightmares," until his mother arrived to comfort him. George's young host, Randall Roden, "was watching, unsure what was happening to his friend. Finally, Barbara pulled him aside and quietly explained about Robin's death. 'It was a profound and formative experience,' Roden believes."

Without an instructive example of how to experience grief, George W. was deprived of the opportunity to learn to mourn, which a child typically learns by watching his parents go through the process. An exercise in holding and integrating the contradictory emotions of love and sadness, mourning is necessary for psychological growth. The capacity to feel sorrow is a prerequisite for the ability to be compassionate, to feel concern for others; managing loss is essential to both personal growth and the development of empathy for others. A child burdened with a primitive worldview, in which others are easily dehumanized either as threats or intruders, or as idealized exemplars of perfect goodness, could obviously benefit from such an opportunity; a child who is instead given the message that one shouldn't feel sorrow is instead implicitly encouraged to hold onto his way of seeing the world. Compassion not only goes untaught, it is discredited, rendered irrelevant. When the population of his world is further dehumanized in this way, the child has a difficult time humanizing others when he reaches adulthood.

The best way to address such a loss is to talk, to interact, to see the parents mourn, to share the loss, to help the child talk about his conflicting feelings—his anger as well as his relief. The apparent silence on the topic within the Bush family half a century ago set a dangerous precedent for the impressionable young George. Viewed through the dehumanizing perspective of childhood, the example of his parents laid the foundation for the development of a powerful, lifelong coping mechanism, grounded in a self-protective indifference to the pain of others.

How ironic, then, that this child should grow up to occupy the presidency at his nation's greatest moment of grief—the period of deep shock that followed September 11, 2001. In his post-9/11 edition of *The Bush Dyslexicon,* Mark Crispin Miller writes perceptively of Bush's "apparent incapacity for any show of sorrow, at least in public. Without a script, he seemed unable to assimilate the tragic aspect of the crisis, or even face it, but would just look right on past it to the happy, happy day of our eventual revenge." Even when Bush did pay lip service to America's grief, it was almost always supplanted immediately by expressions of anger. "If this were a psychobiography," Miller writes, "we might look deeply into Bush's tendency to jump away from grief and straight to rage."

And, as Miller points out, within months Bush was joking about the events of 9/11, and declaring that "all in all, it's been a fabulous year for Laura and me." Whatever grief there may have been appeared to have been washed from his system.

~~~

And what about dad? That question, which hangs over so much of George W. Bush's later development, will reappear throughout the following chapters, but is worth a brief note here. When an infant's needs are unmet by his mother, he turns with great yearning to his father. In George W. Bush's case, the results could not have been very satisfying. As Mrs. Bush's memoir chronicles, George H. W. Bush's approach to early fatherhood was characterized by an endless series of absences. And when he wasn't traveling for business, his famously reserved public persona offers ample reason to believe that he was still detached and unavailable at home. As George would say years later to Yale roommate Clay Johnson, whose parents served as "surrogate parents" to George: "My father doesn't have a normal life. I don't have a normal father." Johnson "could see that Bush felt that he didn't have 'normal access' to his father—but that he wished he had," Minutaglio adds. Elsewhere, Minutaglio notes that George H. W. Bush was such a distant father that he developed the habit of writing letters "to express the intimacy that he could never articulate in spoken words to his children."

In situations where the mother is a child's primary caregiver, the father has less opportunity to have a dramatic impact on the infant's early psychological development. Nevertheless, George H. W. Bush's early absence would have profound implications for his son. The elder Bush's frequent and lengthy disappearances would in some primitive way have been registered by the infant George, as would his expressions of paternal affection when he was around. The repetitive pattern of periods of neglect punctuated by verbal declarations of devotion would thus come to define fatherhood to baby Bush.

The father-son relationship would exert a stronger influence over the child's development as his cognitive abilities developed. At this early stage, George W. Bush likely would have understood his father only as an inconstant presence, whose absences undermined the promises of love and affection the boy quite naturally craved. As we will see, this primitive dynamic registered in infancy would continue to resonate, in an expanding way, throughout his adult life.

# TWO

# AFFABILITY AND DISABILITY

*The more unstable life is the less one likes the small details to alter.*
—Graham Greene, *The Comedians*

THERE'S A LOT to like about George W. Bush. Even his detractors during the 2000 campaign praised his humor, humility, and general affability. His playful friendliness and informality have often disarmed his critics and charmed the media; he winks and kids around, jokes with reporters on the campaign trail, and peppers his unprepared remarks (at least at fund-raisers) with great humor, winning laughs by poking fun at himself or good-naturedly teasing others. Friends and observers of his campaigns describe a demeanor that is at times boyish in an almost schoolyard way, quick with a backslap and a nickname, driven by a restless, often mischievous energy.

Bush's easy affability is all the more striking for its inconsistency. On camera, when addressing the public or the press, Bush often displays a vacant, deer-in-the-headlights stare. At times he seems unable to think in a focused way, or to address complex issues in anything but the simplest possible language—as in October 2003, when he was asked what the U.S. government knew about the bombers of the

Baghdad Red Cross, and he declared that "the best way to describe the people who are conducting these attacks are [sic] cold-blooded killers, terrorists. That's all they are. They're terrorists."

At other times he takes great pains to avoid getting mired in the verbal miscues that have famously undermined his effectiveness as a communicator (except among those who consider them part of his charm). Often this will take the form of relying on pet phrases, which he repeats like so many mantras: "There is no doubt in my mind that Saddam Hussein was a threat to world peace. And there's no doubt in my mind that the United States, along with allies and friends, did the right thing in removing him from power. And there's no doubt in my mind, when it's all said and done, the facts will show the world the truth," he said after the invasion of Iraq. "I am confident we have not executed an innocent person, and I'm confident that the system has worked . . . ," he declared as governor of Texas in 1998.

The enormous discrepancy between Bush's comfort level on and off stage is paralleled by two comparable gaps—between his privileged background and his man-of-the-people image, and between what he says and what his administration does. The accessible, unassuming persona he projects obscures the enormous differences in wealth, class, power, and education that separate him from the average Americans he successfully encourages to see him as one of them, just as his apparent concern for the comfort and well-being of others belies his policies' disregard for those less fortunate than him, at home and abroad.

Such contradictions raise serious questions about the true nature of the president's mercurial good-naturedness, the circumstances of its development, and the psychological functions it serves. As we'll see, these paradoxes started early. Our efforts to identify their roots will take us back to the formative stages of young George's personality, when he lacked the tools to discharge his pain and anxiety in healthier ways. In the conditions of his early childhood, we'll witness the inception of an elaborate disguise, which established the lifelong pattern of displaying a personality that masked the chaos and contradictory motives behind its affability.

The earliest descriptions of George's antic behavior date back to the aftermath of his sister's death, when the private grief of his already distant mother at first left her even less emotionally available to the boy than she had been before. One of Bush's cousins, who also developed an extroverted personality after losing a sibling at an early age, attributed their shared tendencies to their common loss: "We're both clowns. I think kids who lose a sibling often try and find ways to, you know, make things easier on the family." With no guidance in the process of mourning, George took it upon himself to cheer up his grieving mother. Though doomed to fail, he devoted himself to the task as one would care for a parent who was ill, forgoing social interaction with his peers to stay home with his mother. In her memoir, Mrs. Bush recalls overhearing George declining a neighbor's invitation to play because his mother needed him: "I was too much of a burden for a seven-year-old to carry."

Much as Barbara tried unsuccessfully to compensate for her own mother's unhappiness, George couldn't erase his mother's pain, which found vivid expression when her hair turned prematurely white in her grief. His failure to assuage her pain would inevitably have had an effect on the child. Researchers have studied the anxiety a child feels when his mother is told to suddenly make a still, unresponsive face to her child: The child becomes desperate, trying ever more vigorously to elicit a response. As the child's fear of rejection mounts, his need to play increases in intensity. One wonders what Barbara Bush's face must have been like during those years, and what it was like for George to watch his mother's hair turn white.

George's antic personality certainly blossomed in that period, when the stresses on the grieving family—absent father, distant mother, newborn son—made it easy to overlook the behavioral troubles and emotional needs of the oldest child, whose energetic high spirits may have looked to his parents like healthy adjustment. By early grade school, George was known as "Bushtail," a boy who was always on the go. Today that energy level would arouse suspicion of hyperactivity, which often appears in children who resort to physical activity when they're otherwise unable to manage their anxiety. As hard as he may try to force out his anxieties through physical exertion, however, the hyperactive child never addresses the real source of his anxieties, and his need to keep playing or fidgeting only grows, never quite satisfied.

What factors can impede a child's ability to acquire the necessary tools to manage his anxiety effectively? Again we return to the work of Melanie Klein, whose model of infant development grew out of her work analyzing young children using play therapy. (She also looked at anxiety management techniques used by adults.) In 1946, after observing a patient unload his unwanted feelings onto his analyst in an almost invasive manner, she first described the way individuals try to rid themselves of anxiety by projecting discomfort into someone else, who then experiences the discomfort as his own. Klein traced this dynamic of projection back to the interplay between infant and mother, which as we've seen helps the infant learn how to modify the anxiety he projects. Klein's theory has been reaffirmed by recent research into cerebral development, demonstrating that the development of the right brain, which regulates emotions, depends on this unconscious emotional communication between mother and infant. When this process breaks down, and the child's reliance on the primitive tools of splitting and projection fails to render his anxiety less threatening, he often resorts to physical activity that makes the vital communication between mother and child more difficult to achieve. Mother and child can then become trapped in a self-perpetuating cycle of frustration and underdevelopment, the active child growing ever more active as his anxieties mount.

———✦———

A diminished ability to manage anxiety is often just the beginning of the troubles that can result from a disconnect between the mother and the infant. That relationship also plays a central role in the child's development of learning capacities. The child whose projected discomforts are not successfully alleviated and returned by the mother becomes less able to take in information from his caregivers and his environment. The baby derives more than just a sense of self from seeing his mother's emotionally expressive face; research has demonstrated that a properly attuned dynamic between mother and infant is necessary for the healthy development of the frontal lobe of the brain—the locus of our language and problem-solving functions, and the seat of our judgment and impulse control. When a mother dons a stern, restricting facial expression—such as when trying to handle an unmanageable baby—the child becomes more likely to tune out his environment and to have a harder time taking things in.

Unintegrated anxiety also complicates the development of healthy thought processes. Thinking involves the ability to reclaim uncomfortable projections; the child who is unable to hold anxiety must keep these projections external, weakening his ability to think or to solve problems. Complex thinking cannot take place if the child is unable to regulate his feelings. The child consumed by negative feelings, or distracted by the enormous effort required to handle them with only primitive psychological tools, can't get beyond his desperate need to manage his unmanageable anxiety; thus overwhelmed, the child may experience any external input as excessive. The premium placed on internal order leaves no room for growth.

All new stimuli are experienced as a potential threat; new ideas are overstimulating, and curiosity in the outside world is compromised. In the words of noted Klein scholar Meira Likerman, such a child "drastically restricts his ability to take in facts from the world, with catastrophic consequences for his entire mental functioning." If the child is "easily provoked by daily frustrations and hence prone to project excessive aggression," Likerman adds, the unrest affects both how he sees the world and what he sees when he looks at it, "[surrounding] the child with a malevolent, anxiety-inducing world."

The external evidence available to us suggests that George W. Bush's thought process may have been profoundly affected by his need to manage anxiety. If he were a youngster today, the childhood tendencies of young "Bushtail" Bush would probably catch the attention of parents and teachers, who would test him to see if he had Attention Deficit Hyperactivity Disorder (ADHD). The results of those tests would likely shed revealing light on whatever troubles he has had reading, learning, and thinking since childhood.

By early grade school, when he earned his nickname, Bush was already displaying an inability to sit still at school and a capacity to burn off his excess energy with impulsive actions. Those who knew him during his elementary school years recall him as an antic, energetic, and defiant clown who threw a football through his third-grade classroom window after the kids had been told to stay in out of the rain, and used a pen in fourth grade to decorate his face (as a circus clown, of course). But far less was known in Bush's day about the causes of such behavior, which we now recognize as hallmarks of ADHD, which ranks today as the most common neurobehavioral childhood disorder (according to the American Academy of Pediatrics).

A neurologically based condition caused by a neurotransmitter deficiency, ADHD presents in children in various ways. The child may be hyperactive, impulsive, fidgety, or squirmy; he may tend to speak or act before thinking; or he may be easily distracted by things he sees, hears, or suddenly thinks. In children of Bush's generation, the diagnosis of ADHD has come only in adulthood, when the warning signs are often accompanied by more socially acceptable qualities that can mask the symptoms.

The adult with ADHD can be easily distracted, but anticipates or expresses this by constantly monitoring the scene around him; his attention span may be short, but it is intense, and he is able to focus when he must. His disorganization might rarely come to light, because he often makes snap decisions. His lack of interest in abstractions can remain undetected behind his effectiveness as a visual thinker; his fondness for impulsive action and risk taking, in the proper setting, can be read as entrepreneurial drive. Nevertheless, behind these various coping mechanisms, the adult with ADHD is impatient and easily frustrated, has trouble following directions, and has a distorted sense of time.

We have no reason to believe that George W. Bush has ever undergone the testing that could confirm or rule out a diagnosis of ADHD. But much of what we know of the adult Bush's work habits and mental practices conforms to various indicators of ADHD—enough to make it worth considering the likely ramifications of such a diagnosis, even without an official examination. The two biggest problems for adults with ADHD are impulsivity and craving, the latter of which will be explored at length in Chapter Three. Impulsive behavior is often mistaken for decisiveness, but in reality the quick decision is often made because the individual is too impatient to sustain his attention long enough to read all the information, or too uncomfortable at the prospect of complex thought to weigh things sufficiently.

Bush's aides say he "never anguishes over decisions, preferring to gather information, make a decision, and move on," according to a *U.S. News and World Report* cover story. The president is also known for keeping a strictly regimented daily routine, in which short, heavily scheduled workdays with brief meetings are punctuated by regular breaks for exercise. Some would praise this as evidence of a disciplined mind, but it points equally to a desire to minimize the impact of a short attention span, and avoid the impulsive behavior that can otherwise result. As commentators Eric Alterman and Mark Green have reported, Bush's "advisors have admitted that the staff usually limits him to three or four thirty- to forty-five minute 'policy time' sessions per week, about what Bill Clinton engaged in per day. Then, more often than not, the president sloughs off responsibility with the admonishment, 'You guys decide it.'"

The annals of George W. Bush's years in the public eye are filled with examples of restless, impulsive, often childish behavior, especially when he is unaware that he is within range of a camera or microphone. During the 2000 campaign, Bush made headlines when an unnoticed microphone picked up the churchgoing candidate calling a *New York Times* reporter a "major-league asshole." He is often unable to sit still, having difficulty refraining from making faces, reaching out to pinch or joke with people. As Frank Bruni wrote, "The line between effervescence and inanity sometimes escaped him, a fact unchanged by his accumulation of experiences and his entry into politics. As Texas governor, when he held a news conference to address the subject of a fatal heat wave and related forest fires that were ravaging a part of the state, he summoned a Forestry Service official to the microphone by saying, 'Tree Man, get up here!' While the official talked, Bush looked toward the journalists, stuck out his tongue and made a funny face by puffing up his cheeks like a blowfish."

Bush's impulsiveness is also suggested, paradoxically, by his frequent insistence on appearing hypervigilant. Bush made sure it was public knowledge within his father's 1988 campaign that the aide with whom he traveled would "stay in [Bush's] hotel room until late at night to safeguard against rumors about women," Stephen Mansfield notes in *The Faith of George W. Bush,* which quotes a campaign staffer's claim that Bush "wanted everyone to know that nothing [of the kind] was happening." Such exaggerated vigilance regarding appearances suggests that Bush was at least aware that others questioned his ability to control his impulses, and raises the question of whether he worried about his own impulse control as well.

Impulsive, hair-trigger responses to real and perceived threats are also common for people with ADHD, who often act before determining whether the threat they perceive is in fact genuine. And when they don't overreact impulsively, people with ADHD often respond to feeling threatened by choosing to hide or escape. Studies of ADHD adults have revealed that they often change jobs or cities—an obvious element of Bush's professional resume. "I had dabbled in many things," he writes in his own autobiography, *A Charge to Keep,* "but I had no idea what I wanted to do with the rest of my life when I arrived at Harvard Business School," by which time he had "had a taste of many different jobs but none of them ever seemed to fit." What he fails to mention is that after Harvard his professional life grew only slightly more consistent.

The oil industry held his interest for only a decade, interrupted by a failed congressional run; in the next ten years, he would dabble in political campaigning (for his father) and baseball on the way to his first gubernatorial campaign. Some researchers explain the impulsiveness that accompanies ADHD by describing its sufferers as "hunters" who are living in a world of "farmers": "When the hunter sees the prey he gives chase through gully or ravine, over fields or through trees, *giving no thought to the events of the day before, not considering the future* [emphasis mine], simply living totally in that one pure moment and immersing himself in it."

The relentless and primitive rhetoric President Bush has used to describe the hunt for Osama bin Laden is a vivid manifestation of this very tendency. Almost immediately after 9/11, such images began appearing in his repertoire: he spoke often of "tighten[ing] the net" and "smoking al Qaeda out of their caves," of having bin Laden's forces "on the run." A year and a half later, he was still speaking of having to "smoke these al Qaeda types out one at a time."

Even members of his own family noted the trait. On September 17, 2001, Bush attempted to taunt Osama bin Laden with a memorable declaration: "When I was a kid, I remember that they used to put out there in the old West a 'Wanted' sign; it said 'Wanted: Dead or Alive'." Laura Bush found the image so troubling that she asked him to "tone it down, darling." As Bob Woodward reports in *Bush at War,* though, according to Mrs. Bush, "he didn't tone it down. 'Every once in a while, I had to say it again,'" the First Lady conceded.

———◆———

To make matters worse, ADHD is often found to coexist with other learning disorders, the most common belonging to the family of dyslexias. Some dyslexics have problems spelling. Others are mirror readers who reverse letters ("saw" becomes "was"). Others anticipate letters or sounds incorrectly and so misread words, mistaking "battlefield" for "bachelor," "filament" for "firmament." Because the erratic attention span, impulsivity, and restlessness that are the primary symptoms of ADHD can make reading difficult, ADHD can mimic dyslexia, but they are two separate disorders.

Bush's dyslexia is not officially documented, but his reading habits are, and they reveal several earmarks of the disorder. He has said repeatedly, and with a pride that might mask defensiveness, that he does not read newspapers. Sometimes he tries to explain away his habit in partisan terms: he told Diane Sawyer that relying on his advisors to tell him what's in the papers gives him the comforting sense that he "gets his news from people who don't editorialize," which "makes it easier" for him "to digest." But in other instances, he has seemed to suggest a blend of discomfort and disdain for the very act of reading itself: "I glance at the headlines just to kind of get a flavor for what's moving," he said in September 2003. "I rarely read the stories, and get briefed by people who probably read the news themselves."

Elsewhere, Bush has said that his generation of the Bush family— which includes one known dyslexic, his brother Neil—are "not real serious, studious readers. We are readers for fun." (This was apparently true even when the Bush children were growing up: Their home lacked an encyclopedia, according to the mother of a childhood friend of Bush's youngest sister, who regularly visited her friend's house to use her encyclopedia.) He doesn't take notes during debates or press conferences, and has been known to throw down typed briefings and ask his aides to digest the material more thoroughly. As Gail Sheehy and others have described in detail, his speech patterns include pronoun reversal, word substitutions, and the switching of positive to negative meanings, which along with his mispronunciations are all classic signs of serious reading difficulty. Ironically, even after Sheehy investigated his dyslexia in *Vanity Fair,* his response included a dyslexic-style reversal: "I never interviewed her," he said, not only confusing subject and object, but confirming his repulsion at the very idea of becoming object of such scrutiny.

The childhood shame at not being able to keep up with his friends endures throughout the dyslexic's life. Sometimes this shame is expressed as contempt, as in Bush's attitude toward newspapers and the printed word. Bush doesn't seem to take the prospect of dyslexia seriously; he once joked that if he were president he would set up a 119 number for dyslexics—a funny line until one remembers his brother's struggles with the disorder. But if he is in fact dyslexic, the disorder's potential impact on the president extends far beyond his reading habits. Dyslexia is also generally accompanied by an inability to manage anxiety; the escapes of school and reading are beyond the dyslexic child's reach, diminishing his capacity to regulate his feelings. Those feelings include the pain of having a learning disorder—not only the pain of struggling to function, but the frustration of being disconnected from language and from thought, from expression, creativity, books, and words. No wonder he joked with reporters in August 2001 about taking refuge in long walks on his ranch—time he said he would spend "seeing the cows," which would occasionally "talk to me, being the good listener that I am."

Language itself has its roots in anxiety. As children, we develop the capacity to speak and think in words in large part to manage our unpleasant feelings. Language continues to play a role in anxiety management through adulthood; verbalizing our anxieties, through thought and speech, is widely regarded as one of the healthiest ways of dealing with them. An individual who struggles with language, then, must address his anxieties without benefit of one of the most powerful management tools available to him; in other words, a language problem is often an indicator of an anxiety problem. Unfortunately, it's a vicious circle, especially in our early years, because a child who has trouble managing his anxiety is at a disadvantage when it comes to developing language as well.

Bush's troubles with language represent yet another manifestation of the deficiencies in his anxiety-management skills that date back to infancy. Language is born of the anxieties we experience in infancy. The baby experiences his discomfort—the physical discomforts of infancy, or the emotional discomfort of the temporarily or chronically absent caregiver—and first tries to dispel his anxiety through physical means (crying, kicking, and so on). Through his interactions with a nurturing mother, the child subsequently learns that anxiety need not be immediately dispelled, but can be successfully projected onto the mother; her practice of taking in anxiety, processing it, and generating a comforting solution provides a model that the child ultimately internalizes.

Once anxiety has been rendered less threatening, so that a child no longer feels the urgent need to expel it from his mind, he can experience it as a source of thought. No longer overwhelmed by fears that his needs will never be addressed, he is able to use his mind to think about his discomfort in ways that help him tolerate it. By imagining the mother who always comes to feed him, for example, a baby is able to endure the frustration of his hunger as he awaits her arrival. He learns not only to know that something is bothering him, but also to think about what it might be, and how he can manage the situation.

The process by which the mother demonstrates to the child how to transform anxiety into understanding continues well through the time that the baby learns to use words. As time goes on, the child needs to project less and less of his anxiety, as he learns that his own thought processes provide some measure of relief. This provides valuable groundwork for the acquisition of language. Having learned that translating his discomfort into thought can bring results, he is eventually able to project his feelings into words, which contain and give meaning to his feelings as they give them symbolic expression.

When the maternal nurturing process is somehow interrupted, however, the child fails to internalize the means to tolerate his anxiety long enough to understand and transform it; he may even be the object of a depressed or distant mother's projection, receiving images of blame that leave him even more frightened. Still threatened by a fear of being overwhelmed by his feelings, the undernurtured child develops an aversion to anxiety, which he still feels compelled to avoid or dispel unmodified. This aversion, in turn, inhibits his development of language, because he is neither equipped to hold onto his feelings even in symbolic form, nor inclined to believe he can do anything to render them less threatening. Though he will learn to read, write, and speak, such a child's relationship to language will be nonetheless impaired, depriving him of a vital tool for transforming feelings into ideas, and for knowing what to do with the thoughts that cross his mind.

———✦———

These deficiencies placed young George at a distinct disadvantage when he was obliged to fend for himself at two of the nation's most intensely competitive academic environments—his father's alma maters, Phillips Academy (Andover) and Yale. Neither institution was particularly hospitable to a young man with undiagnosed learning disabilities. And both posed social challenges to an anti-intellectual small-town Texan following in the hard-to-fill footsteps of his esteemed father and grandfather, East Coasters who had excelled as both athletes and scholars. As it turns out, George W. Bush seems to have conquered the second set of challenges with skills he developed in response to the first—giving rise to the affable, socially successful, yet isolated personality we recognize today.

The little information we have about Bush's Andover years indicates that he did nothing to distinguish himself academically. In fact, at least one report of his efforts as a scholar supports the idea that he was indeed wrestling with learning disabilities. Assigned to write an essay about the most important event in his life, he chose to write about his sister's death. In an attempt to dress up his language, he substituted for the plural noun *tears* the verb *lacerates*. At the very least, the gaffe suggests an ill-fated collision with a thesaurus; at a deeper level, though, it signals that he was being asked to work at a level that was beyond his comprehension. After receiving a grade of zero on the assignment—to which the teacher added the comment "disgraceful"—Bush wondered how he was going to survive at the notoriously competitive boarding school.

Perhaps to hide or compensate for his academic insecurities (which were likely matched by athletic insecurities, as he was no more accomplished in sports than in his studies), Bush made a name for himself by calling attention to his personality. Bush himself said that he decided to "instill a sense of frivolity" as his personal Andover legacy, and he did so by clowning, calling people names, declaring himself high commissioner of the stickball tournament, and joining the cheerleading squad. As one friend said, "He rose to a certain prominence for no ostensible, visible reason." But behind the glad-handing and nicknaming, the same friend observed, "he just never seemed very warm. . . . He just didn't let people get to know him."

The paradoxical co-existence of familiarity and distance further suggests that Bush's cultivation of his affable personality was motivated by something other than the simple drive to engender social favor and acceptance. As an intelligent person whose access to his intelligence was hampered by disabilities, Bush compensated for his flaws by developing other talents, such as his sense of humor and his uncanny ability to memorize names and faces. People with untreated ADHD can have difficulty functioning as members of a social group, because they find it hard to follow substantive discussion and social interaction. Finding it too hard to grasp thoughts coming from multiple directions, they often resort to telling jokes and disrupt the proceedings; they content themselves with being one of a group of fun-loving people, and avoid more serious interaction.

An ambitious person with ADHD has a problem, then—he has to be the leader to be a member. Otherwise he can't be heard; his outbursts will not be taken seriously. It was fortunate for George W. Bush that he was so energetic as a child, and so much older than his siblings; these chance qualities allowed him to lead, dominate, and even instill a little fear in those around him. And thus he was able to translate this to a leadership position—unfounded by any excellence in performance—first at Andover and then at Yale, where he was president of his fraternity (whose function was primarily to throw parties) and was tapped by the secret society Skull and Bones (which inevitably had much to do with his father's and grandfather's previous membership).

As effective as the trappings of an extroverted personality may have been for Bush, charm and bravado are often tactics used by the intelligent learning-disabled child to hide the shame he harbors about his disability. What looks like gregariousness can in fact be a desperate defense; Bush's remarkable ability to learn names and faces and his propensity for assigning nicknames are likely linked, the latter a common habit of intelligent people who need to compensate for other defects in information-processing. Often the charm starts as a compensatory habit, but soon it morphs into second nature, an integral part of the self. As the child grows into adulthood, the skin gets thicker and thicker, until the individual is safely insulated from any shame over his private incapacities.

The same early learning disabilities that can engender shame can also lead to the development of unhealthy responses to it. Once again, interaction with the mother is crucial, this time in the period—most dramatically during toilet training in the second year of life—when the mother causes her child shame by setting limits, and then must repair the broken bond. Breaking and repairing of bonds is part and parcel of child rearing; in healthy relationships, a pattern is established where the mother understands the pain and shame she has caused, helping the child to regulate his feelings over time. But hyperactivity can get in the way of this process. Bush's adult attitudes suggest that his childhood involved little experience of breaking and repairing; his inability to express contrition, or admit wrongdoing, bespeaks a profound need to deny the possibility of his shame.

The rhythm of breaking and repairing also teaches the child that a negative experience can be followed by something positive; in the process, the child learns to tolerate the bad without having to react violently. This also seems to be missing from Bush's repertoire. When a child doesn't experience relief from his distress, he frequently reacts by defiantly denying outside help or influence, developing a false, grandiose sense of independence.

Both grandiosity and shame are symptoms of the learning-disabled individual's inability to construct an internal world that reflects the complexities of life. Such a child's inner world must be simple, because complexity causes anxiety; when shame is unresolved, compensatory grandiose self-images are allowed to thrive, and magical thinking spawns unrealistic notions that flourish unchallenged. The material world is simplified to conform to his internal worldview. Listen to President Bush's descriptions of the world in which he lives, and you'll probably find that you make your life in a far more complicated place.

Bush's simplified world is populated by cardboard figures who are either enemies or friends, though neither is accurately conceived as what we know a complete person to be. He routinely refers to any ally who stands to help him as simply "a good man," and expresses his judgment of his appointees' and allies' performance simply by asserting that they are "doing a good job." And when he grasps at anecdotal evidence to elaborate, his comments can seem almost mystically vague. Bush has said that his positive impression of Russian president Vladimir Putin, for example, was based on a feeling that he had seen his soul when looking into Putin's eyes, and by the fact that Putin was "willing to wear a cross." If he wears a cross, in short, he must be a friend.

On the other hand, Bush views anyone who differs with him as a potential threat, as Paul O'Neill and others have detailed. It is in this way that opposition gets converted into the enemy and then dehumanized. When Bush discusses his enemies—whether they are the foreign "evildoers" of the war on terror or domestic opponents at home—they generally sound less like real people than like abstractions of his worldview. (Even his wife has been pigeonholed, impersonally, as "a great first lady.") We all have this potential to dehumanize others, for we all once experienced our inner world in terms of people who serve functions—as reflected in children who automatically call anyone who brings them something "mommy," inextricably associating the image of a helpful adult with the idea of "mother." Bush's reductive, absolutist approach to opposition at home and abroad suggests that he has not progressed far beyond this two-dimensional view of those who people his world.

This dehumanization is also disturbingly apparent in Bush's attitude toward the suffering of others. Research has shown that learning disabilities often compromise an individual's capacity to have empathic responses to others. The emotional attachments of a learning-disabled child are experienced as disorganized or insecure, a situation exacerbated by the frustrated mother's ineffectiveness or even neglect. These flawed early interactions scar the template that shapes the individual's relationships for the rest of his life.

Both children and adults with ADHD score low on tests that measure empathy. It's not hard to see why: The various breeding grounds in which empathy is developed—family relationships, socialization, school, even reading—are all compromised when learning disabilities are not diagnosed and treated. People with ADHD are often too impatient to listen to others, thus depriving themselves of a vital component of forming empathic bonds. There is ample evidence that Bush lacks empathy, from his policies to his communication style to attitudes toward people with whom he disagrees. His affability may look like empathy, but ultimately it may have less to do with his relationships with others than with his discomfort with himself.

# THREE

# MESSAGE IN
# THE BOTTLE

*Here are your waters and your watering place.*
*Drink and be whole again beyond confusion.*

—Robert Frost, *Directive*

MELANIE KLEIN OBSERVED that the destructive forces we fear most are those we can turn against ourselves. Dealing with those fears can be a lifelong struggle; if we do not confront them directly, we are likely to project our fears onto external forces that we then feel we must extinguish to be safe. Long before he entered politics, George W. Bush came face-to-face with the potentially deadly self-destructive force that was raging inside him: his compulsion to drink alcohol. Bush turned to alcohol late in his youth, presumably to narcotize anxieties he couldn't bear to confront. But at some point his drinking turned on him, and the drive to drink became a new enemy with a life of its own. To his credit, he eventually set out to solve his drinking problem, but he did so by externalizing the enemy rather than acknowledging that a greater threat than alcohol was the enemy within. It seems highly likely that the inner demons he tried to manage by drinking still bedevil him today.

Considering the uproar over whether or not Bill Clinton inhaled marijuana in his twenties, it's remarkable how little attention has been paid to Bush's twenty-plus years of problem drinking. From his days at prep school (where he was under the legal age) through his fortieth birthday, Bush regularly used and abused alcohol to soothe his anxious soul. He has in various instances described his drinking as heavy, daily, and as an interference with his family life. Perhaps most notably, alcohol fueled a now famous 1973 showdown between Bush and his father. After learning that George W. had been driving drunk with his teenaged brother in the car, the elder Bush summoned the intoxicated 26-year-old to the den of his Texas home. Emboldened by liquor, George W. "rammed through the garbage cans with his car[,] walked in the front door of the house," and challenged his father "to go *mano a mano* right here" as other family watched. Three years later, George W. was once again caught driving drunk near his father's turf—this time in Maine, when he was arrested, at the age of thirty, for driving under the influence. When the incident became public days before the 2000 election, the media's treatment of the story somehow focused more on the possibility of Democratic dirty tricks than on the fact that Bush had managed to conceal the most dramatic evidence of the effects drinking has had on his life—even if another decade would pass before it got bad enough for him to quit.

Is Bush an alcoholic? He has publicly denied it, telling the *Washington Post,* "I don't think I was clinically an alcoholic; I didn't have the genuine addiction," in July 1999. "I've had friends who were, you know, very addicted . . . and they required hitting bottom [and] going to AA. I don't think that was my case." Still, according to former speechwriter David Frum, after reaching the Oval Office, Bush asked for the prayers of religious leaders, telling them, "I had a drinking problem. Right now I should be in a bar, not the Oval Office."

Though a driving under the influence (DUI) arrest has inspired many a drinker to admit a problem and seek help in stopping, there are plenty of drivers with DUI citations who do not identify themselves as alcoholic. Many recovering alcoholics regard alcoholism as a treatable (though not curable) disease that can only be diagnosed by the alcoholic himself. (This may have something to do with the fact that admission of one's alcoholism is considered a necessary first step toward recovery.) Until the heavy drinker describes himself as alcoholic, he suffers from a condition for which there is no treatment. The American Society of Addiction Medicine, on the other hand, offers less room for self-determination: Its definition holds that alcoholism is "characterized by . . . impaired control over drinking, preoccupation with the drug alcohol, use of alcohol despite adverse consequences, and distortions in thinking, *most notably denial*" [emphasis mine].

The historical record, along with Bush's few published comments on his drinking, make clear that he drank in a way that fit most if not all of those criteria. But while it is valuable to know whether or not he was or is an alcoholic, the more pressing question involves the influence his years of heavy drinking and subsequent abstinence still have on him and those around him. Bush's drinking history compels us to consider the prospect that his thinking, behavior, and relationships with his family and the world may be deeply influenced by an alcoholic personality, one that is continually trying—allegedly successfully, though possibly with reduced capacities—to keep the compulsion to drink under control.

———⟶———

I rarely treat alcoholics during the acute stage of their illness; like most psychoanalysts, I refer them to a hospital for detoxification and to Alcoholics Anonymous. Though not a medical program, AA is widely accepted throughout the medical profession as the most effective treatment for alcoholism. Its success rate is low—sometimes placed at 10 percent, sometimes even lower—but it still represents the best hope for recovery. Alcoholism is a potentially fatal, lifelong disease that is notoriously difficult to arrest permanently. Few alcoholics stay sober on their first attempt, and far more die of complications from alcoholism than achieve and maintain long-term sobriety.

I will not treat an alcoholic who is still drinking unless he or she also goes to AA. I have found that active alcoholics are generally uninterested in self-knowledge and incapable of introspection; they value psychic and emotional comfort over the anxiety that self-examination can arouse. Alcoholics Anonymous, on the other hand, places a premium on introspection. The Twelve Steps of the AA program are intended to guide the recovering alcoholic toward self-knowledge and acceptance in the hopes of increasing his chances of staying sober. One of the many slogans in which the AA philosophy is summarized is "to thine own self be true"—ancient watchwords for the examined life.

Bush has said publicly that he quit drinking without the help of AA or any substance abuse program, claiming that he stopped forever with the assistance of such spiritual tools as Bible study and conversations with the evangelist Billy Graham. "There is only one reason that I am in the Oval Office and not a bar," he told the religious leaders whose visit was recounted by Frum. "I found faith. I found God. I am here because of the power of prayer." That may be true—surely all Americans would like to believe that the president no longer drinks, even if we have no way of knowing for certain. If so, he fits the profile of a former drinker whose alcoholism has been arrested but not treated; his abstinence protects him from the crippling effects of heavy alcohol consumption, but he remains in the grip of alcoholic thinking that the program of AA, and the regular practice of its principles, helps its members keep at bay.

Former drinkers who abstain without benefit of the AA program are often referred to as "dry drunks," a label that has been bandied about on the Internet and elsewhere in reference to Bush. "Dry drunk" isn't a medical term, and not one I use in a clinical setting. But even without labeling Bush as such, it's hard to ignore the many troubling elements of his character among the traits that the recovery literature associates with the condition, including grandiosity, judgmentalism, intolerance, detachment, denial of responsibility, a tendency toward overreaction, and an aversion to introspection. By removing the alcohol without treating the "ism," the untreated alcoholic relies on many of the self-serving (though ultimately self-defeating) attitudes and behaviors that characterized his unhealthy approach to life before he stopped drinking.

I've seen this repeatedly in my practice; I've treated alcoholics who are in recovery in AA and alcoholics who are abstaining on their own, and it's easy to tell the difference. Typically, the latter have been far less successful learning to handle the anxiety that they once tried to suppress by drinking. Often they project it onto other people, including me; the typical session with an untreated abstinent alcoholic can be an anxious experience for both patient and doctor, often forcing the doctor to ingest the patient's intolerance for uncertainty. Their rigid attempts to manage anxiety make any psychological insight hard-won. Some can't even face the anxiety of admitting their alcoholism. Without that admission, I have found, even former drinkers cannot truly change, or learn from their own experience.

The pattern of blame and denial, which recovering alcoholics work so hard to break, seems to be ingrained in the alcoholic personality; it's rarely limited to his or her drinking. The habit of placing blame and denying responsibility is so prevalent in George W. Bush's personal history that it is apparently triggered by even the mildest threat; when Jay Leno, on the eve of Bush's DUI revelation, asked him if he'd ever done anything he was ashamed of, he replied "*I didn't*"—and proceeded to tell a humiliating story of his brother Marvin urinating in the family steam iron.

The long years of ducking responsibility and blaming others—before and after he went on the wagon—would have left Bush at an obvious developmental disadvantage. How can someone learn from mistakes if he thinks he never makes any? The individual who attributes his faults and missteps to others deprives himself of the opportunity to grow, to add to his arsenal of thinking skills—from recognizing and solving problems to anticipating the potential consequences of his actions. By limiting his range of capacities over the years, Bush narrows the range of responses available to him when he needs to solve problems today. As his April 2004 press conference made painfully clear, George W. Bush can't bring himself to accept even a modicum of responsibility for either the intelligence failures before 9/11 or the troubled war in Iraq, refusing to rise to reporters' repeated inquiries about mistakes he may have made. "I hope I don't want to sound like I've made no mistakes," he finally said. "I'm confident I have. I just haven't—you just put me under the spot here and maybe I'm not quick—as quick on my feet as I should be in coming up with one."

Blame and denial are arguably as typical of politicians as of alcoholics, though the latter are generally more likely to involve family members in the process. Perhaps the appeal—other than political self-preservation—is as simple and universal as the common desire to get away with something. But blame and denial take on a different resonance when seen from the Kleinian perspective. Blame is in fact a reminder of one's destructive impulse; the individual who hasn't resolved his anxieties surrounding that impulse is particularly motivated to avoid confronting those anxieties, which he can accomplish by shifting responsibility to someone else, or denying it outright.

Drinkers turn to alcohol to suppress anxiety. The untreated alcoholic who has simply stopped drinking treats anxiety as an enemy, and with good reason: He is often more challenged by anxiety because he has lost his time-tested means of numbing its sting. He knows that anxiety is a threat to his abstinence—he fears anything that might send him back to the bottle—but his years of drinking get in the way of learning other methods to manage uncomfortable feelings. Instead of seeking treatment in a Twelve Step program, he turns to less effective means to try to control or avoid his feelings, expending energy that would otherwise be spent more productively elsewhere. He has less energy to invest in the world around him—an encumbrance for most, but potentially tragic in the case of a man carrying the grave responsibilities of the presidency on his shoulders.

These unending efforts to manage anxiety inevitably lead to an exaggerated degree of rigidity in the ex-drinker's thoughts and actions. Because he is so invested in staving off the sources of anxiety that led him to drink, he makes it a top priority to maintain personal control in most—if not all—aspects of his life. (This is the antithesis of Twelve-Step recovery, in which the individual turns personal control, which is regarded as largely illusory, into the hands of a spiritual "Higher Power.")

The rigidity of Bush's behavior is perhaps most readily apparent in his well-documented reliance on his daily routines—the famously short meetings, sacrosanct exercise schedule, daily Bible readings, and limited office hours. A healthy person is able to alter his routine; a rigid one cannot. Bush appears to have chosen a job that cannot bend to rigid routine, yet he managed to spend 42 percent of his first seven months as president away from the White House (as calculated by *Washington Post* reporter Mike Allen), and still averages at least ten visits a year to Crawford alone, imposing his routine of escaping to Camp David or Crawford on the unruly mess of running the country. Of course, we all need rest and relaxation, time to regroup, but Bush appears to need it more than most. And this is hardly a surprise— among other reasons, because the anxiety of being president might pose a real risk of leading him back to drinking.

Along with rigid routines go rigid thought processes—another hallmark of the Bush presidency. We see it in the stubborn, almost obsessive way in which he holds on to ideas and plans after they have been discredited, from his image of himself as a "uniter, not a divider" to his conviction that Iraq held weapons of mass destruction (or, in absence of such weapons, that somehow "America did the right thing in Iraq" nevertheless). Such rigidity of thought is not motivated by simple stubbornness; the untreated alcoholic, consumed with the task of managing the anxieties that might make him reach for a drink, simply can't tolerate any threat to his status quo. Self-protection takes precedence over self-examination; it's safer to hold on to an idea that has served him in the past than to try a new one that might not work. The need to protect the status quo also fuels swift and vigorous responses to any threats that may challenge it—often resulting in responses that are out of proportion to the magnitude of the actual threat. This may help to explain the dramatic contrast between George W.'s response to Saddam Hussein and that of his father, who carefully built a coalition, took action only after Kuwait had been invaded, and then proceeded with prudence and caution once the fighting was underway—the behavior of a seasoned leader who knew he was responsible for countless others' lives, not an alcoholic accustomed to taking dramatic measures to protect his own.

It is probably impossible to know how the former president has felt watching his son's alcoholic behavior unfurl from Andover to Iraq. Alcoholism is a family disease, the conventional wisdom holds; the alcoholic's condition affects every family member, each of whom struggles to cope with the impact that the drinker's behavior has on family life—even if the drinking is in the past.

In my practice, I treat family members of alcoholics more frequently than alcoholics themselves. Over the years, I have observed numerous similarities between families in which there is an alcoholic, most of them stemming from the drinker's unpredictability and the family's efforts to deal with it. Typically, the family never knows when the alcoholic is going to be drunk, but the uncertainty extends beyond mere intoxication; the periods of nondrinking can be just as stressful, as many family members report instances of sudden, inexplicable outbursts or breakdowns.

The most common reaction is to walk on eggshells around the alcoholic, dreading the moment when the anxieties usually or formerly suppressed by spirits inevitably escape his control. This became touchingly clear in the case of Mary, one of my patients. A 43-year-old banker, Mary looked startled every Monday morning at 10:00 when I opened the door to my waiting room. I eventually realized that she reacted the way she did because she thought I looked angry. What emerged in treatment was that her father was an alcoholic, prone to violent, even sadistic outbursts. Growing up, she had never known what behavior of hers might set him off, and the lasting fear of his rages affected her perception of me. When she left a session she took her image of the loving father with her, and left the image of the angry father in the consulting room. But on Monday mornings she would superimpose both images onto me, bringing her apprehension to the surface once again.

I have found that the alcoholic father presents particular challenges to the family unit. His alcoholism undermines his authority in the family. Family members become paralyzed, unable to confront his weakened power for fear of exposing its illegitimacy—which would force the family to change, perhaps to face up to its own participation in the alcoholic situation. They are typically just as unwilling to confront the untreated abstainer, who believes he is doing just fine even as his alcoholic tendencies wreak havoc around him; if he believes that his way to approach problems is sober and thoughtful, however, everyone else goes along with him, reluctant to start a confrontation that could lead to collapse or relapse. Thus, motivated by fear—of being attacked or abandoned by the drinker—the family enables the perpetuation of the disease, whether it is expressed as active alcoholism or untreated abstinence; rather than upset an unhealthy power structure, they sustain it with their denial and collusion.

As the unrecovered alcoholic father busily juggles anxieties in his constant struggle to avoid reaching for a drink, the status quo on which he depends eventually expands to include the entire family unit. When the family is threatened (by anything other than the father's alcoholism), all emphasis is directed toward finding a short-term solution that will preserve the stability of family life, often to the detriment of all other areas. This happens whether the threat is real or imaginary; the alcoholic's damaged internal reality determines the entire family's perception of material reality.

The model of an alcoholic family dynamic bears a telling similarity to the way much of our nation has behaved under George W. Bush—especially since the attacks of September 11. At times, the country has seemed to act like a family with an abstinent, untreated alcoholic at its head, overreacting to vaguely perceived threats by rushing out to buy duct tape or fretting over color-coded alarms. Once the crisis passes, Bush shifts the focus to another alleged danger closer to home—such as the threats to the social fabric posed by gay marriage or stem cell research. Like the alcoholic father who is threatened by the independence of his family members, Bush demands absolute loyalty and conformity, trying to freeze his national family in time—preferably a time before gays demanded their right to marry and women their right to abortion.

In my years of conducting family therapy sessions, I've observed that each family has its own character, a sense of its continuity over time, an identity shared among family members. The alcoholic father, desperately attached to the status quo, clings to his particular conception of his family's identity; the family accepts the self-definition that the alcoholic imposes on it. So, too, our nation. Bush needs to keep his family intact; you are with us or against us, he says. And many of us agree, or at least follow along as if we did.

The behavior of a healthy family is patterned and predictable, committed to preserving its stability even in the face of dramatic changes; any problems are solved using self-correcting behaviors and simple regulatory strategies. Similarly, our nation has been able to maintain its stability amidst so many changes and pressures due in large part to the rule of law, the force of the Constitution, and the power of tradition. In alcoholic families, in which uncertainty isn't tolerated and each threat is treated as a crisis, regulation is compromised and law becomes expendable; overreacting to minor challenges, the alcoholic head of household imposes his need for regulatory behavior onto his family. The alcoholic father is threatened more by dangers he perceives within the family than those outside, because he relies on the internal support to guard his status quo from any external menace. One way that alcoholic families accomplish both ends is to unite against a common enemy, setting aside internal divisions to focus on the peril outside. Thus, the president enjoyed high approval ratings surrounding the invasion of Iraq—until mounting evidence that the war was launched under false pretenses and was bringing a financial windfall to the vice president's former employer made it harder for the nation to keep ignoring its problems at home.

If we are a nation of enablers, allowing our president's untreated alcoholism to shape the national agenda, then special notice must be reserved for the news media. The most delicate eggshells of all have been those walked on by the members of the press. Throughout Bush's first term, the news media have followed a "don't ask, don't ask" policy, treading carefully and lightly around Bush's alcoholism—as evinced by their handling of the DUI revelation—and avoiding any tough question that might sound like a confrontation. Whether they fear that pressing too hard might send him off on a bender, provoke a tantrum, or simply get them excommunicated from further access, the nation's press has maintained a distance similar to what a child would accord an alcoholic father whom direct questioning might push over the edge into collapse or retaliation. Whatever its impetus, their silence rings loudest and clearest of all, like the stubborn denial of the family's most outspoken child; it doesn't prevent anyone else from speaking up, but it doesn't encourage it either.

———

Two questions that the press seems particularly determined to ignore have hung silently in the air since before Bush took office: Is he still drinking? And if not, is he impaired by all the years he did spend drinking? Both questions need to be addressed in any serious assessment of his psychological state.

The first question is inevitable, in my opinion, given his chosen strategy for staying away from alcohol. The family members of alcoholics I count among my patients are far more likely to suspect the abstinent relative is drinking if he or she is not active in AA—particularly those who are characteristically private or secretive. When I'm treating an untreated, abstinent alcoholic, I find myself far more concerned than if the patient is in AA. I may spend as much as half the session wondering if the untreated patient has resumed drinking; I don't feel anything comparable to that level of concern with a patient who is in AA.

When it comes to President Bush, several aspects of his public appearances are enough to give one pause. On a number of occasions, he has appeared almost sedated when he speaks—as if he were calming his anxiety with medication in the hopes of staying away from alcohol. His speech sometimes sounds slow and overly deliberate, in the way drinkers sometimes talk to hide their inebriation. On at least one occasion, the impression has been so clear that speculation has made its way into print: In writing about Bush's halting appearance in a press conference just before the start of the Iraq War, *Washington Post* media critic Tom Shales speculated that "the president may have been ever so slightly medicated."

More troubling, though, are the appearances that arouse suspicion not because of how he talks but what he says. He has repeatedly engaged in confabulation, filling in gaps in his memory with what he believes are facts—most notably on July 14, 2003, when he stood next to Kofi Annan and made up the idea that America had given Saddam "a chance to allow the inspectors in, and he wouldn't let them in." (As the *Washington Post* noted, "Hussein had, in fact, admitted the inspectors and Bush had opposed extending their work because he did not believe them effective."Confabulation is a common phenomenon among drinkers, as is perseveration, which is evident in Bush's tendency to repeat key words and phrases, as if the repetition helps him remain calm and stay on track. Often these phrases are repeated in the context of matters that could clearly challenge any leader's sense of calm—vowing emptily that there's "no doubt in my mind" about issues as perennially complex and morally challenging as warfare and capital punishment.

There may be no decisive evidence, at this remove, to indicate that President Bush has consumed alcohol while in office. But his appearance and behavior in such circumstances are enough to raise a degree of uncertainty on the matter, and to note that the prospect of his returning to alcohol is simply too frightening to ignore. Consider also the motive he offered for his lying about the DUI arrest when it was finally exposed: He said he had done so for his children. Even if one takes that explanation at face value, it is not hard to imagine that the president might similarly justify concealing a relapse "for his country." And if his explanation wasn't true, then there's little reason to believe he wouldn't lie about his drinking again.

Even if we assume, moreover, that George W. Bush's drinking days are behind him, the question remains how much lasting damage may have been done before he stopped—beyond the considerable impact on his personality that we can trace to his untreated abstinence. Any comprehensive psychological or psychoanalytical study of President Bush would have to explore how much the brain and its functions are changed by more than twenty years of heavy drinking. In a recent study out of the University of California/San Francisco Medical Center, researchers found that heavy drinkers who do not call themselves alcoholics reveal that "their level of drinking constitutes a problem that warrants treatment." The study found that the heavy drinkers in its sample were "*significantly impaired* on measures of working memory, processing speed, attention, executive function, and balance." Serious research about long-term recovery from alcohol abuse is still under way. Science has established that alcohol itself is toxic to the brain, both to its anatomy (as the brain gets smaller and fissures between and around the hemispheres get larger) and to its neurophysiology. But recovery does occur with continued sobriety, extending over a five-year period for many alcoholics. Bush claims to have been sober for more than fifteen years, and very well may have improved to pre-alcohol levels. However, even chronic alcoholics who recover their compromised mental functions often suffer lingering damage to their ability to process new information. Important neuropsychological functions are impaired: The new information is essentially put into a file that is lost in the brain.

Former heavy drinkers often have trouble distinguishing between relevant and inconsequential information. They also may lose some of their ability to maintain concentration. All one has to do to observe Bush's inattention is watch him listening to a speech given by someone else, watch his behavior at times on the campaign trail, or consider the obviously desperate effort he makes to retain focus in every speech he gives. Other research into the consequences of drinking has explored whether cognitive improvement among former heavy drinkers is genuine, or merely the result of repeatedly performing a particular task—a question that seems relevant in light of Bush habit of resorting to simple, repeated phrases when facing a new situation.

Clearly, though, anecdotal information is not enough. One study suggests that as many as 85 percent of former drinkers will perform lower on some measure of cognitive function; Bush would put many Americans' fears to rest by subjecting himself to such testing. These things can be measured; rather than rely on anecdotal and speculative information, the American public has a right to know.

Otherwise, we are left to suspect—with reason—that our president may be impaired in his ability to make sense of complex ideas and briefings. His simplistic approach to his job may in fact be as sophisticated as his compromised cognition allows. We all may be a little afraid to find out; after all, he has already held office for three years and has led our nation into war. But if we fail to do so, the consequences may indict every one of us.

# FOUR

# IN GOD I TRUST

No coward soul is mine,
No trembler in the world's storm-troubled sphere:
I see Heaven's glories shine
And faith shines equal, arming me from fear.
　　　　　　　　　　　　—Emily Bronte, Last Lines

Every man is his own doctor of divinity, in the last resort.
　　　　　　　　　—Robert Louis Stevenson, An Inland Voyage

THROUGHOUT ITS HISTORY, psychoanalysis has had a long and un-easy relationship with religion. Freud and Jung both thought that an organized belief in God protected the individual from having to face his fears, both internal and external. Where Jung urged many of his patients to get spiritual protection to help them through frightening situations, Freud was more cautious. Focusing more on the adverse impact of two tenets of religious faith—the adherence to a belief system that is not amenable to reason, and the sense of omnipotence derived from identification with a powerful and benevolent god—Freud argued that the practice of religion can undermine intellectual and psychological development. Melanie Klein agreed with Freud, and identified an element of magical primitivism in the way religion played on fantasies of omnipotence so central to early stages of childhood development.

At its psychological base, religion offers a sense of purpose even as it modifies anxiety. The image of order being created out of chaos, common to the ancient religions that form the basis of Judaism and Christianity, evokes the infant's battle with the chaos of hunger, colic, absolute dependency, and fears of abandonment. From the mother's soothing voice to the predictable rituals of bath and bedtime, order has a calming effect on the infant, an experience we seek to reproduce in various forms for the rest of our lives. The child creates a world populated by powerful forces that bring him relief, the anthropomorphic images of his powerful feelings. The first such images are his parents, who are regarded as all-powerful gods; when the child becomes disillusioned with his parents, he turns elsewhere for strength and comfort—one source of which is organized religion. The adult search for god, then, is a reprisal of the search for order that began in infancy.

Seeking relief from the ongoing chaos that his drinking once eased but ultimately intensified, George W. Bush would have found in religion a source of calm not wholly different from alcohol, as well as a set of rules that helps him manage both the world around him and his private world within. An exploration of the role of fundamentalism in Bush's life will show that the replacement of substances is just one of several ways in which Bush relies on religion as a coping mechanism. Kleinian theory emphasizes religion's capacity to discourage intellectual independence; along these lines we'll see that Bush uses religion to simplify and even replace thought, so that in some ways he doesn't even *have* to think. By positioning himself on the side of the good— of God—he places himself above discussion and worldly debate. Religion serves as a shield to protect him from challenges, including those he might otherwise pose to himself. Having banished disagreement, doubt, and even serious thought, Bush takes solace from a pervasive sense of certainty. Finally, the sheer simplicity of his solutions makes them easy to convey to others, allowing him to convert them readily into changes in government and policy—the arenas in which the impact of his faith is felt most dramatically by the rest of the world.

What is remarkable about George W. Bush's faith, beyond its apparent intensity, is its relatively recent origin. Bush's famous walk on the Kennebunkport beach with Reverend Billy Graham, who asked him if he was "right with God," took place in 1985; within less than a decade, he was the abstinent, multimillionaire conservative Christian governor of Texas, more religious than his parents or any of his siblings. By 1999, he was comfortable enough in his new-found spirituality to write in his campaign autobiography *A Charge to Keep*—the title taken from the name of a painting he hung in the governor's office in Texas because it reminded him that "we serve One greater than ourselves"—that Jesus Christ is the "author of a divine plan that supersedes all human plans."

How did he reach this point? The Bush family tradition has long been fueled by faith, by belief in a God linked closely to moral rectitude. In *The Faith of George W. Bush,* Stephen Mansfield writes that George W. Bush's ancestor James Bush "was possessed of a deep spiritual nature" and became an Episcopal priest. After a traumatic fire on a voyage to South America he said, "Is it not by the courage always to do the right thing that the fires of hell shall be put out?" As a result, "do the right thing" became the Bush family motto, passed from generation to generation. Morality and religion continued to be linked; grandfather Prescott Bush, who was seen as stern and "righteous," was called "the Commandments Man," and George W. remembers how Prescott once publicly rebuked Nelson Rockefeller for divorcing his wife to marry a divorcee.

Yet President Bush's religious orientation represents an important departure from his family. Though certain aspects of the family tradition have been maintained—notably the formality of religious participation—his mid-life conversion to a more fundamentalist approach stands in dramatic contrast to the spiritual life of his father, for example, who lost votes in the 1992 campaign when he couldn't lay simple claim to having been born again. Perhaps George W. Bush was more receptive to the idea of conversion because a combination of circumstances—his learning disabilities, drinking problem, dissolute behavior, and business struggles—had conspired to make him need it more. And a review of the events leading up to Bush's conscious embrace of fundamentalism shows that it clearly occurred at a moment when he was reaching for solutions, in a time of almost desperate need.

The process was set into motion in 1984, a year before Bush's fateful conversation with Billy Graham, when evangelist Arthur Blessitt, renowned for walking around whatever town he visited carrying a twelve-foot-high cross, came to Midland, Texas. Though his father was vice president, George W. Bush had yet to find his footing in business, struggling through a series of bad oil deals amid an industry slump that was affecting the entire region. As he wrote in his memoir, "Midland was hurting. A lot of people were looking for comfort and strength and direction." Bush's own troubles at the time, of course, were more than financial: He was still plagued by whatever fallout his drinking had caused in his increasingly high-profile family.

As Mansfield tells the story, Bush's profile kept him from comfortably joining the other citizens of Midland at Blessitt's events at the basketball arena downtown. Instead, Bush met Blessitt at the Holiday Inn coffee shop, where the evangelist asked Bush if he was confident he would go to heaven if he died that day. When Bush couldn't answer yes, Blessitt posed the following question (worthy of any push-poll Lee Atwater ever designed): "Would you rather live with Jesus in your life, or without Him?" Bush's affirmative response—though hardly surprising—inspired Blessitt to pray for the Lord to "take control of [Bush's] life" and "make [his] home in heaven."

Heaven figures prominently in another important stepping stone that Mansfield identifies in Bush's spiritual path: the conversion of Bush's friend and fellow heavy drinker Don Jones. In 1985, shortly after making a New Year's resolution to quit drinking and read the Bible, Jones had a life-changing experience at home one day after reading the following verse from John: "Unless a man is born again he shall not see the kingdom of God." Despite his encounter with Blessitt and the experience of his friend, however, Bush still was unable to tell Graham that he was "right with God" when Graham asked him the question later that year, though he credits Graham with planting "a mustard seed in my soul, a seed that grew over the next year. . . . It was the beginning of a walk where I would recommit my heart to Jesus Christ." After that meeting, his mother told friends that "George has been born again," and within a year he had joined his friend Jones both in Bible study and on the wagon.

Clearly, Bush was motivated by the search for relief—from doubts about his behavior, his business prospects, and, most important, his drinking—while on the road to conversion. George W. Bush might not be inclined to agree with Karl Marx's observation that "religion is the opiate of the masses," but when he stopped drinking Bush discovered that spirituality could serve as something like his own personal opiate, offering him the means to calm himself in the absence of liquid spirits.

The differences may be less pronounced that you'd think. Researchers have discovered that endorphins, a brain chemical that operates on the same opiate receptors as alcohol—with the effect of suppressing pain—can also be released after deep expressions of religious faith. Perhaps most widely associated with strenuous exercise, endorphins are thus also part of the brain's response to spirituality—not just moments of religious ecstasy, but a steady, calming diet of faith.

Here the link between ADHD, alcohol, and religion becomes clearer: Endorphins modify anxiety and satisfy cravings. Dopamine, an endorphin that facilitates communication between nerves in the brain, is also involved in the "sensation of reward we experience from something we enjoy." According to a study in the journal *Neuron* detailing addictive behavior patterns in the brains of gamblers and cocaine addicts, an area of the brain gets activated in anticipation of winning; the prospect of reward—anticipation of prayer or alcohol—has a calming and focusing effect that is itself addictive. Research from the director of medical genetics at City of Hope Medical Center in California reveals that "certain people have genetic abnormalities in their reward systems" that can "lead not only to potential problems with addictive behaviors but with impulsivity in general."

The brain's response to these chemicals is so powerful that "endorphins have proven to be just as addicting as morphine and heroin," Robert Ornstein and David Sobel report in *The Healing Brain*. In this light, religion can be seen as a system of endorphin-mobilizing ideas relied upon by more addicts than any controlled substances. Indeed, because of the powerful effect of endorphins—some of which are many hundreds of times more powerful than morphine—faith is undoubtedly one of the most powerful ideational suppressors of pain known to man.

From a neurochemical standpoint, Bush's faith serves not only to rectify the wreckage left in the wake of his drinking, but also to numb the pain he drank over (not to mention the sting of missing his favorite chemical relief). But when we numb our pain, even with our body's own pain-killing substances, we sometimes avoid resolving it. Pain is a source of information; being able to feel pain, like being able to feel anxiety, is necessary for the preservation of mental and physical health. The weightlifter's phrase "no pain, no gain" is equally relevant to psychological development; those who avoid emotional pain and its resolution only simplify and limit their understanding of the world.

Religious faith is based on beliefs that are held in the absence of concrete verification—thoughts and feelings that Freud called "illusions" because they are based on the individual's wishing them to be true. Whether religious or secular, these unproven beliefs are often designed to protect the individual from pain. The idea that simply wishing something to be true will somehow benefit the individual can be compared to the placebo effect in medicine. The patient taking a sugar pill sees positive results only because he believes it to be a powerful medication; nevertheless, the relief can be real, seemingly giving rise to some chemical change within the body. The question remains whether the belief itself is accompanied by a chemical change; though the mystery involved in the placebo effect may still be beyond the reach of neurochemistry to explain, the benefits remain nonetheless.

The conscious benefits of belief are easier to assess: Regardless of their basis in fact, beliefs simplify one's intellectual life. They narrow the debate, reducing the number of questions to be answered and possibilities to be explored. This is especially evident with faith-based beliefs that extend beyond the purview of reason, those that depend more on wishes than evidence. And as they order and simplify the believer's universe, they have the same effect on his inner world.

Fundamentalist religion narrows the universe of possibilities even further. It divides the world into absolutes of good and evil, rejecting allegorical interpretation of the Bible for a rigid, literal-minded approach that leaves no room for questions. The view of the self is similarly simplified. Just as fundamentalist creationist teachings deny history, the fundamentalist notion of conversion or rebirth encourages the believer to see himself as disconnected from history. George W. Bush's evasive, self-serving defense of his life before he was born again displays just this tendency. "It doesn't do any good to inventory the mistakes I made when I was young," he has insisted. "I think the way . . . to answer questions about specific behavior is to remind people that when I was young and irresponsible, I was young and irresponsible. I changed. . . ." To the believer, the power of spiritual absolution not only erases the sins of the past, but divorces the current self from the historical sinner.

The impulse to call upon godlike constructs to simplify one's inner world dates back to the primitive fantasies of childhood. "The primitive mind endows its world with agents," writes psychoanalyst Joan Symington. "It makes a god or gods the cause of those events which affect man." The child's primitive mind focuses this capacity on his parents; when the parents are absent or unavailable, the outside world becomes a more dangerous place, and other, equally potent internal gods assume the role of persecutors. Without the parent-gods around to protect him, the forces of evil that populate a child's internal world become more threatening, even demonic; the child must reject the wider world, and fashion his internal gods as ones of exclusion, not inclusion. This phenomenon may help explain the degree to which Bush—a child of wealth and privilege—limited his exposure to the world around him. By his own admission, he didn't "pay attention" at Yale; after college, as the *New York Times* has observed, his "overseas experience was pretty much limited to trying to date Chinese women (unsuccessfully) during a visit to Beijing in 1975." The tendency to see the greater world as a land of gods and demons links with a child's need to pretend, and with the childlike perception of the world as animistic and magical. Children naturally have a sense of omnipotence within their imaginary world—hence the common pastime of inventing imaginary friends, who are under the child's control. These imagined figures are filled with the child's ideas and wishes and fears. They may seem to represent hatred or evil, and therefore be demonic; or they may be filled with the child's reactions *against* fear, and thus be seen as loving, not hateful. The origin is unconscious and subjective, but to the child the figures are powerful. They are at once a source of danger and a requirement for survival. Even when repressed, these thoughts still exert power on the conscious mind.

Pretending frees the mind from the limitations of material reality, facilitating the child's transition from fear to resilience and confidence. If a child perceives his father to be malignant, he can get revenge in adulthood by displacing his feelings through sports and other forms of rivalry. One of my patients symbolically killed her mother every day by imagining that the tennis ball she threw up in the air for her serve was her mother's head. (Her service game improved measurably.)

When a child inflicts his ability to pretend on others, though, problems can arise. The same mechanism that allows the individual to feel a direct connection to God has sometimes enabled my patients to pretend that I will protect them in ways beyond my role as a psychoanalyst—or to imagine that we are developing a romantic connection. When they try to act on such fantasies, the consequences are predictably more severe. Pretending can be a prelude to action, but it must involve thought. If an individual's worldview is founded on pretense, such thoughts are likely to be oversimplified, if not avoided altogether.

The individual who clings tenaciously to unverified beliefs confuses his beliefs with fact, and often inflicts this confusion on others in his struggle to resolve it in his favor. When many people are persuaded to subscribe to the same pretense, of course, it can gain the aura of objectivity; as British psychoanalyst Ron Britton has observed, "we can substitute concurrence for reality testing, and so shared phantasy can gain the same or even greater status than knowledge." The belief doesn't become a fact, but the fact of shared belief lends it the valuable appearance of credibility. The belief is codified, takes hold, and rises above the level where it might be questioned. Shared beliefs can come to define a community; religion is, after all, a communal structure, uniting groups in shared beliefs. In societies where religion is especially powerful, such shared beliefs can actually become law, imposed on others, often restricting their behavior.

Communities are more likely to develop around beliefs when their previous beliefs have been challenged. Witness the environment in the economically depressed former boomtown of Midland, where George W. Bush was just one of many who responded to their shared adversity during the 1980s by developing a newfound commitment to religion. People whose beliefs have been shaken are more susceptible to direction from others, and those who step forward with an air of certainty to offer guidance—even an evangelist dragging an oversized cross in and out of the Holiday Inn—become attractive sources of strength to those yearning for a way out.

Within a primitive society, the fundamentally important survival instinct leads its members to magnify the importance of their own tribe—and to denigrate all others. Other tribes are lumped together as the enemy; one's own tribe functions as an extension of self, and all other tribes are seen as dangers to the self and its survival. A tribe united primarily by tenets accepted only on faith—by shared illusions or wishes, in Freudian terms—thus experiences any threat to its beliefs as a threat to the tribe, and by extension its individual members. The more tenaciously a group arms itself with a fixed belief, the more fragile it becomes when confronted with anything that might cause anxiety or inner conflict. This is true of any belief system, even of mine: psychoanalysts are willing to tolerate all kinds of variations within their ranks, so long as no one utters any doubts about the basic efficacy or value of its fundamental postulates.

As president, George W. Bush has doggedly courted national support for his beliefs, anxious to see them gain stature and become a part of the permanent national creed. He seems to have understood from the start, instinctively, that if simplicity works for him, it can work for many others. His efforts, of course, were aided immeasurably by the national shock of September 11, which found many previously disengaged Americans suddenly hungering for a sense of shared purpose. For Bush, this historical moment offered an opportunity to inflict his beliefs on others. His blend of nationalistic and religious rhetoric, masterfully marshaled by his speechwriters, helped Bush to create a tribe of believers deeply invested in his beliefs, and highly likely to personalize any challenge to them—as the persistent belief in a link between Iraq and Al Qaeda, despite all evidence to the contrary, demonstrates.

There's nothing inherently unnatural about Bush's reliance on his faith for protection. The faith that comes from identification with an omnipotent figure restores a sense of inner peace, protecting the believer from feelings of helplessness or powerlessness. That identification is a two-part process: First we identify the omnipotent figure, then we internalize at least some measure of that omnipotence. The second part of the process is crucial, because ultimately the negative aspects of ourselves—the destructive self described by Klein, or the death instinct that Freud discussed—are the forces we seek to protect ourselves against. We all have unconscious beliefs that protect us from giving too much rein to the darker sides of our internal reality—our aggression and envy, the reality of grief and loss, the knowledge that we are going to die. Calmness is purchased at the price of what Ron Britton calls a "pervasive sense of unreality."

Though his faith gives Bush strength—and makes him stronger, I think, than many suspect—the rigidity of his patterns of thought and speech, and of his schedule, point to a considerable fragility. His fears—of everything from disagreement to terrorist attack—are at times painfully visible, even (or especially) through his denials. He is a man desperate for protection. But what is George W. Bush so eager to protect himself against? His tightly held belief system shields him from challenges to his ideas—from critics and opponents, but, more important, from himself. Just beneath the surface, it's hard not to believe that he suffers from an innate fear of falling apart, a fear too terrifying for him to confront. Though Bush might be loath to concede any insight to the man who brought us the New Deal, there may be nothing he fears more than fear itself.

The adult's ability to process fear is linked to his experience in infancy, when the baby's most threatening terror is a fear of fragmentation, of losing his nascent, fragile sense of self. This dread of fragmentation is a relevant fear for Bush. He's appeared close to falling apart in public repeatedly; after wandering off track while speaking, his statements disintegrate into often meaningless fragments until he finds his way, ends the discussion, or attacks the questioner. In an interview on CNN, impressionist Darrell Hammond—who makes his living analyzing the speech patterns of political figures—aptly described Bush's demeanor when losing his way: "He just decides, *This sentence is worthless to me.* It's like, 'We're working tirelessly to— look, we're tireless. . . . Look, I'm tired of this sentence.'" Bush's discomfort isn't always as phlegmatically charming as Hammond makes it seem, however. On Easter Sunday 2004, when a reporter asked him yet again about the Presidential Daily Briefing in which he was warned of Osama bin Laden's intention to strike the United States, Bush actually laughed—the anxious giggle that so often comes over him when he comes under attack—before settling into a nervous smile and claiming that the memo contained no specific plans. (Days earlier, in response to a similar unwanted question, he had been in full attack mode: "Who are you talking to?" he snapped at a reporter who addressed him only as "sir," instead of "Mr. President.")

For someone so desperate not to lose his way, clinging to a belief (or even a few key phrases), and sticking to them, is yet another way to protect against falling apart. President Bush's press conferences have offered disturbing evidence of this ongoing anxiety—evidence so unmistakable that it's little wonder the White House has proven so hesitant to schedule such events at all. After one particularly disastrous performance in July 2003, the *Slate* political columnist Timothy Noah noted that "Bush seemed jangled"; in a damning editorial the following day, the *New York Times* noted that the president's answers were "vague and sometimes nearly incoherent"—suggesting, perceptively, that Bush was "bedazzled by his administration's own mythmaking."

Indeed, as Noah pointed out, during the press conference Bush depended so heavily on a few repeated phrases that words like "progress," "freedom," "justice," and, especially, "the threat," began to seem like mantras:

> And so we're making progress. It's slowly but surely making progress of bringing the—those who terrorize their fellow citizens to justice, and making progress about convincing the Iraqi people that freedom is real. And as they become more convinced that freedom is real, they'll begin to assume more responsibilities that are required in a free society. . . .

> And the threat is a real threat. It's a threat that where—we obviously don't have specific data, we don't know when, where, what. But we do know a couple of things . . . obviously, we're talking to foreign governments and foreign airlines to indicate to them the reality of the threat. . . .

> I don't know how close we are to getting Saddam Hussein. You know—it's closer than we were yesterday, I guess. All I know is we're on the hunt. It's like if you had asked me right before we got his sons how close we were to get his sons, I'd say, I don't know, but we're on the hunt.

> Well, first of all, the war on terror goes on, as I continually remind people. . . . The threat that you asked about, Steve, reminds us that we need to be on the hunt, because the war on terror goes on. . . .

> I just described to you that there is a threat to the United States. . . .

There is no doubt in my mind, Campbell, that Saddam Hussein was a threat to the United States security, and a threat to peace in the region. . . .

Saddam Hussein was a threat. The United Nations viewed him as a threat. That's why they passed twelve resolutions. Predecessors of mine viewed him as a threat. We gathered a lot of intelligence. That intelligence was good, sound intelligence on which I made a decision. . . .

I analyzed a thorough body of intelligence—good, solid, sound intelligence—that led me to come to the conclusion that it was necessary to remove Saddam Hussein from power. . . . We had— remember there's—again, I don't want to get repetitive here, but it's important to remind everybody that there was twelve resolutions that came out of the United Nations because others recognized the threat of Saddam Hussein. Twelve times the United Nations Security Council passed resolutions in recognition of the threat that he posed. And the difference was, is that some were not willing to act on those resolutions. We were—along with a lot of other countries—because he posed a threat. . . .

Every day I'm reminded about what 9/11 means to America. That's a lesson, by the way, I'll never forget, the lesson of 9/11, because—and I remember right after 9/11 saying that this will be a different kind of war, but it's a war, and sometimes there will be action, and sometimes there won't, but we're still threatened.

Whether one relies on a set of stock phrases in a press conference, or a set of religious beliefs accepted "on faith," the need to cling to a new object can become an act of desperation. George W. Bush has also been known to rely on the much-needed presence of his wife, Laura, refusing to be away from her for more than two days at a time during his father's 1988 campaign. Similarly, Bush's rigid sleep and exercise schedule serves to protect him against the challenges of the unexpected, much as an infant must be protected

against night terrors. Even the war in Iraq barely interrupted his routine: As the *San Francisco Chronicle* reported, Bush left for Camp
David in the first hours of the war, "was not awakened to be told of
the first American casualties Thursday night[,] has kept up his rigorous exercise regimen, and even made time aboard Air Force One on
his way back from a final meeting with allies in the Azores last week
to watch *Conspiracy Theory,* the latest Mel Gibson movie."

So powerful are his fears that he can't even face them. His infa-
mous early advice to Americans less than two weeks after 9/11—
when he told Americans to continue to shop and travel as before, in
apparent denial of the radical measures he was at the same time taking
in response to the nation's newfound vulnerability—suggests just
how simplistically he viewed the situation, closing himself off to
worry and anxiety. Compare his response to that of New York's
mayor, Rudolph Giuliani, who faced his fears, rolled up his sleeves,
and got to work—making people feel far safer than Bush's stilted denial ever did.

In protecting himself from his fears, Bush may believe that he is
protecting the rest of us as well. But the result is quite the opposite.
Denying anxiety is not the same as experiencing and managing it. The
baby whose parents never help him manage his fears lacks the means to
face them and respond accordingly as an adult. The president, who
shows no sign of consciously experiencing anxiety or fear, instead
passes it on to the rest of us—either intentionally (to maintain power
and overcome feelings of helplessness), or unconsciously (to evacuate
anxiety, avoid thought, protect against feelings of mourning and loss,
evade responsibility and guilt, deny the threat of falling apart). To ex-
ternalize his internal terror, Bush bullies others or instills fear in the
hearts of his fellow citizens. In his fear of being, or appearing, afraid,
he may well be one of the most frightened men in America. More and
more, the press finally appears to be taking notice of Bush's behavior:

*American Prospect* editor-at-large Harold Meyerson has recently written that Bush is a president "who had no trouble sending our young people to Iraq but who cannot steel himself to face the Sept. 11 commission alone."

George W. Bush has likely been protecting himself from what he fears, and relying on his simplistic inner world, for his entire life. Certainly, he has been searching for ways to hide from his anguish since his sister's death. Several months after Robin Bush died, while watching a game with his father and some of his business associates, young George alarmed the group when he turned to his dad and said he wished he were Robin—because, he explained, she had a better view of the game from above the stadium than they had in the stands. The charming vision of a child, perhaps—and yet Bush's adult behavior suggests that he has yet to learn to face the meaning and consequences of darker emotions like grief and loss, showing little awareness of the anguish or doubt that a president should feel when sending his nation to war.

Instead, Bush assembles a false and brittle front of bravado out of a few borrowed phrases and gestures of pretend bravado. Similarly, his escapades on the deck of the battleship *Abraham Lincoln* were designed to reassure America that he felt good about the war in Iraq—that he had reached the end of his simplistic inner script, and the "mission" had been gleefully "accomplished." And yet even the Bible, which Bush claims to have studied closely, counsels against such responses: Ever since God angrily silenced the angels rejoicing in the defeat of the armies of Egypt, celebration over killing the enemy and ignoring collateral damage has been part of a long, sad tradition. Rather than learn such valuable lessons from the Bible, though, George W. Bush uses religion to protect himself from challenges, and to reinforce his profound alienation from the pain of loss.

eligion doesn't just replace doubt with certainty; it replaces ambiguity with dualism—something that would make a person like
George W. Bush, whose worldview has likely remained split and unintegrated from infancy, much more comfortable. The world of terrorism, of course, is fertile ground for a perspective divided into good and
evil. In the war on terror—in which Bush's opponent was first Osama,
then Saddam, then terrorists in general—Bush can see himself as the
force of light against darkness. Banishing ambivalence and nuance
from his mind, he envisions himself in a belief system as fixed as his
fundamentalist faith—which can be used to justify all kinds of behavior, since it views the world as full of one kind of infidel or another.

The sense of certainty that Bush affords himself by donning the
trappings of fundamentalism goes beyond the relative black-and-
white clarity of the dogma of his chosen faith. He cloaks himself in
the certainty of being good, absolving the self of responsibility even
for destructive acts, disregarding the possibility that he could make a
mistake. Nearly a year after Bush sent American troops to war on
pretenses now proven false, Tim Russert reminded the president of
how his dogged certainty on the Iraqi "threat" had been adopted—
and acted upon—by the like-minded people around him:

**RUSSERT:** Mr. President, the Director of the CIA said that his briefings had qualifiers and caveats, but when you spoke to the country, you said "there is no doubt." When Vice President Cheney
spoke to the country, he said "there is no doubt." Secretary Powell, "no doubt." Secretary Rumsfeld, "no doubt, we know where
the weapons are." You said, quote, "The Iraqi regime is a threat
of unique urgency." "Saddam Hussein is a threat that we must
deal with as quickly as possible." . . .

**BUSH:** . . . There was no doubt in my mind that Saddam Hussein was a danger to America. No doubt.

**RUSSERT:** In what way?

**BUSH:** Well, because he had the capacity to have a weapon, make a weapon. We thought he had weapons. The international community thought he had weapons. But he had the capacity to make a weapon and then let that weapon fall into the hands of a shadowy terrorist network.

Bush's confidence in his goodness, and in his being right, derives from the certainty of his convictions, religious and otherwise. But certainty, which has to do with refusal to make the important distinction between belief and knowledge, comes with a price: It is only when one is uncertain, when one relinquishes a belief after finding out that it is false, that one acquires new knowledge and coping skills. One must give up the lost belief in order to see how internal fantasies distort experience and compromise psychological growth. A more realistic worldview provides an opportunity to solve problems in new ways, as one becomes better able to differentiate between internal fantasy and external fact. An inflated since of certainty, on the other hand, can actually diminish an individual's authority, which is typically based on compromise and self-awareness. Bush's troubling inability to deal effectively with opposition, and get along with the world, arises directly from this handicap.

Certainty, when it replaces doubt, also replaces the capacity to think—making it somehow easier to act. Thoughts and ideas may persist, but the apparatus to think them is completely dismantled because it can only function as a simple machine. The rigid mind faced with challenging circumstances is like a simple water pump suddenly asked to analyze and purify the water it delivers, or to ponder whether it's even necessary for particular crops. A simple pump cannot do all that.

It just keeps pumping, asking us to trust that its water is healthy and life-giving.

———➤———

The presidency of the United States would seem to be an odd career choice for someone so threatened by ambiguity and complexity. But George W. Bush has displayed no doubt about his decision to pursue the office—or to pull out all the stops running for a second term. "Given the rambling non-answers the president gave to questions about Iraq and the economy," the *New York Times* observed after Bush's July 2003 press conference, "it was interesting to hear how focused he was when someone asked how, with no opponent, he planned to spend $170 million or more on the primary. 'Just watch me,' Mr. Bush said concisely. There is one area in which the president's thinking is crystal clear."

In fact, Bush's ascension to political power is the aspect of his life in which his obsessive need for order and embrace of Christian spirituality are perhaps most explicitly—and troublingly—intertwined. Bush has been surprisingly explicit in declaring that he sees himself on a mission from God, and it is his belief in that divine assignment in which we see the most potent combination of politics, psychology, and faith at work.

Bush's certainty in his religious mission was the premise for his run for the presidency. Before the 2000 election, writes Mansfield, Bush told Texas preacher James Robison, one of his spiritual mentors: "I feel like God wants me to run for president. I can't explain it, but I sense my country is going to need me. . . . I know it won't be easy on me or my family, but God wants me to do it."

Of course, Bush knew his audience, and these could simply have been the words of a politician rehearsing what he would have to say to the religious right to get elected. (And then again: "I always laugh when people say George W. is saying this or that to appease the religious right," Bush cousin John Ellis told biographers Peter and Rochelle Schweizer. "He *is* the religious right.") Or he could have been trying to extinguish the doubt that would understandably strike someone with only six years of public service (and little more than twice that many years of divine service) seeking the most powerful elected office in the world. From what we have observed about his psychology, however, it's apparent that Bush needed to believe that he was in fact answering whatever call from on high he understood himself to have received.

Bush has continued to cite divine instruction to explain his actions since assuming office. As reported in Israel's *Haaretz News,* Bush said, "God told me to strike at al Qaida and I struck them, and then he instructed me to strike at Saddam, which I did." Though his administration insists that the war on Iraq is not a religious war, at least one high-ranking official says otherwise: Lieutenant-General William Boykin, the deputy undersecretary of defense, who shares the president's views on Bush's divine destiny. "He's in the White House because God put him there," Boykin said after claiming that our "spiritual enemy will only be defeated if we come against them in the name of Jesus." Boykin is also reported to have described the war as a struggle between Christianity and Satan.

The White House has officially distanced itself from Boykin's assertions, yet has refused to censure him. So perhaps Boykin is indeed God's deputy—not just from his perspective, but also from the president's. Certainly, most of this administration, from Bush on down, is populated by fervor-struck men like the general, whether religiously, ideologically, or both. And Bush is clearly of a mind that if God has chosen him, then the blessing extends to the nation that Bush has been chosen to lead. Among the many implications of being so "chosen" is the status that every other nation is not. This is a solipsistic, ultimately dangerous, way of thinking. The mental hospitals used to be full of people playing Napoleon. Now the merchandising machine of the religious right offers little toy action figures of George Bush in his flight jacket, so that the true believers can play American Avenger—and no doubt encourage their children to do the same.

For Bush's faith is nothing if not evangelistic. The world knows of the force of his religious influences; the White House has never seen so many Bible study programs and regular prayer meetings as it has under Bush, and religious leaders are always well received. He has appointed other deeply religious people to his cabinet and as top advisors; he has made the promotion of faith-based initiatives a central tenet of his presidency, and urged the federal government to support faith-based institutions from religious schools to charities. He opens every cabinet meeting with prayer and a daily reading from *My Utmost for His Highest.*

Bush wants the rest of us to believe the way he does; it's an extension of his mission as a Christian and as a politician. In his last year as governor, while he was running for the Republican presidential nomination, he declared an annual "Jesus Day" in Texas, urging "all Texans to answer the call to serve those in need. By volunteering their time, energy or resources to helping others, adults and youngsters follow Christ's message of love and service in thought and deed." Bush has a very personal stake in his spiritual mission, demonstrated by his response to the outcry after he told a Jewish reporter that Jesus was the only way to heaven: "It was, of course, picked up and politicized," he said. "You know, 'Bush to Jews: Go to Hell.' It was very ugly. It hurt my feelings." The feelings of millions of Jews, of course, went unmentioned.

Bush's evangelism also pays political dividends. The more voters he manages to convince that he was chosen by God to lead the nation, the more likely he is to be re-elected. In soliciting the voters' mandate, Bush is seeking consensus verification of his otherwise un-verifiable tenets of faith—tenets on which he has based both his presidency and his personal salvation. Bush's countless steps to blur the boundary between church and state are merely extensions of his efforts to order his internal chaos through the rigid doctrines of religion. Unfortunately for those who don't share his convictions, he is less sensitive to the personal stakes others might have in keeping those boundaries intact. Nor is he particularly tolerant of others' own quest for salvation: He dismissed born-again Texas death row inmate Karla Faye Tucker's plea that her spiritual conversion should spare her from execution on the grounds that such conversions are common in prison—and somehow less genuine than his own conversion amid the personal prison of despair fueled by alcoholism and business failure.

Now he plays all of this out on the world stage. The almost prophetic warning of imminent danger that accompanied his call to the presidency has evolved into the politicization of evil with which he has waged his wars. The Biblical struggle of good and evil has resonated throughout his discourse since 9/11, from his repeated use of the term "crusade" to his characterization of the terrorists as "evildoers" and grouping of Iraq, Iran, and North Korea as the "Axis of Evil." At the same time, he presents the United States as nothing more than a nation of wholly innocent victims. The evildoers hate "us" solely because they envy our freedom, our way of life, our God. "They hate progress and freedom and choice and culture and music and laughter and women and Christians and Jews and all Muslims who reject their distorted doctrines." In externalizing evil this way, while absolving America of responsibility, Bush has transformed his unintegrated infantile worldview into a starkly combative (and primitive) foreign policy.

Bush's rhetoric highlights how he identifies the concepts of himself as president with both God and America: For him, these three appear to have become somewhat interchangeable. Unable to mourn the dead

of 9/11 enough to allow for a full investigation of how it happened—
and what responsibility we might have had—he blindly attacks the
"enemy" he perceives to be everywhere, a terrorist suddenly hiding
under every rock. The more we spread freedom—allegedly, the very
thing we think the enemy envies—the more enemies we create. And
the more closely we align ourselves with the angels, beyond reproach.

Resolve and fear are not separate, however; killing others increases fear of being killed oneself. Melanie Klein proposes that we
are all unconsciously subject to the biblical Law of Talion, a psychological version of "what goes around comes around" or "he who lives
by the sword dies by the sword." The prospect of divinely ordained
retribution makes the destructive person more frightened. The more
Bush sends American troops to spread violence around the world, the
greater his fears of retribution will be, and the greater his need to resort to violence once again. In trying to heighten security, he actually
is heightening his sense of danger. And by making our world seem
more dangerous, he creates a permanent, self-fulfilling justification
for his behavior.

When a child attacks his mother, in his fantasy he splits her into
pieces. I witnessed this phenomenon with particular vividness in
one patient of mine, who had a recurring childhood fantasy of
blowing up her parents' house with her chemistry set. In college,
she told her friends that her parents were dead. But when she had to
give speeches later in life, she froze: suddenly, everyone in the audience looked like her mother. What happens is that the attack on a
whole, rather than annihilating it, fragments it into smaller pieces
that all are poised to retaliate.

Bush is doing much the same thing in the war on terror—with
one important difference: The fragmenting is taking place not just in
his own head, but in a world he has plunged into battle. His war on
Iraq has had the effect of multiplying Bush's enemies around the
world, from the European allies he rejected to the Iraqi terrorists

whose numbers have mushroomed in the wake of his preemptive war. The result is inevitable: George W. Bush has created a situation in which he (and thus his followers) will feel, and be, perennially persecuted. Increasingly frightened of the inevitable recourse of his actions, he shuttles between a series of staged and heavily protected settings; even during his fall 2003 trip to Great Britain, our staunchest ally, Bush and his advisors were sufficiently daunted by the threat of protest that they canceled the president's plans to address Parliament.

And still he wraps himself in rectitude, externalizing terror and denying his own destructive tendencies. His unconscious awareness of Biblical law, which promises that he will be held to account for his actions, may haunt him deep inside. And yet, when asked by Tim Russert to explain the atmosphere of international contempt for him, Bush took refuge in the only source of solace he knows: stubborn consistency. "Heck, I don't know," he shrugged. "I think that people—when you do hard things, when you ask hard things of people, it can create tensions. And I—heck, I don't know why people do it. I'll tell you, though, I'm not going to change, see? I'm not trying to accommodate—I won't change my philosophy or my point of view."

# FIVE

# OUTLAW

*In one hand I've a Bible—In the other I've got a gun*
*Well, don' you know me? I'm the man who won.*

—The Eagles, "Outlaw Man"

WHEN FREUD WROTE in *The Future of an Illusion* that "every individual is virtually an enemy of civilization," he identified a central fact of human nature: Society creates laws, but individual members of that society resist them. By their very nature, laws are not a product of instinctual life or personal desire; they are created to protect people from each other. As they promote the growth and protect the survival of the group that creates them, laws challenge individuals to combat their instincts and live under legal authority.

The Law of Talion, the Biblically cited psychic law of retribution, serves a similar function. By instilling a fear of discovery and retaliation, it helps us control our destructive impulses. George W. Bush's refusal to accept blame for any wrongdoing suggests a consistent desire to live outside the Law of Talion. Like most forms of denial, the idea that one remains safe from attack by denying wrongdoing is at best a temporary defense, but it provides an illusion of safety that can be used to justify one's actions.

The Law of Talion is just one of many laws of both the state and the psyche that Bush's actions appear to defy (or at least deny). A review of his family and personal histories, as well as his presidency, reveals a long and rewarding pattern of evading the law and making up rules to justify destructive behavior. From the alcohol-fueled indiscretions and questionable business tactics of his first four decades, to his more recent conduct in office—abrogating "more international treaties in the first year of his presidency than any other executive in American history" (according to biographer Stephen Mansfield), and exhibiting a flagrant disregard for the truth—Bush has comfortably and repeatedly conducted his life outside the laws of the land and the psyche. What's more, he seems to do so with an absence of remorse or internal conflict that places him even more at odds with the civilization he has been entrusted to lead and protect.

Once again, the Kleinian model of the development of the infant's worldview holds the key to understanding the psychological processes at work. The individual who projects his destructiveness, rather than integrating it into his worldview, is more likely to fear getting caught than to experience guilt about not living up to internal standards. His inner world, in extreme cases, is peopled by sadistic and vindictive figures; as psychoanalyst Roger Money-Kyrle has said, "they suggest a pack of devils rather than a God of Love." An adult with this developmental defect tends to regress from the need to recognize that he can love and hate the same person; such an individual finds it necessary to project hate outward, and to cling to feelings of persecution in defense against guilt, or a need to make reparations to loved ones for any harm he might have caused.

Freud identified two character types he encountered clinically among individuals who disregarded the law: criminals who possessed what he called "an unconscious sense of guilt," and people who felt normal laws didn't apply to them, whom he termed "the Exceptions." The latter type comes close to what we know of George W. Bush.

The Exception is someone who felt deeply injured in early life, and therefore feels entitled to live outside the limitations that apply to ordinary people. Bush's simplified, conflict-free approach to his inner life exempts him from the normal trials and tribulations that come with responsibility. As we'll see, Bush was further protected by his family—not just by its wealth, but by its history of disregarding laws and its skill at rescuing young George when needed.

B ush was born into a family that was simultaneously of the law and above it, steadily accruing the power to legislate even as its actions moved further from the law. His mother is descended from President Franklin Pierce, his grandfather Prescott Bush served in the U.S. Senate, and his father is a thirteenth cousin, twice removed, of Queen Elizabeth II of England. Though the family's considerable wealth and privilege would eventually contribute to young George's seeing himself as an "Exception," the manner in which the Bush family amassed its fortunes had at least as great an impact on the development of his worldview. Historian Kevin Phillips details the Bush family's often-ambiguous relationship with the law in *American Dynasty,* a damning and invaluable historical look at the familial influences on our president's psyche. "Four generations of building toward dynasty," Phillips writes, "have infused the Bush family's hunger for power and practices of crony capitalism with a moral arrogance and backstage disregard of the democratic and republican traditions of the U.S. government."

Perhaps most notable among the "clandestine arms deals and European and Middle Eastern rogue banks" that Phillips describes are Prescott Bush's dealings, along with his father-in-law George Herbert Walker, with Nazi Germany. As numerous historians have documented, Prescott Bush had deep financial ties with key Nazi businessmen as late as 1942, when the U.S. government forced him to stop doing business with a number of German industrialists. Not only did he violate laws of morality by putting economic needs ahead of moral ones, his profitable business enterprises violated both the letter and the spirit of the federal Trading with the Enemy Act. But Prescott Bush's actions were ultimately overlooked, if not rewarded, as he made the transition from outlaw to "of-law": within a decade, he had been elected to the U.S. Senate, where he was serving when Andover accepted his grandson.

As a high school student, George W. Bush reportedly sold fake ID cards to his fellow Andover students, making a personal profit while helping others violate the drinking-age laws. But it wasn't until he went to Yale that he began running into direct trouble with the law—even as he drew closer to the law-making establishment. In late 1966, weeks after his father was elected to the House of Representatives, he was arrested for disorderly conduct in New Haven. The following fall—a time when he was deeply involved with his secret society Skull and Bones, which boasts countless leaders of industry and government among its members—he was detained and questioned by Princeton police for similar disorderly behavior. That fall also brought controversy to the DKE fraternity, of which he was president, for its practice of burning pledges with a hot branding iron. The imbroglio made the pages of the *New York Times,* where Bush was quoted as dismissing the wound as "only a cigarette burn."

In later years, Bush would downplay these incidents as harmless college pranks. And his denials might be less troubling if they didn't fit so neatly into his lifelong pattern of implying that he has never done anything wrong. Dodging responsibility can be seen as a typical component of his problems with alcohol, which no doubt played a central role in all three circumstances. For George W. Bush, drinking and evading responsibility have always coexisted—a fact that became dramatically clear when his DUI arrest was made public in the closing days of the 2000 presidential race. As reporters scrambled to investigate his background more closely, parsing his on-the-record remarks about his past, they discovered that he had spoken about his previous arrest record with extreme care—in an obvious (if ultimately unsuccessful) attempt to avoid being caught in a lie.

Living outside the law, denying responsibility, and keeping secrets were all linked early in Bush's experience, and there's little evidence that this has changed. "Once ensconced in their offices at 1600 Pennsylvania Avenue," John Dean writes in *Worse Than Watergate,* Bush and Cheney "quietly closed their doors, pulled the shades, and began making themselves increasingly inaccessible to the media and Congress while demanding complete control over government information. Government under a virtual gag order became their standard operating procedure."

This behavior appears to have reached a zenith in the days following the 9/11 attacks, when Bush set into motion secret "continuity of government" plans. "With little notice, and no announcement, men and women throughout the federal government in Washington . . . were transported by Military district of Washington helicopters and buses to one of the two East Coast underground facilities," Dean writes. "What started as precaution soon became permanent," remaining secret until March 2002. As Dean points out, "It is difficult to trust a co-presidency hell-bent on enhancing its powers through secrecy, demanding that it be held unaccountable, and willing to mislead the nation into a war."

Living outside the law turns any questioner into a policeman in Bush's mind. He behaves more and more like a criminal who sticks tenaciously to his story, often in the form of random stock phrases that may or may or not apply to the point at hand. In his April 13, 2004, press conference, he laced his answers to a variety of questions with the same few epigrams: "prior to 9/11 the country wasn't on a war footing" (the same sound bite, word for word, that Condi Rice had delivered to the commission on April 8), or "now is the time to talk about winning this war on terror," or "a free Iraq will change the world."

From his Skull and Bones membership to his time in the White House, Bush has carried on the family tradition into which he was born, one that Phillips describes as "the culture of secrecy . . . deceit and disinformation [that] have become Bush political hallmarks." As his grandfather's business history made evident, the Bush family lived by its own private laws. His father continued the tradition, functioning outside the law while ostensibly living inside it—serving as the head of the CIA, and participating as vice president in the Reagan administration's efforts to cover up wrongdoing in the Iran-Contra scandal.

All families have their secrets and their private language and culture; as a family therapist, I find myself learning a new language with each new family with whom I work. But having a private, family-specific culture is one thing; carrying on a tradition of living above the law is quite another—especially within a family of lawmakers and presidents.

⌇

What we see in the combination of political power and amoral behavior common to the Bushes is a sense of omnipotence—both psychological and social. Omnipotence has its psychological roots in early childhood. All children pass through a stage characterized by delusions of omnipotence, which is typically followed by a period in which reality intrudes and we begin learning about our limitations. When this progress is somehow impeded, however, the omnipotent fantasies of our early childhood can expand into adult delusions of being an exception to the laws that govern everyone else.

Ironically, the seeds of omnipotent thinking are planted in the period of life when the infant is actually quite powerless, plagued by fears of falling apart. Though he may depend on his caregivers for feeding and comfort, the infant constructs an internal reality with an entirely different power structure. Omnipotent fantasies help the baby cope with the helplessness and frustration caused by his limited ability to manipulate his environment: When his mother is present, he tries to make his needs known without use of language; when she is absent, he hallucinates her to keep her near and cries when he wants her to return. When she answers his cries and appears, ready to feed him, change his diaper, or otherwise address his physical needs, the baby sees this as evidence of his omnipotence: He speaks and the world reacts, assuaging his fears of disintegration. His mother—or whoever is responsible for his care—is expected to understand his wishes and do his bidding appropriately. Life is simple, and he is all-powerful; there are no laws governing the universe other than the satisfaction of his demands.

No limitations, no accountability: It's a recipe President Bush might recognize. "The interesting thing about being the president," he explained to Bob Woodward in *Bush at War,* is that "I don't feel like I owe anybody an explanation." He continues in that frame of mind when dealing with the 9/11 Commission, agreeing to attend only in closed session under the watchful eye of his vice president, and refusing to take an oath to tell the truth. He remains outside the laws of history and responsibility. In an unconscious mockery of his mother's hatred of the search for truth—whether about her husband who was so often away from home, or about her dead child, or even about her own mother—Bush blocks others' attempts to investigate him the way his mother must have blocked him when he was a child.

Of course, the infant is not as omnipotent as he would like to believe. Inevitably, his needs are not met as promptly or effectively as his delusions lead him to expect. As he comes face to face with reality, he learns that he doesn't control his mother's thoughts and must solve his own problems by discovering other methods to manage anxiety and meet his needs. The discomfort of confronting his own limitations often inspires aggressive fantasies of attacking the caregivers on whom he depends. These destructive fantasies usually begin to disappear by the end of childhood, as the infant's delusions of omnipotence are modified by the limitations of reality—a process central to intellectual growth and development. But for some individuals who fail to outgrow the infant's defenses of splitting and projection, and thus never develop the capacity to feel concern about hurting a loved one, this primitive, pre-moral destructiveness can persist well into adulthood.

What happens when reality intervenes and a child's wishes actually come to pass, even through no action of his own? If a sibling rival should actually die, for example, it may only cause the omnipotent fantasies to persist—perhaps linked with guilt and a sense of responsibility. The nature of such feelings of hostility is that they must continually be both satisfied and denied. Satisfaction can come in derivative ways, such as sadism and mockery; denial can take the form of narcotizing the hatred with alcohol or other means, even including religion. Still, that omnipotent sense of power persists in the unconscious. I had a patient who was brought to the clinic at age sixteen for disemboweling three pregnant sheep on his father's farm. He had never relinquished his unconscious hatred of his own mother for having so many children after he was born. His behavior came as a total surprise to the family, who had heretofore regarded him as a model big brother.

Another source of delusions of omnipotence can be a troubled relationship between infant and mother, one in which the child's dependency needs are regularly unmet. If the child's cries should go unanswered too often, he will stop asking for help. Instead, he compensates for the failing relationship with his caregiver by developing an ability to act more independent than he in fact feels or is capable of being. This pose of competence presents a defense, a camouflage, against the child's dependence—a phenomenon not uncommon in first-born children, who often prematurely turn their backs on childhood needs and act like a "big boy (or girl)" taking care of the next in line.

The Bush family's push toward self-reliance, evident in the available portraits of George W.'s childhood, helps explain how he came by his familiar outgoing personality. Beneath the boyish bravado, though, his adult autonomy is actually illusory; the harder he tries to deny his dependency, the more clearly he expresses it—through drinking, through being born again, even through his habit of making public jokes at his mother's expense. In one oddly telling public service announcement released in September 2003, Bush is asked by a young audience member whether his family took meals together during his childhood. "I did eat with my family," Bush answers, "so long as my mother wasn't cooking." Then Barbara herself reveals the purpose of the ad: "It's not good making fun of your mother—even if you are president. But it is good to have dinner with your kids. We know the more often children have dinner with their families, the less likely they are to smoke, drink, and use drugs."

He also make jokes at the expense of his wife (on whom he so clearly depends), telling reporters that she has gone back to Crawford "to sweep the porch, because the president of China is coming tomorrow." But his ultimate expression of dependency is his insistence on appearing with Cheney before the 9/11 Commission, a position so baldly cowardly that he proved utterly unable to defend or even attempt to explain it.

Omnipotence is also expressed as the sense of invincibility often seen in adolescents, who need to deny any dependency on their parents and disregard safety laws when engaging in certain behavior. Adolescence is associated with recklessness, with the delusion that one is immune to injury, exempt from the restrictions of others. Bush's willingness to risk arrest by driving while intoxicated demonstrates that he lived outside those laws at least until he quit drinking, behaving like an adolescent who never felt the consequences of his actions. Laura Bush recounts an episode that illustrates how he later transferred that adolescent dependency to his wife: After she criticized a

1978 campaign speech he gave—before he quit drinking—he acted out his aggression by driving their car through the wall of their garage. Alcohol itself fuels feelings of invulnerability similar to adolescent fantasies, even as it makes the individual more vulnerable to physical harm.

Adolescent omnipotence evolves into adult grandiosity, but they share a common pathology: Like the adolescent who feels he is never going to die, the grandiose adult denies the possibility of death, indulging instead in fantasies of immortality. Most adolescents behave this way at one time or another—driving too fast, drinking too much, taking too many risks in the spirit of assumed invincibility. The adult version of grandiosity can link to magical delusions in less perilous ways, from buying lottery tickets to investing in a new sports car. Unless we spend our entire paycheck on the Lotto, though, or endanger ourselves and others by totaling the car, we're in no danger of having these acts dominate our lives.

The same cannot be said for George W. Bush, who has brandished his "Wanted, dead or alive" mentality brazenly since September 11. By all appearances, Bush sees himself as the sheriff who can save the day. When he says he is going to hunt Osama bin Laden down and get him—along with destroying all other terrorists one by one—he appears to believe it, his magical thinking telling him that the agents at his disposal can do anything. He repeats his taunts over and over, like a child who says "I'm gonna get you" to a scary parent figure. To many, his insistence may seem to be an attempt to inspire confidence in others; far more likely, though, it's simply an outward manifestation of his own grandiosity.

There's no clearer example of magical thinking than the "Mission Accomplished" banner that served as a backdrop to Bush's flight-suit photo op on the *Abraham Lincoln*. Beyond the obvious wish that proclaiming victory would somehow magically convince people the war was over, the event displayed Bush's grandiose aspirations at their most extreme. He was even able to convince the military and secret service agents charged with protecting the president to let him risk his life landing in a jet plane on an aircraft carrier in time of war—and then, as John Dean has noted, "did nothing to dispel the illusion that he had piloted the plane to the deck." In truth, Dean notes, Bush was "a passenger in a pilot's costume." The action-figure toys made of Bush in his flight suit are inadvertently accurate interpretations of his behavior, the concrete personification of a childish fantasy.

Magical thinking never takes consequences into consideration, for every action based on magical thought is expected to have a positive outcome. The danger of magical thinking comes when one acts as if the magical beliefs are real, as in Bush's justification for invading Iraq. Did Bush make the link between Saddam Hussein and al Qaeda because Dick Cheney and others convinced him that he could fool Congress into justifying the war, as his critics have suggested? Was he trying to divert attention from the troubled economy, or from his failure to heed warnings about 9/11? Or is there another possibility—namely, that he actually *believed* the two were linked because he wanted so badly for it to be true? And since he can't accept that the result of acting on this belief will be anything but positive, his ability to assess and acknowledge the damage done is compromised in ways that the mounting death toll in Iraq and Afghanistan cannot transcend.

One aspect of magical thinking is the simplification of terms. In his major speech announcing the invasion—as in so many other speeches he has given since 9/11—Bush used sweeping phrases that simplified the emotional landscape of the situation. We were going to war against the "enemies of freedom," "rolling back the terrorist threat to civilization," challenging an "aggressive tyrant [who] possessed terrible weapons." All complexities were reduced to dichotomies: good versus evil, peace versus violence, civilization versus chaos—all grandiose variations on the us-versus-them division that shapes a mind-set like Bush's from infancy onward.

Defensive in nature, omnipotence is a means to protect us from self-recognition—from facing our complexity, our vulnerability, and our mortality. Omnipotence typically breeds arrogance, another defense against vulnerability. Kleinian psychoanalysts Wilfred R. Bion and Eric Brenman have each written that arrogance involves an unconscious alliance of various emotions—destructiveness, cruelty, and narrow-mindedness—that is often expressed as obstinate curiosity. What better description of the promise to hunt down terrorists one by one, no matter what it takes or how many innocent lives or countries get trampled on? By identifying with and drawing strength from our hopes and fears after 9/11, Bush can feel justified in unleashing destruction on Iraq: He is free to be cruel in the name of goodness. Bush's arrogance shines through his patriotic bravado and chest-thumping speeches, where it is often applauded; but it can also be seen in his nervous laughter, which betrays his underlying fear.

In political terms, Bush's omnipotence has proved to be a powerful weapon—for it appeals to the omnipotent fantasies in all of us. From the honest businessman who claims too many deductions on his taxes, to the loyal housekeeper who feels justified in stealing a little something, we all feel at least in part that we should be exempt from certain rules or limitations of life to make up for early injuries to our self-love. When Bush presents himself as someone willing to do anything he feels necessary to right the wrongs done to us, he may only be responding to his childhood fantasies of triumph over helplessness, but we can identify nonetheless. By shamelessly talking big, living large, and carrying an enormous stick, Bush takes his omnipotence to an extreme, but it is the extreme of a universal attribute we all share. He says the things we want to say and is indignant about the things we're all indignant about. This knack for tapping into our basic vindictive impulses has a nearly universal appeal (though, of course, we don't all act on our fantasies of killing the umpire).

Though his arrogance makes him popular, it comes at a price. Wilfred R. Bion points out that the part of the personality that hates internal law—the laws of reality, of time, of responsibility, of loss—hates external reality as well. It attacks links made in the mind, undermining the capacity to think and organize that comes from facing reality and its limitations. Living outside the law of mature responsibility becomes both the midwife of omnipotent fantasy and the mortician of the capacity to think.

In its paranoid fantasy that Saddam Hussein was a sponsor of terror, and that the United States is the nation chosen by God to protect the world from that threat, the Bush administration has tapped into the part of our personality that hates external reality and prefers to cling to a simplistic, secure worldview. And in Bush's constant antagonism toward the press—his press conferences and public statements are peppered with warnings about "trick questions" and not-so-veiled threats to punish skeptical questioners—the president has made it clear that he far prefers the refuge of his own blinkered worldview over the awkward challenges and intrusions of the truth.

The ability to process complex thought—to differentiate between our own omnipotence and the challenges of the real world—is one of the capacities that help us distinguish fact from fiction. And it is in Bush's failure to make this distinction—deliberately, unconsciously, or both—that his comfort with living outside the law is perhaps most apparent. George W. Bush's inability and/or unwillingness to maintain fealty to the truth is so central to his presidency and political life that it has inspired a growing number of courageous, important books, most notably Al Franken's *Lies and the Lying Liars Who Tell Them* and David Corn's *The Lies of George W. Bush*. As Corn writes: "So constant is [Bush's] fibbing that a history of his lies offers a close approximation of the history of his presidential tenure." Lest the reader dismiss Bush's behavior as mere politics as usual, Corn reminds us that the "honest-man routine" was central to Bush's campaign: "a candidate who rises to power by denouncing lies," he points out, "warrants more attention when he engages in dishonest behavior."

The ease and frequency with which Bush misrepresents the truth gain new resonance when seen in the context of a personality that considers itself exempt from the laws that govern others. Why doesn't he tell the truth? Because he doesn't have to. Bush gets away with lying not because he is good at it—he's not—but because in his formulation there's nothing to get away with: The laws of accuracy mean little or nothing to him. In this light, his simplified worldview is especially important: His capacity to identify and convey the truth relies on a mental apparatus so primitive and misguided that he may well be unable to recognize its limitations and mistakes. Though there's no way of knowing for sure—even for him—we've seen enough of his personality to suspect that he may actually believe many of his dubious claims; encumbered by a self-serving, underdeveloped way of seeing the world, he simply lacks the tools to differentiate telling lies from speaking the truth.

This is not the place for an exhaustive review of Bush's many misrepresentations, a service that has been performed effectively elsewhere by Franken, Corn, Ivins, and others. Thanks to their efforts, we know that Bush has distorted or lied about his military service, his business dealings, his arrest history, his Texas political record, his campaign opponents, his rationale for war, and the ramifications of his policies for starters. What is perhaps even more startling is the certainty with which he denies what is all too obviously a way of life for him. "I have been very candid about my past," he claimed in 2000, at a press conference after the revelation of his DUI arrest (about which he had been anything but candid); after the event, he boarded a campaign plane he and his handlers had dubbed Responsibility One.

It's striking how freely Bush has engaged in distortion or deception—that is, defied the authority of truth—on questions that have to do with defying other forms of authority. Take the matter of military service, for example—particularly government-sanctioned mandatory service. Bush has repeatedly misrepresented his military service in the National Guard, from which he has been accused of going AWOL before cutting short his required service time. Not only was he able to call on family friends to get himself exempted from fulfilling his requirements, he even exempted himself from telling the truth about what service he did perform.

The next authority he successfully evaded after the military was the Securities and Exchange Commission (SEC). Bush's late and faulty compliance with SEC requirements surrounding his profitable sale of Harken Energy stock in 1990 has been well documented, as has the likelihood that he benefited from insider information. Here, too, he compounded his dishonesty by offering conflicting explanations and ultimately misrepresenting the conclusion of his run-in with authority, claiming to have been exonerated in correspondence from the SEC that specifically said this was not the case.

This flagrant flouting of authority—of the law—took place before he essentially became the law, first as governor and then as president. Not surprisingly, it has continued throughout his time in office. According to Bob Woodward, he has even defied the authority of the Constitution—by taking money allocated for Afghanistan and diverting it to fund his planned invasion of Iraq. Others have assembled lengthy litanies of Bush's many broken public pledges, campaign and otherwise, documenting the ease with which Bush says one thing and does another. What is relevant here is the continuity between his past defiance of authority and his current failure to live up to his word. Now that he holds office, the authority he defies is his own. His broken pledges bring to light his failure to respect and execute the authority he has been granted. His attitude suggests that he feels this is his right, whether by birth, by law, or because of his perceived "Exception" status.

As David Corn reports, when Bush was pressed on a broken tax pledge in Texas, he responded with a dismissive "there are pledges all the time," as if he were free to violate any pledge he might have made. More recently, he dodged Diane Sawyer's questioning about the failure to uncover WMD in Iraq with a rhetorical question of his own: "So what's the difference?" Not only was Bush revealing his belief that he didn't believe there truly *was* a difference—he was also challenging her to call him on his sudden, unilateral disavowal of the very claim he had used to justify the invasion. It was a challenge he must have felt safe in making; after all, to a man so blithely able to dismiss one of the central premises of his foreign policy, what possible obligation could there be to be honest and forthcoming in a television interview?

The more closely we look at George W. Bush, the more clearly we see a man who cannot live within the constraints of his own ascending power. Here is a businessman who missed four consecutive SEC filing deadlines for reporting his Harken stock trades. Here is a candidate who alleges that his opponent "will say anything to get elected," and then proceeds to do the same himself. Here is a contested winner of the Florida popular vote who says "we have a responsibility to respect the law and not seek to undermine it when we do not like its outcome" and then complains that "the court cloaked its ruling in legalistic language." Here is a president who proclaims, "We must uncover every detail and learn every lesson of September 11th" and then fights the commission formed to do just that. Here is a man who declares, "I take personal responsibility for everything I say," and then evades and dissembles when the media try to hold him to his promise.

In his response to Diane Sawyer, Bush displayed once again his familiar contempt for anyone who would dare hold him responsible for his actions. Other examples are equally flagrant. When asked about German Chancellor Schroeder's belief that Bush was violating international law by preventing France and Germany from investing in post-invasion Iraq, Bush sarcastically quipped, "International law? I better call my lawyer!" If international law can be so easily dismissed, one wonders just what the president does take seriously. Lawyers are for people who live outside the law—who violate laws and have the misfortune of getting caught. Of course, Bush doesn't really feel the need to call his lawyer; he lives above the law, not outside it. The laws that apply to others are irrelevant to him. He doesn't seem himself as breaking laws, but as transcending them.

This contempt for anyone who might challenge the individual's notion of his being an Exception is a predictable psychological consequence of living above the law. This is accompanied by a subtler vein of contempt for those who obey the law. By leveraging a small investment in the Texas Rangers into a multimillion-dollar windfall, Corn notes that Bush the businessman "became independently wealthy because he was part of an enterprise that pushed for higher taxes, that violated property rights, and that benefited from corporate welfare"—even as Bush the politician made a career depriving others of the same opportunities by carrying the banner of tax cuts, property rights, and welfare reform.

In her own interview with Diane Sawyer, the president's mother hinted that this vein of contempt for the common man may be a family trait. With the Iraq war dawning, Mrs. Bush told Sawyer that she would watch "none" of the televised war coverage. "Why should we hear about body bags and deaths and how many, what day it's gonna happen?" Mrs. Bush mused. "It's not relevant. So why should I waste my beautiful mind on something like that?" Those body bags, of course, would soon be filled with the remains of law-abiding soldiers who volunteered for military duty, sent off to their death by a president who had used family connections to avoid seeing military action decades before.

Thus far, the president has avoided making such impolitic comments about our men and women in uniform. But he has revealed comparable contempt through his actions, turning his back on the flag-draped coffins that commemorate the suffering caused by his war, and joking in public about being unable to find WMDs under his White House desk. His self-mocking behavior—aimed to blunt press criticism—reveals yet again how he turns his back on the bloodshed brought by his false claims.

---

Predictably, the world doesn't always agree with an individual's delusion that he deserves to be treated as an Exception. When this happens, he may rely on others to come to his rescue. For Bush it was his father, or his family name, that frequently saved him—from the family friend who engineered his berth in the National Guard to his father's former chief of staff who engineered his triumph in the Florida recall (with a little help from his dad's Supreme Court appointee, Clarence Thomas). Even the Harken Energy deal, which set young Bush on the path to financial independence, itself depended on his name. As John Dean points out, George Soros, who owned part of Harken, has said of Bush's involvement: "We were buying political influence. That was it. [Bush] was not much of a businessman."

This reliance on rescuers underscores how the individual living outside the law can actually be dependent in unexpected ways. Though not consciously dominated by rules, he is nevertheless dominated by the need to stay safe and secure while living outside them. Consider the experience of another of my patients, a heroin addict in her early twenties who left home at fifteen to get away from her controlling mother. She traveled around the world, feeling totally free. Yet her addiction gave the lie to her sense of autonomy; unable to live without her fix, she ended up enslaved to her habit much the same way she had felt enslaved by her mother. Bush has a similar quality: Though he appears to be free to make his own decisions, he is a slave to special interests as he formulates those decisions, and to his self-preserving mantras as he tries to explain them. He appears free from the constraints of law, yet is a slave to his coping mechanisms—and to the rescuers who save the day when all else fails.

A person who is always rescued misses out on both the opportunity and the impetus to grow. His potential to develop internal controls and regulators is compromised; his aspirations are as unrealistic as the rest of his life. Likewise his solutions: When a problem confronts Bush, finally breaks through the bubble of Crawford-land, he can offer only nostrums, or impractical measures (a Homeland Security bureau that excludes the FBI and CIA; a domestic SWAT team to stop corporate fraud). His approach to problem solving recalls the child who thinks that wishing can make it so, that things will get better and problems will magically go away: *Saddam is captured, therefore America is safer than ever.* With magical thinking always available to provide the desired results, genuine thinking can be put off until the real world dispels the illusion.

The individual who lives outside the law ultimately stops seeing the world as being real. Problems are not only simplified, they become dismissible. The dangers of arsenic in drinking water can be ignored; damage to the environment can be overlooked; concrete claims about Iraqi WMD can simply be forgotten. Even Kenneth Lay, a former business colleague, longtime correspondent, and Bush's single biggest campaign contributor before the 2000 election, can be dismissed as merely one of many contributors—a blatant attempt at outright denial he unleashes so frequently that it might be called

KWD (the "Kenny Who?" Defense). Until March 2004, Bush had denied ever receiving a memo warning of the possibility of 9/11-style attacks; once the details of the August 6, 2001, PDB could no longer be denied, he simply shifted gears and began to deny the memo's significance.

Since new knowledge poses a threat to his fixed ideas and fixed worldview, an Exception like George W. Bush must narrow his horizons in order to avoid the kind of discordant information that might threaten his sense of omnipotence and cause psychic discomfort. Not only does he fear *discovery*—the threat that ultimately motivates stonewalling techniques such as the KWD and his refusal to turn documents over to various investigatory commissions; more deeply, he fears *discovering,* having to take in any evidence that his way of seeing things is flawed—the kind of evidence he might encounter, for example, if he were so bold as to pick up a newspaper on his own.

Bush's tunnel-vision omnipotence may ultimately make him dependent on others to solve his problems. But he fights that image—and creates a facade of independence—by playing the role of the rescuer. The man who acts like a savior, of course, has a far easier time convincing himself and others that he doesn't need to be saved. He becomes the *deus ex machina* for others. This is a piece of deception and delusion that Bush and his handlers have mastered. When he swoops into Baghdad on Thanksgiving, he looks like a war hero, though he is anything but. He plays the role of the rescuer—the provider with the prop turkey, produced for showing, not serving—though such shallow acts of bravado obscure his true life story in which he was rescued so many times himself. The ultimate personal cost is that Bush inhabits an unreal world whose laws are dominated by his magical expectations that things will work out the way they do in the movies. With his ability to solve problems thus compromised, he risks ending up like the movie character-turned-real person in Woody Allen's *The Purple Rose of Cairo,* who had only fake money to pay his restaurant bill. Bush's theatrics may fool others, but it is unlikely that he can completely fool himself.

Despite his efforts at denial, Bush's dependency on others must dog him like an addiction. And like an addict warding off feelings of fear and desperation, a person living outside the law must continue to do so—to refresh the feeling of invulnerability necessary to ward off the limitations of reality. The more he manages to lie without consequence, the more outrageous his lies must become.

It's this kind of mindset that allowed Bush to take his narrow, hotly contested election to the presidency and treat it as a mandate for radical change. Deluded by his fantasies of omnipotence, yet somehow also aware that his "election" was actually his biggest rescue yet, Bush must have felt compelled to up the ante higher than he might have if he had won the popular vote. Unable to accept any doubt about the legitimacy of his presidency, he promises bipartisan cooperation when he gets to Washington—then does whatever he wants, asserting his legitimacy by venturing further and further from the law. None of this is necessarily conscious; denying his dependency, denying the lie of his omnipotence, he lies not only to others but also to himself, about what he does, what he knows about himself, and how he feels inside.

Ultimately, Bush cannot afford not to believe his lies. Living outside the law requires the use of major psychological defenses to maintain one's personal sense of safety, and to retain a feeling of omnipotence, unburdened by blame or internal conflict. The simplest and most readily accessible way to achieve this self-regulation is that first, primitive defense mechanism—the projection of destructive behavior. He must maintain the split between good and bad with increased vigor, always at the ready to eliminate anyone who disagrees with him.

One danger of extensive omnipotent fantasies is that they eventually make a figure like Bush feel invulnerable: Dominated by what psychoanalyst Meg Harris Williams calls the "temptations of ignorant omnipotence," he ends up overlooking the inconsistencies in his own stories. After Bush was forced to make the August 6, 2001, DPB public, for example, he tried to claim that there was nothing specific in it. During his April press conference, like Condoleezza Rice before him, he tried to claim that "there was nobody in our government, at least, and I don't think the prior government that could envision flying airplanes into buildings." And yet moments later he explained that he had requested the terrorism briefings because of earlier alerts about the July 2001 Genoa G-8 conference—alerts, it turns out, that had warned the president that "Islamic terrorists might attempt to kill President Bush and others by crashing an airliner into the Genoa summit."

And yet, paradoxically, he must keep the enemy around, for psychological as well as electoral reasons. The eminent psychoanalyst Vamik Volkan has written that we need an enemy to rally the community around a "chosen trauma." Almost immediately after 9/11, Bush began speaking of the war, in grandiose terms, as a kind of epic and eternal struggle; by July 2003, as the Iraq war was quickly proving to be more difficult than initially advertised, he was reduced to repeating that "the war on terror goes on, as I continually remind people." Making the war against terrorism perennial keeps him in power, by keeping that terror externalized. When your enemy is as real as a dirty fugitive in a hole, and as resilient as the threats behind America's recent Orange Christmas—the orange-level terror alert that was declared at the start of the 2003 holiday season—it's easy to get away with living above the law.

Yet the Orange Christmas itself reveals how Bush's efforts to live above the law come full circle. Shortly after apprehending Saddam Hussein on December, Bush seems to have seen the world as once again a much more frightening place: As if cowering at the prospect of the Law of Talion's threat of reprisal, he put his nation under a state of elevated alert and anxiety (to match his own?)—then disappeared from December 22 until his January 1 quail hunt with his father, while America suffered through the Ten Days of Terror.

The one law the president cannot evade, it seems, is the Law of Talion.

We've seen Bush's sense of omnipotence threatened before—in the hours following the attacks on the World Trade Center and the Pentagon. All of us were understandably frightened, but Bush's fear at first appeared paralytic: He continued reading to the third grade class he was visiting for a full twenty minutes after he was told that the first tower had been hit. Then he fled for an entire day, serpentining across the country until the coast was clear and he finally made it back to Washington. The government issued the cover story that Air Force One was targeted for attack that day—a claim later proved to be false.

The attacks of 9/11 must have undermined Bush's sense of omnipotence, recalling his early childhood feelings of humiliation and inadequacy. After he recovered, though, his language was stronger than ever; now, suddenly, he felt emboldened to promise that he would rid the world of evil itself. The "war on terror" has occasioned some of the most overtly grandiose and omnipotent proclamations ever uttered by an American president. "This conflict was begun on the timing and terms of others. It will end in a way, and at an hour, of our choosing," he declared at the National Day of Prayer and Remembrance at the National Cathedral three days after the attacks. "It is the calling of our time to rid the world of terror," Bush said at a U.S. Attorneys Conference in November 2001. Ridding the world of terror, of course, is an order beyond what is humanly possible—as is the attempt to predict the end of such an effort with certainty. Such claims can make for sweeping, even inspiring rhetoric, but their essential hollowness cannot be denied; Bush's bold pronouncements ultimately serve as echo chambers for the fear of vulnerability their grandiose excesses cannot hide.

Bush's efforts to disguise his fears have proven to have many layers. At the surface is his trademark bravado—a boyish glib enthusiasm for war, marked by schoolyard jibes like his challenge to "bring 'em on"—a sentiment belied by the unprecedented security measures with which he surrounds himself. At the next level is his denial of war's devastation—his apparent lack of any concern for civilians killed in war, or of any meaningful recognition of our own fallen servicemen and women. Such denial is but a step away from malign indifference and abject cruelty—the sadistic impulse explored in the next chapter.

Finally, when his fear of the reckoning dictated by the Law of Talion becomes too great for him to handle, George W. Bush evacuates his fear by spreading it throughout the nation he fears he cannot protect. The terror of which he promises to rid the world is in fact a different fear altogether: his intractable dread of his own individual punishment. And now that Bush has, in his grandiose imagination, identified himself with the entire nation, the nation has become the target for the personal retribution he fears is his due. As anyone who experienced the heightened levels of anxiety with which the nation brought 2003 to a close can attest, when Bush feels threatened, we all feel vulnerable. Tragically, that's probably an appropriate response.

# SIX

# THE SMIRK

*There are only two styles of portrait painting; the serious and the smirk.*

—Charles Dickens, *Nicholas Nickleby*

Long before he led our nation into war, George W. Bush exhibited an appetite for destruction. As a child, Bush inserted firecrackers into the bodies of frogs, lighting the fuses and blowing the creatures up. As president of his fraternity at Yale, he used a branding iron to maim young pledges. As governor of Texas, he was observed smirking over the executions of death-row inmates, many of whom were later found to have received inadequate legal protection.

Bush's tendencies toward sadism now play out on a bigger stage, with more resounding results. He orders bombings in Baghdad and proudly shows off the horrifying photographs of the bodies of Saddam's sons, almost daring the world to look away. He gets an even larger audience for the video footage of Saddam Hussein's humiliation in captivity, then demonstrates a very personal sense of triumph at his capture and glee at the prospect of his execution. Closer to home, the self-proclaimed "master of low expectations" behaves more like a master of dashed expectations, raising voters' hopes that he will demonstrate the compassionate side of his advertised brand of conservatism, then silencing them with righteous indignation when he repeatedly refuses to make good on his promises.

Bush's trademark smirk makes his sadism easy to spot today—unless, of course, the image has become so familiar that we no longer notice it. There was a day, not long ago, when Bush watchers were alarmed by the frequent, seemingly involuntary display. He flashed it perhaps most memorably in the presidential debates of 2000, when the pleasure he took in putting Texas criminals to death was clearly visible for all the world to see and hear: "Guess what? The three men who murdered James Byrd, guess what's going to happen to them? They're going to be put to death." At once arrogant and cowardly, the smirk heard round the world put the nation on notice that the act of inflicting pain—and the good fortune of having a job that allowed him to do so within the laws of the land—brought Governor Bush a certain pleasure that he couldn't quite stop himself from expressing.

The smirk drew enough attention in Bush's first presidential campaign that his handlers and defenders scrambled to explain it away, downplaying it as nothing more than a nervous tic. They were partially right; the smirk can be accurately interpreted as a sign of anxiety, which we now know runs perpetually beneath the surface of almost everything Bush does. But as real as that anxiety is, so is its source. The Bush smirk conveys both the pleasure he derives from inflicting pain, and the defense he mounts against the discovery of that pleasure—a disclosure of the sadistic impulse, and an attempt to deny the destructive self he cannot bear to acknowledge.

Though the sadist is by definition driven to administer pain in such a way that he can see and enjoy the effects of his efforts, he doesn't necessarily recognize the pleasure he derives from the pain he inflicts. If his compulsion is not consciously recognized, he may experience sadistic pleasure simply as indifference. Witness Bush's callous declaration to the National Security Agency in 2002: "I'd rather have them [American troops] sacrificing on behalf of our nation than, you know, endless hours of testimony on congressional hill." Such indifference serves as both an expression of sadistic pleasure and a defense against it: the very offhand nature of the coldly dismissive remark testifies to the speaker's lack of engagement.

On a conscious level, the sadist may experience his drive as vindictiveness, or as a desire to assert his power over the weak and defenseless (which is often vindictiveness directed at a more vulnerable target). He may also see his motives as greedy destructiveness, a wish to possess everything for the self and destroy it for others. Of course, some of these motives are more socially accepted than others. Many Americans celebrate the revenge Bush has exacted on Saddam Hussein, and others appear to accept domestic policies that place the weakest members of society at risk. Less universally embraced is the urge to hoard the earth's resources at the expense of the planet that we see in Bush's relentless pursuit of oil.

Lurking beneath the conscious justifications for sadistic behavior, however, is a dangerous perversion that holds the sadist in its grip. Despite the telltale smirk and the delight he sometimes demonstrates when speaking of the harm he has inflicted, Bush likely remains in denial about his sadistic tendencies and their pervasive influence on his actions. As a review of both the psychological underpinnings of sadism and the many ways in which they have come to the surface in Bush's life will reveal, he engages the nation both as agent and victim in a perilous psychodrama that rages far beyond his control.

Almost all of us have sadistic elements in our personality. During childhood, it is normal for us to evacuate our hateful feelings by attacking others. In traditional, Freudian psychoanalytic theory, sadism is viewed as a fundamentally anal phenomenon, which gets expressed in ideas about cruelty or dirt. Anal character was first described by Sigmund Freud and Karl Abraham—and later by Eric Erickson—after they observed that a particular triad of characteristics regularly occurred together: orderliness, parsimony, and obstinacy. The baby who is excited by having a bowel movement grows angry when that pleasure is denied him by his mother, who insists it be cleaned up and flushed down the toilet. The child then develops these character traits—a set of defenses against the urge to make an anal mess, a natural function he comes to see as a cruel attack on his mother. That is the basic essence of anal characters: Children who once enjoyed anal pleasures, and now find them prohibited, go overboard prohibiting them on their own.

What is important here is the link between anal tendencies in childhood and sadistic fantasies in adulthood. The anal child's wishes to inflict harm are often expressed through wishes to smear, to make sneak attacks from "behind," to play dirty tricks. The anal phase of development is usually mastered by the age of three, but children may return to anal solutions for their troubles throughout their lives. After discovering that his father is too dangerous to engage in direct rivalry, for example, such a child may retreat from his oedipal fears of his father into fantasies of anal attacks on less threatening representations of the father—such as animals or other children, with whom the child frequently alternates his cruelty with periods of great kindness. These alternating cycles may carry into adulthood: in a man's compassion toward his friends or colleagues one minute, followed by verbal abuse the next. Or the individual may contain the incongruity—by cultivating an extremely neat outward appearance, for example, that obscures his inward feelings of being "dirty."

Melanie Klein expanded on Freud's ideas about the anal and oedipal nature of sadism to include the child's envy of his mother's power as well. She identified the mother's role in helping the baby differentiate between "normal" and destructive aggression. Klein thought that a very hungry infant is unable to tell when his aggression is justified, and when it is destructive or murderous. The responsiveness of the mother is the key variable; if the mother fails to acknowledge and respond to the child's destructiveness, the child fails to learn the appropriate limits, and his aggression toward his mother is unchecked. Unable to contend with his dependency on his mother, the child feels a need to attack anything that reminds him of her power over him.

Sadistic fantasies are also a common expression of sibling rivalry, so the death of a sibling can serve to ignite the fuel of a child's existing sadistic tendencies; having played the role of the killer in his fantasies, the surviving child fears retaliation, and may temper the expression of his sadistic impulse, adding a smile or a wink so he can deny his actual dangerousness.

From his childhood on, a great deal of evidence suggests that George W. Bush harbors just such tendencies. One need think only of young Bush's invasive torture of frogs to see how this can be played out. Another story, which I heard firsthand from an Asian-American high school classmate of Bush, reveals a sadistic sense of humor in full bloom. After Bush called him by the nickname "Chief" for an entire year, the young man—an anomaly at what was then a mostly white school—confronted Bush and told him the derogatory nickname hurt his feelings. Bush apologized instantly—but then, the following day, called him "Cochise."

By the time he was branding college lowerclassmen in fraternity hazing hijinks, Bush's jocular sadism had metastasized into the infliction of real physical pain—"branding each initiate just above and in between the buttocks with the red-hot tip of a wire coathanger." His attempt to downplay the wounds as "only a cigarette burn" offers some insight into his frame of mind surrounding the incident, as does a much later defense he offered an interviewer when he claimed the procedure never left a scar. Such attempts to minimize his actions almost defy listeners to confront Bush with the obvious question: What kind of person would actually burn someone else with a lit cigarette?

(And, as my own experience with a patient who burned herself repeatedly with cigarettes made sadly clear, they do leave scars—every last burn.)

———✦———

Now that he is president, Bush can express his sadistic impulses in subtler ways. He has institutionalized his sadism, which he metes out as revenge or vindictiveness against political opponents. He humiliates members of Democratic congressional committees by locking them out of the political process, allowing them to speak only through the committee chairmen. He betrays Senator Edward Kennedy—to whom Bush's father had awarded the highest possible medal from the Bush family library—by ostentatiously soliciting his cooperation on Medicare, then signing a bill that gutted all of the senator's hard-won compromises.

The anal/sadist individual may also project his anal anxiety onto others he perceives as being dirty, a process that gives rise to its own set of anxieties. Bush is noticeably fastidious about his appearance, insisting on proper dress at all times—as if all his dirt has been banished, projected into the nation's enemies (who spend their time, as he constantly contends, hiding in "holes in the ground)." But Bush has also used his administration to evacuate his "dirtiness," by playing "dirty tricks" on others—passing the Patriot Act and Medicare legislation in the middle of the night, for example, or appointing accused racist Charles Pickering to the federal bench over the Martin Luther King holiday break. John Dean, who knows about presidential dirty tricks, claims that the Bush administration "plays even rougher with its enemies than Nixon's." According to Dean, this reached a low point in the White House's highly controversial disclosure that the wife of a Bush critic was a CIA agent. "Planting (or leaking) this story about Valerie Plame Wilson is one of the dirtiest tricks I've seen in lowball/hardball politics," Dean writes. "I thought they played dirty at the Nixon White House, but this is worse for two reasons. Nixon never went after his enemies' wives, and he never employed a dirty trick that was literally life-threatening."

More subtle is the sadism that Bush expresses by teasing voters with promises he doesn't fulfill. He acts as if he is promoting the greater good, then delivers much less—a pattern of raising and then dashing hopes that he repeats too frequently to be written off as mere accident. Molly Ivins and Mark Dubose highlight the cruelty of several of these events in *Bushwhacked,* a book that dares to hold Bush accountable for the pledges he makes to others. His sadism is most evident in the stories they tell of assistance he falsely promised to ease people's suffering—reaping the political rewards of making a $15 billion humanitarian pledge to fight AIDS with money that had already been earmarked for it (despite his own threats to siphon it elsewhere), or grabbing credit for providing low income heating assistance when, again, he was simply releasing funds he had tried unsuccessfully to cut. Ivins and Dubose also detail the travesty of Bush's assault on the meat inspection system—designed to prevent the torturous illness that ensues when contaminated meat reaches the public—which gained new relevance when an isolated case of mad cow disease was discovered in the meat supply.

People with AIDS, impoverished families living without heat, and the elderly and infirm (who are especially vulnerable to contaminants in the food supply): all classic powerless victims of the sadist's cruel impulses. Most fit the profile of the undesirable "other" who would scarcely be surprised to be on the receiving end of Bush's indifference, if not his outright contempt. "I don't understand how poor people think," President Bush told Reverend Jim Wallis, the leader of the Call to Renewal group of churches, after the 2000 election. Three years later, Wallis told *New York Times* reporter Elizabeth Bumiller that Bush had failed as a compassionate conservative. According to Bumiller, as president elect Bush had "appealed to [Wallis] for help by calling himself 'a white Republican guy who doesn't get it, but [would] like to.'" Apparently six years as governor of Texas wasn't sufficient to give George W. Bush an idea of the depredations of poverty.

But the fall and winter of 2003 saw Bush unleashing the false-promise tease on one of his core constituencies (albeit one that may remind him of the father he is unconsciously driven to destroy): American combat veterans. On a visit to Walter Reed Medical Center in the week before Christmas to look after his own medical needs, Bush came across a group of veterans to whom he claimed "a commitment [to] provide excellent health care . . . to anybody who is injured on the battlefield." These men and women were soldiers in the war on terrorism on which Bush has staked his presidency and the reputation of our nation.

And yet for months Bush's promises had been belied by reports of shoddy treatment coming out of the military's medical system. Bush had opposed expansion of the Pentagon's health-insurance system to include the National Guard and Reserve, and attempted to cut the budget for military family housing and medical facilities. The result, as UPI reported in October, was that "hundreds of sick and wounded U.S. soldiers including many who served in the Iraq war are languishing in hot cement barracks here while they wait—sometimes for months—to see doctors. . . . The National Guard and Army Reserve soldiers' living conditions are so substandard, and the medical care so poor, that many of them believe the Army is trying push them out with reduced benefits for their ailments."

An *Army Times* editorial in the summer of 2003 exposed Bush's empty praise for the military: "Talk is cheap—and getting cheaper by the day, judging from the nickel-and-dime treatment the troops are getting lately. For example, the White House griped that various pay-and-benefits incentives added to the 2004 defense budget by

Congress are wasteful and unnecessary—including a modest proposal to double the $6,000 gratuity paid to families of troops who die on active duty. This comes at a time when Americans continue to die in Iraq at a rate of about one a day." The editorial contained numerous examples, including various cuts in funds for building and even for basic pay. "Taken piecemeal, all these corner-cutting moves might be viewed as mere flesh wounds," the editorial concluded. "But even flesh wounds are fatal if you suffer enough of them. It adds up to a troubling pattern that eventually will hurt morale—especially if the current breakneck operations tempo also rolls on unchecked and the tense situations in Iraq and Afghanistan do not ease."

At the heart of this record of distorted and broken pledges is an all-too-evident indifference to the suffering of others, a passive manifestation of innate sadism. A hallmark of grandiosity, indifference reveals the individual's unconscious fear of conferring reality to other people. The indifferent individual seeks to avoid any recognition that others are autonomous or beyond his control, thus protecting his fragile sense of omnipotence from the fear of vulnerability and humiliation at the heart of his omnipotent delusions. Though passive in appearance, indifference functions as an active expression of triumph, a denial of the humanity of his victims.

George W. Bush's indifference is especially—startlingly—overt at moments when the times seem to call for expressions of concern and compassion. Around the time of the first anniversary of 9/11, his priorities were revealed in a rare interview he granted to *Runner's World* magazine. "I try to go for longer runs, but it's tough around here at the White House on the outdoor track," he told the reporters. "It's sad that I can't run longer. It's one of the saddest things about the presidency."

Similarly, on January 1, 2004—when 130,000 American troops were in Iraq, the United States was in the grips of an Orange Alert, and Iran had been devastated by a tragic earthquake that left more than 40,000 dead—the president was asked by reporters about his New Year's resolutions. In his response, he made a gesture toward the recent discovery of America's first case of mad cow disease—but reported that a second crisis was preoccupying his mind: an injured knee that was forcing him to cut back on his jogging. "My New Year's resolution this year is to work—stay physically fit to the point where I can run—in other words, rehab my knee," he said. "I miss running. The elliptical machine is good, but it just doesn't have that same sense that running gave me. So that's one of my resolutions— which may require eating less desserts, kind of getting a little trimmer, to take the pressure off the knee." Later in the interview he came closer to acknowledging concern for the suffering in the world, but could scarcely muster specifics: "It's going to be a year in which the world will become more peaceful and more people will be able to find work, and that's important." The indifference and detachment that are such a part of his personality have made it impossible for him to think in specifics, to feel genuine compassion, or even to remember the American losses in the war on terror unless reminded.

Despite his lip service to the compassion he promised voters, Bush's actions reveal the attitude of a man out of touch with the world's pain. Consider the days after September 11, 2001. Millions of Americans sprang into action; I know that half my patients gave blood within the week, and many of the residents of Washington, D.C., where I live and practice, applied to help with the clean-up at the Pentagon. What was Bush's advice at the time? He told us to hug our children and to fly more; he bemoaned the prospect that America might "let the terrorists achieve the objective of frightening our nation to the point where we don't conduct business or people don't shop." The childhood roots of Bush's defensiveness are obvious: He uses bravado and indifference to prove that terrorism has no effect. It was as if he wanted to impose his own inability to mourn onto the rest of us. And Bush seemed decidedly removed from the nation's pain during the lead-up to the war on Afghanistan; while the nation and his new hometown were mired in shock and grief, Bush left town every weekend for a month. He spent the day before the strikes began watching the University of Texas football game.

And it wasn't long before Bush began demonstrating his willingness to exploit the tragedy of 9/11 for his own political benefit. In an appalling joke he used repeatedly in his fund-raising speeches during the months following 9/11, Bush recast the tragedy as manna from political heaven: "I remember campaigning in Chicago and one of the reporters said, 'Would you ever deficit spend?' I said, 'Only—only—in times of war, in times of economic insecurity as a result of a recession, or in times of national emergency.' Never did I dream we'd have a trifecta." (Strangely, there appears to be no record of his using this campaign line in Chicago—yet another of his many misrepresentations of the historical record, which so often read as attempts to deny his own shame.) And by 2004, his trip to Ground Zero four days after 9/11 was being co-opted for his own self-aggrandizement, when his campaign decided to use images from his appearance (some real, some simulated with actors impersonating rescue workers) in its first major TV ad of 2004.

———❦———

Can such behavior be explained as a simple product of the abstractness of war? Hardly. Bush's indifference to human life found its most dramatic expression during his years as governor of Texas, when he presided over more executions than any governor in American history. Even as he continued to refuse her pleas for clemency, Bush felt able to mock Karla Faye Tucker in conversation with conservative reporter Tucker Carlson: " 'Please,' Bush whimpers, his lips pursed in mock desperation, 'don't kill me.' " That widely reported moment may have shown him at his most sadistic but Bush's role as executioner in chief has allowed his sadism to come out in a surfeit of other ways. He was heard making offhand comments or asides about several other victims, reportedly giggling when asked how he could send to death a prisoner whose attorney had slept through his trial. And he bragged about how difficult it was to escape the Texas death chamber, boasting that state law gives death-row inmates "one bite of the apple"—only one chance to make an appeal, even if new evidence turned up after the trial that might change the verdict.

Beyond providing a venue in which Bush could mete out the ultimate punishment, the Texas death chambers functioned as a tool he could exploit to spread fear. The sadist spreads fear for two important reasons: to inflict emotional pain and to assert and retain his power. Bush continues to express his sadism by instilling fear in others (when he isn't busily denying it). Consider the moment in the 2003 State of the Union address when he suddenly leaned over the lectern and almost whispered: "Imagine those nineteen hijackers with other weapons and other plans—this time armed by Saddam Hussein. It would take one vial, one canister, one crate slipped into this country to bring a day of horror like none we have ever known. We do everything in our power to make sure that that day never comes." Using the language of the sadistic bully, Bush had cruelly evacuated his own fears into everyone who was watching: that night, the state of the union was terrified.

In the same speech, Bush admitted to the cold-blooded murder of suspected terrorists who had yet even to stand trial. "All told, more than three thousand suspected terrorists have been arrested in many countries," he intoned. "Many others have met a different fate. Let's put it this way—they are no longer a problem to the United States and our friends and allies." *Let's put it this way:* Behind the forced familiarity of his tough-guy talk was the unmistakable message that Bush feels he can "put it" to anybody, and in any way, he wants. His threat is also an admission of his comfort with living outside the law, with what Princeton philosopher Peter Singer calls "killing people without any judicial process at all." As Singer has remarked, Bush "appeared to be proud of that fact."

What is at work here is a variation on the primitive anxiety-management tool of projection learned in infancy. Bush projects his fear into others so he doesn't have to experience it—bringing him one step closer toward neutralizing his own destructiveness and thus insulating himself from guilt or responsibility. The sadist expresses his sadism for both his pleasure and his protection; by evacuating his sadistic impulses, he can escape the fear that he might turn those impulses against himself with self-destructive results. As with so much of Bush's psychology, the goal is to maintain an inner life free from conflict—in this case, the conflict that can come from having to confront a desire to murder his father (in Freudian terms) or destroy his mother (as Klein would suggest).

For Bush, dropping bombs in the name of a "just" war offered a way to dispel tension while affirming the illusion of goodness that is jeopardized by inner conflict. By constructing an enemy, the individual constructs himself as good. By externalizing danger, Bush supports his idealized image of himself as an agent of good, one who speaks to and is aligned with God. If the object of his attacks is a known sadist, all the better: His own sadism may escape detection. But to keep the source of danger outside, the war on terrorism must continue to expand.

---

Indeed, the war in Iraq provided the most conspicuous expression of Bush's sadism. At the simplest conscious level, Bush's obsession with capturing Saddam Hussein was about payback—wreaking vengeance upon the man who had tried to assassinate his father. But Saddam fits into the pattern of Bush's sadism in several ways. At least up until his capture, Saddam served as a focal point for Bush's spreading fear. The 2003 State of the Union message is a case in point: as if what happened on 9/11 weren't terrible enough, Bush used Saddam to turn our pain into a fantasy of even greater pain, diminishing the real tragedy of 9/11 while trying to elevate his personal anti–Saddam vendetta into a new national crusade.

In the summer of 2003, Bush approved the widespread dissemination of the brutal and graphic pictures of Saddam's murdered sons. The gesture sent a vivid message about his insensitivity to the spectacle of violence and destruction. The fact that these were bad men—even very bad men—doesn't mean that showing their pictures everywhere wasn't a sadistic act. What it does mean is that Bush was eager to show the world the graphic remains of the enemies he had conquered. This is more interesting in light of the embargo on pictures of the arrival at Dover Air Force base of the flag-draped coffins of our own fallen troops—images that, when made public, revealed the toll of Bush's sadism on his own people. As his dealings with American war dead have made clear, Bush's behavior strongly suggests an unconscious resentment toward our own servicemen, whose bravery puts his own (nonexistent) wartime service record to shame. In past conflicts, respectful photography of the returning casualties of war offered a fitting tribute; in the Bush administration, such displays are prohibited for political reasons—and the result is a sadistic, symbolic negation of the troops the president sent into war under false pretenses.

By now it has become tragically clear that Bush built his case for war on Iraq upon the sands of deception. A year before the invasion, while still claiming publicly to be looking for a diplomatic strategy for handling Iraq, he privately told a group of senators: "Fuck Saddam, we're taking him out." The belligerent outburst—a throwback to Bush's hot-tempered days working on his father's campaigns—was arguably his last moment of candor on the topic. Bush subsequently lied about the threat Iraq posed with nuclear weapons and WMD, misrepresented its ties to al Qaeda and the 9/11 attacks, hid the fact that his administration began preparing for the invasion almost as soon as he assumed office, and denied in public that such preparation was underway. (As Woodward has since established in *Plan of Attack,* days after September 11—if not earlier—Bush was already determined to do something about Saddam Hussein.)

So much energy was spent spreading misinformation to justify the war that one wonders not only what was really behind it, but also why Bush felt the truth was so terrible that it had to be concealed. In fact, the psychological function served by the vilification and removal of Saddam Hussein virtually *required* Bush to hide it—from the nation and from himself. Incapable of safely confronting the true extent of his own sadism, Bush had to project his sadism onto an enemy of his own creation—one he entered the White House ready to demonize and destroy; one whose annihilation would serve to protect his own fragile, deluded sense of self.

Falling back on the primitive infantile apparatus of splitting off an unmanageable part of the self and projecting it into the environment, the sadist detaches his destructiveness and assigns it to someone else. In Saddam, Bush found the ideal vessel for his projected sadistic self. Because Saddam is already a known murderer—and a cruel one at that—he serves as a natural receiver for the sadism Bush must deny in himself; people see Saddam's sadism so clearly that Bush's can be easily overlooked. At the same time that he provides a ready home for Bush's projected sadism, Saddam supplies an easy target on which Bush can inflict harm. By destroying Saddam, Bush seeks to destroy the part of himself that is too sadistic to accept.

Such a symmetrical strategy may seem irresistible, even ingenious—yet it is doomed to fail. The destruction of the projected sadistic self is itself a sadistic act, an expression of the impulse the individual seeks to deny and destroy. It cannot quench the appetite for destruction, only perpetuate it. And so the president's psychic troubles play themselves out on the world stage, creating a vicious circle of escalating violence and an eternal search for new enemies.

And none of this has gone unnoticed by the public. Indeed, the pronounced parallels between Bush and Saddam may well have promoted a wider understanding of Bush's destructive self, rather than hiding it. As suggested by the many circulating photos of Bush's face digitally merged with Saddam's image—a computer trick that reveals a dramatic pictorial understanding of the process of projection—satirists instinctively understand that there is a pot-calling-the-kettle-black aspect to the showdown between Bush and Saddam. After all, during his years in the CIA and the Reagan administration, Bush's father essentially helped create Saddam by aiding his rise to power and arming him with the some of the weapons that he was later punished for having. In this case, it seemed, the pot (or its father, at any rate) had handed the kettle black paint.

As an undeniable sadist who gave full, unrestricted expression to his most perverse and violent urges, Saddam Hussein offers a clear illustration that the sadistic impulse leads to ever escalating levels of paranoia and cruelty. Allowed to spread his destructiveness without restriction, the sadist becomes deaf to his own unconscious—even while maintaining his sensitivity to the emotional lives of others, the better to inflict his torture. In order to tolerate his capacity for cruelty he must silence his humanity, deny the forces of love and compassion that might rein in his excess. He may lose the ability to distinguish between love and fear—the predictable, if extreme, expression of his inability to integrate the conflicting emotions in his primitive worldview.

The psychoanalytic theorist Otto Fenichel described how the deluded individual can confuse the arousal of fear with the expression of love. In the context of the president's family, we're reminded of Barbara Bush, "the one who instills fear"—and left to wonder about George W.'s efforts to outdo her by revealing the grotesque evidence of how *he* punishes (Saddam's) bad sons. Barbara Bush's grown-up son appears to have adopted a similar attitude toward the entire nation of Iraq, as if telling its people "I am killing you to make you free"—an attitude with which they are sadly already familiar after decades of Saddam's rule. Any glimmering of guilt can be avoided by evoking a higher authority. Bush draws strength from God or from America—goodness personified—and then feels free to practice cruelty in the name of goodness. Carried to its extreme, such a deluded leader may "omnipotently hijack human righteousness and conduct cruelty in the name of justice," Fenichel wrote in 1944, when the world was in the grips of another sadistic tyrant.

Bush's sense of omnipotence is highly individual, as is often apparent in his unscripted remarks about the war on terrorism and Iraq. "I made the right decision for America," he tells Diane Sawyer defensively when she pushes him on the phantom WMD. Saddam is not the outlaw who attempted to assassinate our president, but "the guy who tried to kill my dad." Bush's triumph, such as it is, is the triumph not of an entire nation but of a single-minded individual; he has narrowed his perception to protect himself against his personal psychotic catastrophe, to sustain the subjective, self-righteous illusion of goodness he uses to shield himself from psychic pain.

Ultimately, sadism is a perversion of good and bad. The sadist's world is split into good and bad out of necessity—out of the need to be sure that nothing bad happens to something good or ideal. The real sadism comes not from the splitting of good and bad, but from the perverse linking of the two—the confusion of love and fear, of leadership and torture. The simplest example of this link is the idealization of democracy, as it was used to justify the destruction of a five-thousand-year-old culture, allegedly for its own good. Bush's sadism has masked itself as an heroic attempt to liberate the Iraqi people from a brutal dictator.

The sadism that motivated the war is evident in Bush's lack of a plan for postwar Iraq: The invasion was an end unto itself, not (as advertised) a means toward achieving a safer and more equitable Iraqi society. Within months of Pearl Harbor, Franklin D. Roosevelt had a comprehensive plan not only for conducting the war, but also for rebuilding after the war was over. Where was the plan for Iraq when George W. Bush's invasion began? For its roads, schools, housing, food, water? The answers to those questions require compassion, forethought, a sense of responsibility, and a willingness to make reparations for damage done. Unfortunately, a man who has spent his life trying to evade guilt and responsibility is unequipped to take seriously the damage his aggression can inflict. Planning for the future consequences of present actions is simply not in Bush's psychic vocabulary; his delusions of omnipotence appear to prevent him from thinking about the future as anything but victorious.

After the ceasing of "major combat operations," and the consequent failure to find weapons of mass destruction, the Bush administration's rhetoric underwent a noticeable change; suddenly the stress was on the idea that "after decades of oppression," as the president told a press conference in July, "the people of Iraq are reclaiming their country and are reclaiming their future." But Bush's failure to plan for Iraq's future belies any claim that the war was undertaken to solve the problems of the Iraqi people. The masquerade of humanitarianism makes the vindictiveness all the more sadistic.

And yet how can we be surprised at how ill-prepared Bush was to repair the damage inflicted on Iraq, when he shows no more interest in repairing the damage his policies have inflicted here at home?

Dismantling the social safety net, undermining laws that protect the environment, squandering the surplus, advancing such transparently political initiatives as attacking gay marriage and sending astronauts to Mars, using dwindling resources that might otherwise be spent on health care, housing, and jobs—all of these hallmarks of the Bush presidency exemplify his characteristic inability to take responsibility for his actions and take steps to minimize their disastrous results. From his draconian tax cuts to his relaxation of ecological and safety standards to his hundreds of billions of dollars of voluntary, unbudgeted military spending, Bush's barrage of initiatives have served as the domestic equivalent of the bombs dropped on Baghdad—launched in the name of goodness, with no provisions for repairing the ruin left behind.

The more clearly we perceive the vast international charade that Bush engineered to justify his war on Iraq, the harder it is to accept at face value his claims of economic stimulus, energy production, and the many other excuses he has propagated to justify his flights of domestic economic, social, and environmental cruelty. Like the explosives Bush unleashed on Iraq, the time bombs he has planted in our future were inspired by the perverse combination of destructiveness and denial, righteousness and recklessness, that marks the sadist mind-set. Our nation will be dealing with the devastation left in Bush's wake for years to come; with the tragic exception of our soldiers and the innocent men, women, and children in Iraq, the heaviest burden of his sadism will ultimately be ours to bear.

# SEVEN

# TWISTED TONGUES

*Though I speak with the tongues of men and of angels and have not charity, I am become as sounding brass, or a tinkling cymbal.*

—1 Corinthians 13:1

"Is OUR CHILDREN learning?"

"I know how hard it is to put food on your family."

"Our nation must come together to unite."

Bush's struggle with the English language has spawned a cottage industry of books and Web sites that document the president's astonishing capacity for misstatement. But when a reporter cleverly dubbed him "The English Patient," his joke tapped into more than the ease with which Bush's verbal gaffes can be mined for laughs. Sadly, the president's malapropisms aren't as funny as they might be—at least for those who recognize the seriousness of the problem underneath the humor. Bush's blunders are symptomatic of a patient in dire need of help; his abuse of language can be seen as the psychic equivalent of a smoker's persistent cough—easy to overlook, perhaps, but all too frequently a warning that something in the patient has gone very, very wrong.

By now, most of us are familiar with the notion of the Freudian slip, the misstatement that reveals an unconscious fantasy that undermines or contradicts the meaning that the speaker presumably intended to convey. Amateur analysts of Freudian slips have had a field day with countless examples of Bush's gaffes. His most obvious statements—"there needs to be a wholesale effort against racial profiling, which is illiterate children"; "I will have a foreign-handed foreign policy"; "I am a person who recognized the fallacy of humans"—lend themselves almost too easily to anyone looking for evidence of Bush's racism, the duplicity of his foreign policy, or the absence of compassion in his "compassionate conservatism." Nevertheless, sometimes the most facile interpretations offer an element of truth, and it would be foolish to overlook the often-frightening implications of statements such as "Security is the essential roadblock to achieving the road map to peace," "There is no doubt in my mind that we should allow the world worst leaders to hold America hostage, to threaten our peace, to threaten our friends and allies with the world's worst weapons."

Nor is it wise to ignore the hints of suppressed emotion—including prejudice—that can be revealed through language. The Bush family has a history of condescension toward people of color, usually captured in spontaneous remarks. At the 1988 Republican convention, as he was preparing to accept the presidential nomination, Bush's father was overheard pointing out his three Mexican-American grandchildren to President and Mrs. Reagan: "These are Jebby's kids from Florida—the little brown ones." Bush later tried to dismiss the remark as a term of endearment, but many Hispanic organizations were offended by what they felt was his insensitivity.

Condescention toward people of color is something to which George W. Bush has clearly given some thought—conscious or otherwise. In a comment about Iraqi self-government during his April 13, 2004, press conference, the president spontaneously ventured that "Some of the debate really centers around the fact that people don't believe Iraq can be free; that if you're Muslim, or perhaps brown-skinned, you can't be self-governing or free. I'd strongly disagree with that." The remark appeared to come from out of the blue; it's hard to imagine who was thinking of the Iraqi problem in such terms—except, apparently, for the president himself. To a psychoanalyst, Bush's words clearly smacked of projection; as in the 1950s, when self-conscious white people protested that "Some of my best friends are Negroes," the denial seemed designed to reassure the speaker himself, not the audience.

Bush's verbal challenges represent much more than the occasional ill-chosen word or jumbled phrase. Other syntactical tics are just as common in his repertoire, though less entertaining and less likely to draw attention: his tendencies to repeat phrases, deflect questions, offer evasive answers, lose his thoughts in tangential speech, make quips, tell lies, even appear to lose momentarily the ability to respond. While one could argue that many politicians share one or two of these traits, it's difficult to name a single politician who exhibits all of them. When viewed together, they form a pattern of related linguistic misfires and abuses that raises startling and profound questions. Not surprisingly, Bush's wayward way with words reminds us once again of the deficiencies of the learning and coping mechanisms he uses to try to tame the chaos that rages in his mind. Moreover, closer inspection suggests that Bush doesn't just struggle with language; he perverts it, in ways that reveal a capacity for indifference and contempt that reverberates far beyond the written or spoken word.

Given the scale of Bush's ongoing efforts to manage both anxiety—in which we have already traced the roots of language—and his apparent learning disabilities, it should come as little surprise that both have had a significant impact on his use of language as well. His familiar use of pat phrases and stock expressions suggest that he is compelled to use language less to express than to control; he seeks to manage the message, both by limiting what he says and deflecting others' attempts to engage in dialogue.

The president often attempts to wave away difficult questions by reaching into his storehouse of empty platitudes—and sometimes the results have no apparent relation to the question asked. In May 1999, when he told Diane Sawyer "I do know that mothers and dads have got to say and understand the most important job they will ever have, they will ever have, is to love their children," his words appeared to make sense—until you remembered that Sawyer's question had to do with standing up to the gun lobby, not child rearing. Other times he just talks tough; the familiar "you're either with us or against us" mind-set scarcely invites debate or dissent.

This defensive use of language likely reflects the enormous amount of hidden effort Bush must expend to manage his anxiety. The trouble he has in managing his thoughts makes them that much harder to express. As experience has taught him, his disorganized thought processes can reveal themselves too easily through his misstatements, tangential digressions, and other aspects of his speech. Relying on repeated phrases allows him, however feebly, to control what he says, limiting his potential for serious verbal missteps. At the same time, the strategy also minimizes input from others, which could require him either to depart from his script or to place further demands on his thinking. Bush may adopt a tough-guy posture, but his real reasons for blocking the possibility of dialogue may have more to do with his inability to tolerate complexity.

Consider also his performance in press conferences, another venue in which he manages anxiety by managing input. The rare prime-time press conference President Bush gave on March 6, 2003, on the eve of the Iraq invasion, appeared carefully choreographed—so much so that at one point the president himself seemed to admit as much, as if to defend himself. ("This is a *scripted* . . . ," Bush said; the room burst out in laughter before he could finish his thought.) In another press conference thirteen months later, a flustered Bush rushed past a difficult question by saying he had some "must calls" to make.

The press conference is a duty the president generally avoids, and approaches only with apparent great discomfort. As he casually confessed at the Associated Press annual luncheon on April 21, 2004, "I kind of like ducking questions, and I would be glad to duck any questions, like my mother once told me to do." His responses generally conform to a number of different input-control strategies. He turns his awkward and memorized answers to any question into a question itself, and then answers *that* instead of the original one. His struggle to stay on message—evident in his consistently rigid responses, and his unwillingness to deviate from prepared and often superficial answers whether or not they address the questions that have been asked—represents yet another front in his ongoing battle to manage anxiety by limiting input. And when he does deviate, he falls back on his affability defense, poking fun at reporters to buy time to get back on track—or ending the briefing entirely.

Bush is anxious to limit new input, because any new information that challenges his beliefs can make him anxious about the choices he has already made. In this light, his handling of the issue of Iraqi weapons of mass destruction (WMD) appears to demonstrate the great lengths to which he goes to manage his anxiety, even before we consider the likelihood of his willful misleading of the public. Assume, for the sake of argument, that Bush actually did believe at some point that Saddam Hussein possessed such weapons. Once he made the decision to believe this was true, any information to the contrary would be too threatening to consider. Unwilling or unable to entertain information that would cause cognitive dissonance—such as the evidence discrediting the claim that the Iraqis had attempt to purchase African uranium—he avoids revising or revisiting old decisions until the anxiety around their validity becomes too much to tolerate.

The conscious limiting of input is also common among adults with ADHD, who are constantly struggling with the impulse to respond to new stimuli—a phenomenon that manifests itself as distractibility and difficulty maintaining focus. We see efforts to counteract this trouble in Bush's heavily scripted public appearances, which emphasize the repetition of simple phrases to facilitate his staying focused. Experience has shown that he is unable to be spontaneous without running the risk of losing his way, getting fouled up and fragmented in his discussion of an idea. The examples are almost too numerous to mention. Take his remarks at a news conference in New Hampshire during the 2000 primaries, when he was asked his thoughts on the information superhighway. Unable to respond to the question directly, he began rambling and eventually spun out of control "with the flailing of a nervous, befuddled student," as Frank Bruni of the *New York Times* reported. On another occasion, Bruni recounts, he astonished the reporters covering him with a "marvel of free-floating pronouns and absent antecedents," saying, "When I was coming up it was a dangerous world and we knew exactly who the 'they' were. It was us versus them and it was clear who 'them' was. Today, we're not sure who the 'they' are, but we know they're there."

But defensiveness shouldn't be confused with helplessness. Regardless of how often his misuse of language betrays the severity of his struggle, Bush has learned to deploy language as a very effective defense against a wide variety of perceived threats. In this respect, his years of special effort spent trying to think and speak clearly have helped him turn his awkward relationship with language to his advantage. By all appearances, he has come to regard language as a tool that can be used to communicate messages wildly divergent from their surface meaning. From his boyhood creation of an affable, joking persona within a distant, grieving family, to his youthful efforts to distract others from his learning disabilities, to his adult investment in the denial surrounding his drinking problem and questionable business skills and practices, Bush has historically used language to hide while appearing to reveal. Protecting the secrets of his simplified private world, he has spent a lifetime deploying language as an instrument of indirection—even misdirection—in the guise of expression.

Ironically, this use of language requires more management than the kind of spontaneous speech that causes him so much anxiety. Nevertheless, this disconnect between word and meaning can be exploited in a variety of linguistic perversions, all of which are familiar components of the Bush arsenal—serving Bush's wide assortment of political and psychological agendas. Ultimately, of course, the particular anxieties and responsibilities he has used words to evade in the past may be telling—but they are less important than his use of language in the present, now that his words are among the most powerful in the world. We review his record of perverting the language—its function as well as its component words—to learn more about the patterns of thought and behavior that he is now bringing to the presidency.

Although the term "perversion" has historically been associated most closely with sex, in recent years psychoanalysis has increasingly applied it more generally to the process of turning away—as in turning away from truth, or from what is right. In traditional, sexual terms, the term "perverse" is used to describe practices that turn away from the biological purpose of sexual intercourse—to join together to produce something generative—and substitute some other goal. On a more abstract level, we can see a similar dynamic at work in the perversion of a conversation, for example: If one participant thinks the purpose of the dialogue is to reach an agreement or understanding, and the other is willfully trying to block such an effort, the latter is perverting the conversation by turning away from the goal of communication and thereby denying its generative purpose.

Some patients try to pervert the goals of analysis by ignoring its very purpose; rather than proceeding as if they are in the doctor's office for help with their problems, they reverse therapist-patient roles, acting as though they are actually there to help the doctor. Bush often attempts a similar reversal with reporters. In December 2003, when Diane Sawyer pressed him on the question of Iraqi WMD, his response was a chilling and memorable attempt to pervert the very premise of the conversation:

**SAWYER:** Fifty percent of the American people have said that they think the Administration exaggerated the evidence going into the war with Iraq, weapons of mass destruction, connection to terrorism. Are the American people wrong, misguided?

**BUSH:** No, the intelligence I operated on was good sound intelligence. The same intelligence that my predecessor operated on. The, there is no doubt that Saddam Hussein was a threat. . . .

**SAWYER:** Again, I'm just trying to ask, these are supporters, people who believed in the war who have asked [whether it was right to state] as a hard fact, that there were weapons of mass destruction[,] as opposed to the possibility that he could move to acquire those weapons still.

**BUSH:** So what's the difference?

Bush's tendency to pervert difficult conversations—to distract his questioners from the truth—is a hallmark of his dealings with what he sees as a generally hostile press. Even when cooperating with a generally nonconfrontational portrait of the president, such as Alexandra Pelosi's human-interest documentary *Travels with George,* Bush launches his trademark charm offensive on the young filmmaker (and daughter of House Democrat Nancy Pelosi), preempting her questions with his own inquiries about whether she is having a romance with a certain reporter. It's a classic Bush gambit: Engaging in a perversion of the relationship between reporter and interviewee, the candidate literally disarms the interviewer, using his patter to make it almost impossible for her to get through to him.

Bush's avoidance of press conferences is precedent-breaking: he has held only eleven solo conferences in the first three years of his presidency, just over half the comparable total for Ronald Reagan, the next most reticent president of the television age, according to Ken Auletta's eye-opening *New Yorker* profile of the White House press team. When Bush does go before the cameras, he tends to discourage follow-up questions, rooted in part in fear that his verbal limitations allow him only to rebuff challenges, not rebut them. His familiar practice of sticking to scripted answers during press conferences, for example, represents more than self-protective deflection—it amounts to a willful perversion of the search for truth. His difficulty with reasoning has bred indifference toward it. While this pattern of secrecy and selective disclosure is consistent with the Bush family tradition—from his parents' handling of his sister's illness to his father's behavior in the Iran-Contra episode—his use of language can be seen as feeding his personal need to pervert the truth, to protect against being intruded upon, to mock any attempt at genuine discourse.

This perversion takes many forms, one of the most obvious being projection. Considering Bush's dependence on projection as a psychological defense, it's no surprise that he relies on it as a rhetorical device as well. Bush engages in projection every time he repeats his shopworn phrase "They hate our freedoms," which he used as a justification for the encroachment on our own civil liberties written into the so-called Patriot Act. Though Bush is hardly the first American politician to reply on this unconscious process, rarely has a leader relied upon it as pervasively as he does. Consider his defiant claim at an October 2003 press conference: "This nation is very reluctant to use military force. . . . Military action is the very last resort for us." As James Carville reminds us in his book *Had Enough?* Bush once famously observed: "there are some who would like to rewrite history—revisionist historians is what I like to call them." Bush, of course, speaks through the biggest "revisionist historian" megaphone of all, and with such regularity that he probably doesn't consciously realize what he is doing. His presidency has afforded him endless opportunities to rewrite history on a grand scale, projecting onto an enemy the responsibility for the war he started.

Silence can represent another form of turning away, a refusal to make public one's thoughts or actions. Bush's refusal to volunteer the facts about his DUI arrest is just one example of how language can have as big an impact in its absence as in its presence. More recently, his failure even to mention Osama bin Laden or the controversy over Iraqi WMD in his 2004 State of the Union address was so obvious that it generated almost as much attention as what he *did* say (notwithstanding his baffling attempt to distract us by making the fight against illegal steroid use a top national priority). During the Bush family's summer safari, when Bush was caught on film shielding his daughters' eyes from the spectacle of elephants copulating in the wild, the result was more than just a funny photo op: It was a metaphor for the president's favored strategy for dealing with the unsettling truths of the world.

He turns away from the truth, not just by using words as part of his missile defense, but by using them to obscure facts. The resume Bush distributed during his unsuccessful 1978 congressional race listed his first venture into the oil business, the ill-fated Arbusto partnership he funded with millions from family and friends, "even though it didn't start operations until March 1979, several months after he lost the election," Craig Unger notes in *House of Bush, House of Saud*. Interestingly, Arbusto and its failed successors are nowhere to be found in his official White House biography; as John Dean observes, this document "is notable in that between his graduation from Harvard Business School in 1975 and his work helping run the Texas Rangers baseball team, his only reported activity is working on his father's 1988 presidential campaign." Whether by including false information or by omitting unpleasant truths, Bush uses language to craft an image of himself as someone who never participated in the businesses and elections he lost.

When he's not using language—or the absence thereof—to turn away from the truth, Bush often uses it to turn away from debate. In this context, Wilfred Bion makes a useful distinction between the "language of achievement" and the "language of substitution." The speaker who employs the language of achievement is interested in considering possibilities—in encouraging discourse—as a responsible prelude to action. The speaker who relies on the language of substitution, on the other hand, paints his conversational partners into a corner, leaving no room for substantive dialogue, erecting verbal barriers to any further substantive dialogue.

Bush's words often serve as a prelude to action—such as bombing Baghdad or cutting health care. But they are deployed in a way that invites no further interaction. Bush's use of absolutes to justify the war in Iraq—and to question the patriotism of any opposition— is typical of this pattern; the receiver of the language is given no room to think, simply to join up "with us" or choose the only other option, which is to be "with the terrorists." The language of substitution comes in particularly handy when there is a clear opponent to involve in the process. Consider Bush's characterization of Al Gore as a candidate "who will say almost anything to get elected." The same, of course, could certainly have been said about Bush—but once Gore started verbally defending himself, he fell inevitably into the trap, "saying anything" just as Bush had predicted. If you're looking to stifle communication, not encourage it—to use language as a defensive weapon against the language of others—it's hard to find a better role model than George W. Bush.

The language of achievement is based on a willingness to have dialogue, to be uncertain about one's conclusions. The language of substitution, on the other hand, substitutes verbal tricks and false choices for the honest work of conversation. Word for word, the language of substitution may look like language of achievement—as when Bush extols the virtues of freedom and his desire to see it spread throughout the Middle East. Bush's use of the word *freedom,* as his behavior makes clear, has nothing to do with freedom itself—he cannot even tolerate the freedom to disagree.

In an observation that has special relevance to President Bush, Bion refers to "the usurpation of the domain of reality (scientific facts) by the moral outlook, and of scientific laws by moral laws." As Bion writes, the temptation to replace thought—reasoned judgment—with the simplistic prejudgments of morality can spread like a cancer through the mind of the susceptible personality. A dogmatic reliance on "knowing what is right and wrong" becomes a substitute for thinking—as in Bush's late-2003 interviews with both Tim Russert and Diane Sawyer, in both of which he insisted that it was right to invade Iraq, *regardless of what the facts showed,* because Saddam was evil and we needed to get rid of him. This is the mentality of an evangelical minister like Elmer Gantry—a man through whom the light of God shone, but who could take nothing in. It is the mentality of the Barry Goldwater slogan that defined the conservative movement: "In your heart you know he's right." As for what's in your mind—well, never mind.

The language of substitution is essentially the language of intimidation—a Bush specialty. It is also a language of false action, false thought. But Bush has demonstrated versatility in his perversion of language, which just as often involves burnishing it with a positive, idealizing spin. This is a tool he trots out whenever he discusses children, nature, or even animal species. In one memorable instance, his idealization imagery was capped off with a slip of the tongue: "The public education system in America is one of the most important foundations of our democracy. After all, it is where children from all over America learn to be responsible citizens and learn to have the skills necessary to take advantage of our fantastic opportunistic society."

As the record shows, however, when Bush starts talking this way it's a safe bet that he's damning with loud praise—preparing to hide destructive actions behind a veil of positive terminology. All too often, any public praise he offers a group or a program is just a prelude to his undercutting the object of his praise. In 2002, he used the State of the Union platform to hail the achievements of the Ameri-Corps program as "good works [that] deserve our praise . . . deserve our personal support . . . deserve the assistance of the federal government." In the speech, Bush promised a 50 percent increase in the program; the following year, however, he cut AmeriCorps funding by 80 percent. In 2004, he made a passionate plea for the importance of space exploration, unveiling election-year plans to return American astronauts to the moon on the way to Mars; only weeks later, he cut off funding necessary to keep the Hubble satellite telescope operative (and failed to mention the Mars initiative in his State of the Union address). One wonders if the pattern of unfulfilled promises of love and support remind him of the absent father of his boyhood; whatever the case, it reveals an unconscious contempt—not just for the program about to be gutted, or for the listeners he is deceiving, but for language itself.

Bush's attempts at humor often harbor further traces of his contempt—both for the people he ridicules to get laughs, and for the whole notion of honest, generative discourse, in which his mind is too disordered to participate. Teasing an overly inquisitive reporter for having "a face for radio," he silences the humiliated individual while putting other reporters on notice that he's willing to attack if they push too hard. During a joint appearance with Jacques Chirac in May 2002, one reporter asked him to explain the view "that you and your administration are trying to impose America's will on the rest of the world"—and then proceeded to finish his question in French. "Very good," Bush jibed haplessly. "The guy memorizes four words, and he plays like he's intercontinental. . . . I'm impressed. *Que bueno.* Now

I'm literate in two languages." Even this pale comeback did the trick; few would remember Bush's actual attempt to answer the question, but everyone remembered the moment when he closed down the showoff reporter who tried to upstage him in front of Chirac.

The reporters may laugh it off—an expression of their anxiety—but the device conveys a contempt for the seriousness of their undertaking. A very clever patient I treated years ago would fend off the anxiety that my interpretations caused by making light of them. Once, I clearly caught her off guard when I informed her of my vacation schedule; the following day she announced that she was already planning to be away for a longer period around the same time. When I suggested that she was protecting herself against the surprise of my announcement by presenting her plan as a kind of fait accompli, she replied that it was more like *feta cheese*—a quick-witted association than served to dismiss my serious concern, if not the whole therapeutic process. Expressing her aggression in a safe way, the punster kills conversation with a smile, mixing the metaphoric with the concrete to kill her conversational partners with a laugh while protecting herself from feared retaliation.

Bush uses humor to achieve similar ends when he is caught off guard or is about to be taken too seriously. In *Ambling into History,* Frank Bruni describes Bush using his foot to draw an imaginary line, then jumping back and forth over it, saying "Off the record. On the record." By turning the reporters' questions into a comical charade, he makes fun of their claim on his thinking, while precluding any substantive discourse with symbolic humor—just as my patient did with her pun. He does this frequently, with great ease—consider again the "I guess I'll have to call my lawyer" response to suggestions that Bush's Iraq policies violated international law.

Bush is an equal-opportunity put-down artist; few people or subjects are exempt from his mockery, which reveals the startling breadth of his indifference, if not hostility. The often-repeated "trifecta" joke, a favorite on the post-9/11 fund-raiser circuit, demonstrates that even the tragic attack on America, along with economic hardship, are fair game—particularly if they can be used to deflect blame for the deficit spending at the heart of the joke. None escapes his putdowns—including his wife, whom Bush called "the lump in the bed next to me" at a summer 2003 event. (Bush's attempts to soften the tone a moment later—"She is a—she's a remarkable person. . . . She has been calm and steady in the face of significant crisis. She can smile, she can listen. She is a fabulous First Lady for the United States of America"—was so painfully hollow and patronizing that he could just as well have been talking about the White House pets.)

But humor isn't the only roadblock to dialogue in Bush's arsenal. Another is the use of serial simple sentences, by which he (and his crafty speechwriters) often manage to reduce the most complex situations into simple, declarative sound bites. His style of stringing together simple declarative statements into run-on sentences has been called "biblical," worthy of the old-testament litanies of *begats;* what this linguistic device truly begets, however, is an ongoing public monologue in which ideas are simply restated, no longer expanded upon. His summary of the Florida recount is one famous example:

> As I recall, the facts are these: On election night we won. And then there was a recount and we won. And then there was a selected recount as a result of different legal maneuverings, and we won that. And I believe one of these days, that all this is going to stop and Dick Cheney and I will be the president and the vice president.

Another comes from his televised address announcing the war in Iraq:

> My fellow citizens, the dangers to our country and the world will be overcome. We will pass through this time of peril and carry on the work of peace. We will defend our freedom. We will bring freedom to others and we will prevail.

And a third (among many), from his postwar address to the United Nations in September 2003:

> Events during the past two years have set before us the clearest of divides: between those who seek order, and those who spread chaos; between those who work for peaceful change, and those who adopt the methods of gangsters; between those who honor the rights of man, and those who deliberately take the lives of men and women and children without mercy or shame.

No doubt this pared-down recitative style suits his verbal capacities as well as his agenda; the fact that a series of such statements can so simplify and distort the truth so grossly demonstrates that even the simplest language can be used to "obsfucate," as Bush once said, rather than illuminate.

⟶

Just how does Bush benefit by using these devices? First, they allow him to pervert the official version of the truth until it resembles more closely the version of events that he and his handlers think voters want. Second, they allow him to hide his own faults and mistakes by locating points of attack outside himself, deflecting responsibility while accusing opponents of the very failings he himself manifests. Calling himself a "compassionate conservative," for example, allows him to label critics of bills he passes as obstructing goodness, even though the record indicates that his compassion is in short supply. (Indeed, the "conservative" half of the label might be questioned by some on the basis of Bush's radical social agenda, and by others on economic grounds.) Third, the disconnect between language and meaning makes it easy for him to hide his plans under profoundly misleading labels. Bush's "Clear Skies Initiative," for example, doubles the allowed levels for sulfur dioxide, the substance responsible for acid rain. His "Healthy

Forests Initiative" relaxes restrictions on the rate that forests can be cleared; it might be more accurately referred to as "Leave No Tree Behind." As if George Orwell hadn't exposed the Newspeak strategy fifty years ago, Bush has brazenly attempted to advance his political agenda using such linguistic perversions that up-end the relationship between supporters and opponents, allowing him to accuse advocates for clear skies and healthy forests of being their enemies.

Bush's use of language has been widely discussed, at times to brilliant effect. As Mark Crispin Miller told the *Toronto Star,* Bush runs into trouble only intermittently, and that the content of the material he stumbles over is usually revealing. "He has no trouble speaking off the cuff when he's speaking punitively, when he is talking about violence, when he's talking about revenge," Miller said in late 2002. "When he struts and thumps his chest, his syntax and grammar are fine. It's only when he leaps into the wild blue yonder of compassion, or idealism, or altruism, that he makes these hilarious mistakes."

Washington psychologist Renana Brooks, in an important summer 2003 essay in the *Nation,* draws on her own close analysis of the president's syntax to identify what she considers a "mastery of emotional language" behind Bush's apparent bumbling. She describes several linguistic techniques with which he instills a sense of dependency in the listener. Of particular interest is his use of "*empty language* . . . statements that are so abstract and mean so little that they are virtually impossible to oppose," and a "*negative framework* . . . a pessimistic image of the world" that ultimately discourages the listener from trying to question or oppose Bush's positions.

Bush's pessimism again recalls FDR's famous remarks about fear, the "nameless unreasoning, unjustified terror which paralyses needed efforts to turn retreat into advance." Bush is the person who feels the terror, and uses language as part of his externalization process. These few sentences from an April 12, 2004, appearance with Mubarak in Crawford illustrate both what Brooks calls the "negative framework," and what I describe as his desperate, unconscious need to evacuate his own inner terror:

> We recognize that the starting point for a prosperous and peaceful Middle East must be the rejection of *terror*. Egypt has taken a firm stand against *terror* by working to disrupt the activities and capabilities of the region's *terror*ist organizations. These are the policies of a nation and a statesman that understand the threat that *terror*ism poses to all of us—to my nation, to his, to all the Arab states, to Israel and to the future of any Palestinian state. *Terror*ism must be opposed and it must be defeated. And I'm grateful for President Mubarak's support in the global war against *terror*.

Who can argue with that? But how can one defeat a word?

By highlighting Bush's indifference to meaning and communication—which our bemused disbelief often lulls us into overlooking—Miller and Brooks, among others, are helping draw the nation's attention to the most disturbing aspect of Bush's use of language. Like the travesties of misrepresentation he uses to disguise his attitudes toward the skies, the forest, or the children his budget cuts so cruelly leave behind, the patterns Miller and Brooks identify underscore how Bush perverts language not just to evade, but also to control. His tendency to hamper discourse, in other words, it has the effect of steering it—and it's no coincidence that the result is often to his advantage.

Such attempts to control the dialogue can take many forms. As we've seen, Bush uses language to attack ("a face for radio"), dismiss ("I better call my lawyer"), distract ("Kenny who?"), intimidate ("Bring 'em on")—asserting his power and authority along the way. Of course, whenever he is touting his power to others, his message is also directed ultimately toward himself, constantly reassuring himself that he's in control. This is clearer when he positions himself as having divine authority—as in March 2004, when he told an audience in Los Angeles, "God loves you, and I love you. And you can count on both of us as a powerful message that people who wonder about their future can hear," such as when he asserts his god-like power by speaking of "my" army or "my" country, or makes references to God, Jesus, and his divinely ordained mission. The fractured syntax of comfort sends a strong hidden message of power: *Don't worry about your future. God and I are taking care of it for you.*

It may be hard to imagine someone with the self-confidence to equate him with God; yet such *hands off—I'm handling it* messages are generally the product of fear. What does George W. Bush fear? He probably couldn't answer, though any analyst could identify a number of possibilities worth investigating, most involving the prospect that his lies, his limitations, or the less healthy aspects of his personality might be exposed.

Ultimately, though, both the process of spreading fear and the effects of the fears themselves may be of more immediate relevance than the fears themselves His perversion of language reflects his disregard for other peoples' words—and what are laws, after all, but formations of words? In Bush's troubled perception, law is as easily perverted as any other language. Furthermore, when he detaches language from meaning, he deprives the electorate of its voice—of the very words with which the nation can shape and register its dissent. Though the apparent humor of Bush's verbal blunders may lull us into taking our own words no more seriously than he appears to take his, our complacency distracts us from a legitimate danger. If we adopt a similar attitude to our own language, our words will be as profoundly robbed of their meaning as his have been. The result: Our dissent is quieted, if not entirely silenced, out of fear that it lacks authority or relevance.

Though his self-effacing stance encourages and invites us to laugh along, Bush's contempt for language is no laughing matter. We cannot afford to follow his example. If we "misunderestimate" him, we underestimate ourselves as well—and we do so only at our own, and the republic's, grave peril.

# EIGHT

## OEDIPUS WRECKS

*Loyalty might also become betrayal—of the self and the world outside the circle of blood.*

—Tobias Wolff, *Old School*

**W**HAT DOES IT mean to be a son? In the Bush family, ultimately, it means loyalty. Although thus far George W. Bush's presidency has arguably been more successful than his father's, George H. W. Bush was—at least until he got into the White House—a tough act to follow. Before he was elected president, the elder Bush had served with distinction as a fighter pilot and war hero, had been a successful businessman, had served in Congress, was named ambassador to China, headed the CIA, and served for two terms as Ronald Reagan's vice president. But follow George W. did—to Andover and Yale (and DKE and Skull and Bones), into the oil business, and into politics, all with significantly less initial success than his dad. "I want to be a fighter pilot because my father was," the younger Bush announced, and he followed his war hero father into the cockpit, though there was little chance for heroism in the skies over Texas. He even tried to follow his father to the altar, getting engaged at the young age of twenty just as his father had (although George W's youthful engagement was called off).

The parallels between *pere* and *fils* are all the more striking because they appear to have been undertaken at least somewhat voluntarily, or at least without explicit encouragement from the elder Bush. Though he cites "barely hidden pressure for [George W.] to emulate [his] father," biographer Bill Minutaglio reports that "family and friends said [that] much of what his father expected from the first son was implicit, assumed, never articulated." "Dad was shy," George W. told Minutaglio. "I never had a sense of what his ambitions were for me." Interestingly, Bush illustrates his point to Minutaglio about his father's reticence by describing his father's restraint on the topics of sex and condoms: "We never had 'the talk.' He never told me to wear a raincoat or anything." (Apparently this had changed by the time of the 1988 Republican convention, when the *Hartford Courant*'s David Fink asked the younger Bush what he and his father talked about when they weren't talking politics. "Pussy," Bush answered.)

Fathers, sons, and unmentionable penises: These have long been among the theoretical cornerstones upon which psychoanalysts have organized their understanding of the mental development of boys. Bush's relationship with his father, as with every boy and his father, has something to do with the penis—its size, strength, integrity, and symbolic meaning. We cannot hope to understand the mind of George W. Bush without exploring his relationship with his father. And to assess the influence of the relationship between the first and second Bush presidents, we cannot afford to overlook the powerful symbolic value of some of psychoanalysis's most common (though easily abused) constructs.

Despite its sophistication as a method for studying the mind, psychoanalysis is rooted in our primitive selves, in primitive desires and needs, some of which are expressed by our anatomy. Psychoanalysis strips away sophistication and focuses on the most primitive elements of the self, on the basic components of emotional life. And to a boy—the essential boy—what makes him feel he is a boy is his penis. If the president's penis seems like an uncomfortable or even humorous topic of discussion, remember that the president himself brought it up—even if his father was too embarrassed to do so.

There is a deep link between a boy's fear of his father—or his father's size and strength—and his fear of bullies. One way to manage this fear is to mimic the father, to identify explicitly with his image or style. If the boy has deep rivalrous and aggressive feelings toward his father, he may exaggerate that identification and become a bully himself. Bullies identify with their projected image of father, but lack the substance to back it up. Bullies rely on fear, building confidence as they find that most people don't want to confront them.

George W. Bush bullies with sarcasm, among other weapons in his repertoire. And there's much more evidence of his residual need for his father. This desire is typically focused on the father's symbolic role in defining manhood for his children. It is this powerful representation of the father's masculinity that the boy wants and fears. When those wishes are repudiated, some boys defensively idealize their father—more commonly if their father is abusive or away from home. An indifferent father can excite heightened desire in a young boy, and lead him to envy and emulate all the trappings of father's masculinity, in an effort to cope with his father's absence.

It is clear by now that, despite his affectations of humility, President Bush is profoundly competitive, driven to win at any cost, eager to be on center stage. Numerous reporters have noted that Bush avoids giving them any opportunity to "peacock"—his revealing term for upstaging him at a press conference. It is as if in his mind he turns every reporter into a potential father figure who might outshine him—the way his father's reputation did at Andover and Yale. He uses his role as president, along with his strength of will, to have his way. His cabinet members are all potential fathers (many even worked *for* his own father) whom he has rendered harmless by making them do his bidding with the rest of the world. Bush himself may have refused to be an extension of his father—despite his deep desire to make him proud—but the elders on his team, Cheney, Rumsfeld, and Powell among them, are very obviously serving as extensions of himself.

Ultimately, it's not surprising that the elder Bush never had "the talk" with his son; both men have made clear their discomfort over discussing personal matters. And, of course, George H. W. Bush's absence from family life has been well documented and openly discussed as a key influence in his sons' development. "Even when we were growing up in Houston, Dad wasn't home at night to play catch," Jeb Bush told Minutaglio. Though his father was captain of the Yale baseball team, it was George W. Bush's mother, Barbara, who played catch with him.

Though a child's mother has a more profound and immediate parental impact on his early childhood, Bush's father's isolation from his children did have one unmistakable effect: it magnified the influence that their distant, disciplinarian mother had on their development. In traditional family structures, the father has the task of helping his children separate from their mother; in families like the Bushes', he serves a protective function, helping children feel less dominated by her. In traditional families, the father lays down the law—even the Ten Commandments are essentially laws made by fathers for their children. But in the Bush household, Jeb told Minutaglio, "Mom was always the one to hand out the goodies and the discipline. In a sense, it was a matriarchal family."

Melanie Klein described the impact that an indifferent or absent father can have on his children. Rather than helping to wean son from mother, the distant father can simply expect, or insist on, the independence that he would in other circumstances play a role in developing. The son of such a father will often develop the appearance of strength and autonomy, but such a performance can be premature, not yet grounded in the qualities of compassion and consideration that are necessary for genuine strength. Waiting in the wings to get noticed, the child closes down and never talks about what he is feeling—particularly if he faces challenges expressing himself, as the linguistically troubled young George W. must have.

Such silence on emotional issues creates fertile ground for certain archetypal father/son patterns, most notably the father/son rivalry that Freud labeled the Oedipus complex. As described by Freud, the Oedipus complex is about ambivalence—about love and hate toward each parent, as well as toward the parental unit (and toward parental intercourse in particular), and about the strivings to obtain the desired parent (usually the parent of the opposite sex) at the expense (the destruction or symbolic murder) of the other. Though each oedipal configuration is different, the traditional oedipal dynamic involves the boy's desire to surpass his father in the eyes of his mother. What the boy experiences is his own aggression projected into his father; namely, he fears the father's judgment and wrath. This can be even more pronounced when the father is perceived as withholding his love and approval, as in the case of an absent father like George H. W. Bush.

As he works through these conflicts, the boy can rediscover love for his father; as he re-owns his aggression, he may also develop concerns for the father based on fears of having hurt him. These fears are accompanied by feeling a need to repair any damage he might have done. All boys go through some version of this process—though the reparative phase of the process is less pronounced in a boy like young George W., who is constitutionally less capable of claiming his aggression or working through ambivalence. In these boys, the aggression remains unchecked, though it may be redirected. The boy may focus his aggression on the parental unit, attacking it by engaging in delinquent behavior (such as teenage drinking) that mocks the positive outcome of parental intercourse by embodying incorrigible evidence of their failed union. The aggressive impulse can also be expanded into a general urge to break things, a drive that can continue long past childhood. In adulthood, in other words, Oedipus wrecks—whatever he can get his hands on.

As any parent of a son knows, one thing that every little boy loves to get his hands on is his penis, the focal point of another common developmental phase that is particularly pronounced in boys with overactive fantasies of grandiosity. In this phase of "phallic narcissism," the boy of three to six years old has a sense that his penis is the biggest and strongest in the world, and that it should be admired by everyone around him. Most boys go through this phase in one way or another, and some even manage to get perspective on it. But there are those who fear shame or humiliation, who have perhaps been shamed by the inattentiveness of their parents, who compensate by becoming the cock of the walk—or, more accurately, the cock with the walk, the walking penis, who embodies his phallic narcissism in his erect posture and fastidiously developed and maintained physical strength. We see traces of this in the adult George W. Bush's compulsive devotion to exercise; he is so obsessed with making sure his body remains unequalled, unbent by age or aggression, that even only a month after the attack on the Twin Towers—a tragedy that takes on new symbolic resonance to an individual who seems never to have completely outgrown this stage of childhood phallic narcissism—he needed to remind reporters that he had just run a mile in under seven minutes. And eighteen months later, he looked even stronger when he landed on the USS *Abraham Lincoln* in his hypermasculine flight suit, standing proudly before the fraudulent "Mission Accomplished" banner.

An oedipal perspective on adult phallic narcissism would suggest that a son exhibiting such behavior is seeking to defeat his father by exhibiting his superior strength. We've certainly seen this in the second Bush's pursuit of his father's nemesis and would-be assassin, Saddam Hussein. Now that George W. is the most powerful man on earth, he has the entire U.S. military to function as his penis, and he swings it around with fierce power. Not only has he defeated the enemy his father could not, but he presents force and might enough to impress even his own father, the great scholar-athlete whose achievements were previously beyond the son's limited reach.

A man like George W. Bush seeks his father's approval as much as his defeat. The neglected son of an absent father, unprotected from his mother's disciplinarian ways, simultaneously yearns for the father's love even as he resents its being withheld for so long. What's more, given the younger Bush's need to defend his fragile sense of self, this yearning raises strong feelings of vulnerability, making it too painful for him to face. Thus, George W's oedipal aggression toward his father is heightened by a defensive hostility, rooted in his fear of being humiliated for needing his father's love and approval, that he directs elsewhere—often at the weak and needy, who remind him unconsciously of his own unacceptable needs. The result is an individual who is driven to impress, emulate, and outperform the father he unconsciously holds responsible for his own past and potential future humiliation. At the same time, he is highly motivated to unleash his considerable destructive resources on symbolic reminders of his father's strength and his own weakness.

And it's hard for the rest of us to avoid getting caught in the crossfire.

Every boy needs his father. But the elder Bush's frequent and prolonged absences during George W's childhood doubtless left young George with feelings of longing and rejection more powerful than he was equipped or prepared to handle. The boy needed his father to help him separate from his depressed, controlling, and unsympathetic mother; given his physical and emotional distance, though, his father was unavailable or unable to respond to the boy's cries for help. To a child who in his pained confusion knows no better than to conclude that there is something wrong with him, this leads almost surely to humiliation.

As we've seen, the young George W. Bush exhibited a variety of defenses—teasing, inflicting cruelty on animals, and developing the appearance of affable independence—that could mask the sting of his father's rejection. Despite whatever self-protecting impulses he may have used to deny his dependence on his rejecting father, the younger Bush continued to rely on him (and his family name) nonetheless. He relied on his father's help throughout his life, from getting into schools, the Texas Air National Guard, and a series of business deals, to getting bailed *out* of the Texas Air National Guard (to campaign for an Alabama friend of his father's) and out of businesses he failed at running. Though he relied on such help, the combination of yearning, rejection, and rivalry would have inhibited Bush's ability to feel or express any true gratitude. Thus, Bush lived a kind of dissociated existence, accepting his father's help without acknowledging his dependence.

Dissociation brings with it complications both subtle and obvious. The obvious complication is that the dissociated individual is out of touch with his feelings; he can be unknowingly sadistic, unremorsefully deceptive (as when he says with apparent sincerity that he will leave no child behind, even as his plans involve cutting funding and closing schools in poor districts). A subtler complication is that dissociation renders empathy for others impossible; the individual cannot feel the suffering of anyone else, because he can't perceive it emotionally. Bush has long protected himself from experiencing his own suffering through drugs like alcohol, or God, or the expulsion of his own feelings of humiliation. Such self-protection may succeed on the surface, but ultimately it echoes the indifference that his father displayed toward him—a disinclination to act compassionately when someone else is in obvious pain. The pain of the families and the world after the attacks of 9/11 was far more obvious than the internal pain of a little boy riding his bike around Midland hoping his father would take note, but it wasn't obvious to this president because of his chronic dissociated state.

Dissociation, though, only goes so far; the humiliation a figure like Bush feels because of his dependence on his inattentive father must still be evacuated. He accomplishes this by projecting his self-hatred into others, whom he then degrades and attacks. These feelings of longing are never examined—the prospect of it is too frightening—so the adult's understanding of the need for a father's love and power is limited by the primitive perspective of the child's unconscious. His attempts to reverse his humiliating dependency have even led him to publicly dismiss his father's influence, unconsciously attacking his father's potency altogether: As Bob Woodward reports, Bush has said of his father that "He is the wrong father to appeal to in terms of strength. There is a higher father that I appeal to."

The young phallic narcissist, who locates his power in his penis, will understand his father's power in similar terms, misinterpreting a desire for his father's love and attention with a desire for his father's penis. The two are not the same, of course, but the confusion can be alarming, especially to an individual already struggling with shame. A figure who misunderstands the nature of his longing in such terms, tellingly, would be likely to locate his degraded view of his self in homosexual men—men who are able to give and take love from other men. He develops contempt for these reflections of a split-off part of himself, and expresses his contempt by attacking others.

George W. Bush's record suggests that he finds homosexuality extremely threatening; after all, he put forth as a nominee for the

Presidential Advisory Council on HIV and AIDS an individual who "described homosexuality as a 'deathstyle' . . . and AIDS as a 'gay plague,'" according to Eric Alterman and Mark Green's *The Book on Bush*. So great is Bush's discomfort with homosexual behavior that he advocates a constitutional amendment whose goal is to stigmatize and limit the basic human rights of gay people. The link between such feelings of self-hatred—derived from the longing for a strong relationship with his father—and a hatred of homosexuals suggests an important insight into George W. Bush's character.

Bush's fear of appearing weak, however, affects more than his stance on gay marriage. A wide array of his domestic policies punish elements of society whose weakness reminds him unconsciously of his own, just as his familiar bravado attempts to drown out his feelings of self-doubt. But his need for his father's power continues. He needed it to assume the office of the presidency, which he gained by the hand of his father's Supreme Court appointee and his former chief of staff. And he needs it to perform in office, where he is surrounded by veterans of his father's administration—the surrogate father figures on whom he relies.

Bush's reliance on his father's advisors should not be mistaken for deference, however. The popular theory that Bush is a puppet of Cheney and crew overlooks the psychological fact of Bush's need to assert his independence, limited though it may be. He has invested too much in his struggle against his father to function as a puppet of his father's former staff. If anything, he perpetuates the competition by getting more of what he wants from them than his father ever did. His administration has certainly been more effective at imposing his vision on the nation and the world than the first Bush White House ever was. Despite his detachment, Bush has chosen figures from his father's past in order to correct the humiliation he felt at the hands of his own distant father, not to repeat it. Witness the almost obsessive demands of absolute loyalty that he places on his elder inner circle:

Bush is extracting from his alleged puppeteers the unconditional devotion and reliability his father could never provide.

We see in Bush's personnel choices a clear example of the son emu-
lating his father, a defense common among neglected sons trying
to protect themselves from the humiliation and resentment that come
with limited paternal support. Viewed in this light, the consistency
with which the younger Bush slavishly followed the path first taken
by his father becomes more telling: his desire to excel at the same institutions and endeavors as his father was all the more urgent, because
it reflected a deep-seated attempt to confirm his own worth and deny
his dependence. At the same time, of course, the son's attempt to better his father by outperforming him has classic oedipal overtones.

At first, George W.'s attempts to rival his father's accomplishments
were largely unsuccessful. His limited intellectual capacity doomed
his chances of achieving the level of academic distinction his father
achieved at Andover and Yale, and he had to settle for the cheerleading
squad at the prep school where his father was a varsity star. His venture
into the oil business was lackluster at best—at least until he profited
from his controversial sale of Harken Energy stock. And though both
Bushes lost their first political campaigns, George W's defeat kept him
out of politics for sixteen years before he ran successfully for governor.

Nevertheless, Bush had ways of coping with his failure to measure
up to his father, making a name for himself outside the classroom at
Andover and Yale. Yet, he was sufficiently haunted by his academic
shortcomings that he left the Northeast with a strong anti-intellectual
bent. During the 2000 primaries, Bush was quoted as saying that too
many Ivy Leaguers just "sit down and decide for everyone else what
they should do." He had returned to Texas to get "away from the
snobs," he said, but continued to decry the "intellectual arrogance" he

countered in the Ivy League, which he considered populated by people who felt "so guilty they had been given so many blessings in life—like an Andover or a Yale education—that they felt they should overcompensate by trying to give everyone else in life the same thing." He was not going to be driven by guilt or by gratitude just because he got to go to Ivy League schools as a "legacy."

"I don't remember any kind of heaviness ruining my time at Yale," Bush said, despite having graduated the week Robert Kennedy was assassinated and only two months after Martin Luther King had been murdered. His campus experience seems to have been untouched by the outside world. "I had fun at Yale. I got a lot of great friends out of Yale. And I didn't pay attention. I guess there were some people who paid attention, some of whom you've obviously been talking to. But I didn't want to be friends with these people who felt superior."

Bush's gripe about people to whom the interviewer had "obviously been talking" suggests a paranoid streak—a turn of mind that would also explain his habit of accusing reporters of asking "trick questions," as he has done eleven times in the very few press conferences held in the first three years of his presidency, according to a tally in *Harper's* magazine.

Such paranoid accusations—accusing others of behaving as though they are superior, when Bush in fact feels superior to them—are typical examples of projection, the primitive defense mechanism by which an individual endows others with his own negative attributes. Secrecy, elitism, and indifference go together, all stemming from the pain he must have felt as a child, excluded from the inner worlds of both his parents.

Even more telling is the attitude that surrounded his return to the Ivy League, when he was accepted to Harvard Business School. Bush received a Harvard MBA though he originally told his parents he didn't want to attend and had applied only to prove a point: "I just wanted to let you know I could get into it." The efforts to win his parents' praise and attention continued (and continued to be denied) well into adulthood.

It's not hard to imagine the level of residual pain that must have surrounded the learning-disabled George W.'s failure to live up to his father's academic record; rather than admit defeat, Bush chose to demean the whole enterprise. We can also see an element of scorn in his bid for athletic notoriety at Andover, where his father was remembered as a baseball star. George W., on the other hand, mockingly appointed himself stickball commissioner, the post he turned to his profit by using it as a platform to sell fake ID cards. Of course, George W.'s eventual role as front man for the partnership that purchased the Texas Rangers offered the chance to enjoy the appearance of a more legitimate victory over his dad's baseball record (even if his father's recent election to the presidency likely helped make the deal possible). But even that victory had an edge: the younger Bush, who could never be the baseball star his father was, ordered up fake baseball cards with his name and picture that he would pass out at Rangers games. Such a blatant illustration of oedipal competition is perhaps even more touching when one learns what regularly happened to the simulated souvenirs of Bush's would-be baseball heroism: according to Minutaglio, the floor of the stadium men's room was "littered with Bush baseball cards" on the nights he passed them out.

The image of our current president's picture on dozens of fake baseball cards—an adult variation on the stickball fake IDs—being stepped upon on a wet public bathroom floor presages the artifice of Bush's "Mission Accomplished" banner more than a decade later. Though the chicanery of the banner's claim (and the denials of responsibility for it) is arguably no less hostile, the scorn inherent in the pantomime of his father's war heroism is now delivered without a sense of humor. As events have subsequently made clear, Bush's aircraft carrier stunt had the making of a fraud perpetrated on the entire

U.S. military—indeed, on the general public, if not the citizenry of the war-torn world.

Elsewhere in the younger Bush's mock military heroics, however, we see a glimpse of the pain of the oedipal struggle. When Bush visited the desperate U.S. troops on Thanksgiving, on some level the trip reflected an attempt to offer the paternal comfort he yearned to have himself: he was a war-hero father figure coming home to his sons in uniform, making it possible for them to express the yearnings he could never freely express. Even in such an emotional holiday setting, though, the promise remains as essentially false as those he received from his own father—as anyone who tried to eat the display turkey in his photo op would have found out.

Nevertheless, George W.'s emulation of his father has been a resounding success on a number of fronts, if the striking similarities in their character are any measure. George W. has certainly proven himself as secretive as his father, closing off access to his papers as effectively as the elder Bush buried evidence of his ties to the bin Laden family. (In fact, as Dean points out, the younger Bush's audacious moves to restrict access to presidential papers could well protect both father and son.) And he is perhaps his father's equal in not admitting to mistakes or White House wrongdoing; his refusal to acknowledge the dramatic change in his story about Iraqi WMD from one State of the Union to the next offers a silent echo of his father's handling of the Iran-Contra affair, who claimed he was "not in the loop" prior to the revelation of evidence that clearly showed otherwise.

On a larger scale, Bush identifies with his father on deeper and more perverse levels—including the smiling indifference we can imagine characterized his absentee father's approach to parenting. He says that he supports the brave firefighters of New York, yet cuts their funds so drastically that the president of the firemen's union boycotted the first commemoration of 9/11. He behaves much the way his father must have with his family, dropping in to George's Midland house, saying his *I love you*s, then leaving to find another oil well. They are both experts at leaving people in need behind. Bush treats America the way one can imagine he himself felt treated by his seductively rejecting father. Like the father who promises to come to his child's little league game and is then detained by business, he says one thing and does another.

Klein disciple Wilfred Bion has written about the absent mother, referring to her as the "no-breast." The young George W. Bush was also saddled with an absent daddy—a "no-penis"—throughout his developmental years. Bush is not there when the body bags come back to American shores; he is not there to interact with the press at his staged press conferences. When his prized national security advisor, Condoleezza Rice, testified before the 9/11 Commission on April 8, Bush was watching on television from his Crawford ranch (it was his thirty-third visit there since becoming president); afterward, he had an interview with the *Ladies Home Journal.* At times of mourning and loss, the nation needs a strong paternal presence—not someone who is indifferent or absent. But in these moments George W. Bush can only impersonate his father; to me, it seems that he is living out his idea of what a father does, in a kind of mock identification.

The president appears to be following his father's example at home as well. There's little evidence that he is any more engaged with his daughters than he is with the rest of us—in the past three years he has asked little of his daughters, who have little to do with him in return. As Ann Gerhart writes, "There is plenty that the Bushes don't ask their daughters to do, that much is clear. Jenna and Barbara have not been asked to campaign. They have not been asked to rein in their adolescent rebellions. They have not been asked to appear even nominally interested in any of the pressing issues affecting this world their generation will inhabit. . . . These girls have all the *noblesse* with none of the *oblige*." They are free to be whoever they want—so free in fact that they don't even know how to dress respectfully for a state affair. When Jenna accompanied her mother on a ten-day European trip promoting Afghan women's rights, she was dressed in a slovenly way—even for a college student. Reporters had expected that she would change clothes on the plane, but she did not. When reporters gathered round at the Paris Airport, she hid out of sight behind her mother's Neiman Marcus dress bag. She had the appearance of a child who has never been told that she has certain obligations in life, even if she doesn't like them.

In his autobiography, Bush admits to reversing parental function with a pride that is hard not to find disturbing: "I may have been a candidate for Governor, but I didn't have much status at my house. I will never forget one night in 1994. After a long day on the campaign trail, I went to pick the girls up at a party at eleven PM, well past my bedtime. They had ordered me, 'Do not come in,' so I sat outside waiting and waiting as other parents walk in and out to retrieve their children, until mine finally came to the car thirty minutes later." In this story, he sounds so clearly intimidated by his daughters that it's easy to overlook the fact that in 1994 they were barely thirteen—and that 11 P.M. was *his* bedtime, not theirs.

Years later, Gerhart writes—on Christmas Day 2000, the day before the family had plans to visit his parents in Florida—Jenna fell ill and required an emergency appendectomy. Only her mother was present at the hospital for the procedure; her father paid a visit later that evening. "The next day, he went on vacation to Florida just as he had planned," according to Gerhart. "As he boarded the plane, reporters inquired about Jenna's condition. 'Maybe she'll be able to join us in Florida,' the president-elect said. 'If not, she can clean her room.' The reporters stared at him, stunned." Rather than a concerned father, he sounded like a boy with a fit of oedipal pique, annoyed that his daughter spoiled his plans. It was as if he saw her illness as one of his own acts of defiance—as an attempt to get her mother to herself, perhaps, or even as an unconscious echo of his sister Robin's illness years ago, which stole his mother away from him for long periods of time without his understanding why.

Without knowing more about Bush's relationship with his daughters, it's impossible to decode either story with total authority. As a parent who felt neglected as a child himself, Bush may be susceptible to one common pattern, envying the love his children are shown— and then, when it becomes too painful to watch, revisiting the sins of his own parents by depriving his children. Whatever the case, we're left with the question of whether Bush is simply detached, or more profoundly dissociated—unable to recognize what his children need from him, in much the same way that he has proven unable to provide what Americans genuinely need.

B ush's habit of treating the nation with the same disregard his father showed him suggests that he is far from conquering the residual rage left in the wake of his childhood neglect. In this instance, imitation should not be mistaken for flattery; like the fraternity pledgemaster hazing freshmen the way he was once hazed himself, the younger Bush identifies with the aggressor who caused him injury in order to pass that injury along to another victim. Bush's identification with his father is a way to manage his oedipal rage; rather than extinguishing his anger, though, this process only obscures or redirects it, allowing his unresolved hostility to exert a powerful force in his decisions and actions.

Though it appears to be under more firm control now than in his youth, George W. Bush's temper has been well documented. Biographer Bill Minutaglio notes that Bush's face is prone to "wash over with anger," and reports that at the New Orleans GOP Convention in 1988 he "publicly [admitted] something that he had never admitted before, that he was wrestling with ways to rein in his sputtering rage." During Bush's first gubernatorial campaign, Minutaglio also reports, his impulses were under the careful watch of his advisors: "The strategy was to make him more Texan than Ann Richards and also to extinguish any anger." It's unlikely that campaign advisors can truly extinguish any anger, a difficult process that requires more humility and introspection than our current president appears to have at his disposal. More likely, the spontaneous eruptions of Bush's anger—which by this point he had ceased to narcotize with alcohol—were simply brought under some semblance of control. But the vindictiveness of Bush's treatment of others—from the defecting Senator Jim Jeffords (whom he shunned on several public important occasions after Jeffords had opposed Bush in the Senate) on down—indicates that his anger is far from resolved.

As the journalistic record reveals, the younger Bush's anger has at least occasionally been directed explicitly at his father. In 1995, for example, when he learned his father had resigned from the NRA, George W. hurled his glasses across the room, and cursed so loudly when he called his father that his mother threatened to hang up the phone.

And the element of oedipal rage gives meaningful resonance to the anger that erupted in the twenty-six-year-old George W.'s drunken invitation to go *mano a mano* with his father. Interestingly, the tension of that scene was broken only after brother Jeb, who had witnessed the argument, revealed that George had been accepted into Harvard Business School—his first significant achievement that wasn't already on his father's list of successes.

Today, Bush's anger appears to be fueling his oedipal determination to defeat his father—not simply by outperforming him, or by vindicating his losses, but by destroying parts of the elder Bush's legacy. In many respects, in fact, the current Bush presidency is a mockery of his father's, characterized by positions that his father fought against. He has squandered the economic surplus of the 1990s with what his father once called "voodoo economics." His Iraq war "coalition" was an affront to his father's internationalist policies. Even his pursuit of Saddam Hussein can be seen as a contemptuous repudiation of the first Bush presidency's military moderation.

The most effective and absolute way for one man to defeat another is through brute strength. For the little boy, who lacks such power, defeating his father can loom as a frustrating and potentially humiliating challenge. So he compensates with grandiose fantasies— identifying with a superhero who has the power to defeat the enemy (with whom he must share his mother), or lionizing his father and turning him into a hero, or feeling powerful by overvaluing the appendage that he believes makes him a man. Many parents can remember their sons waving their penises around and proudly declaring their strength, and we see derivatives of this in adult men who emphasize the size of everything from their car to their football team to their capacity to consume beer. As commander-in-chief, Bush now has the largest symbolic penis in the world to wave around, with aircraft carriers larger than any SUV to help him fulfill his superhero fantasies and "defeat the evildoers."

Defeating the evildoers who humiliated his father—whether he is relentlessly criticizing and attempting to destroy all of Clinton's successes, or bombing Baghdad to settle a family score with a barely competent ex-tyrant—has proven an effective way for this President Bush to disguise his own wish to defeat his father . . . even from himself. He must be good, he can tell himself; after all, he's protecting daddy, by beating daddy's bogeymen. Thus, he attacks his father's attackers, externalizing his murderous rage, even as his aggression lays waste to the international coalition his father helped build. George W. Bush is so profoundly conflicted, it's no wonder he needs so much time off.

———✦———

But Bush doesn't have to leave town to be absent, as Paul O'Neill's look inside the Bush White House has confirmed. Bush's father was AWOL from the family; now Bush is an AWOL president, and not just when he is in Crawford. He turns away from truth, from what is important; he is, in O'Neill's phrase, the "blind man in a room full of deaf people." But his absence is more than a passive lack of presence; it is a malign indifference, a repudiation of the commitment to public service that his family worked so hard to make central to its reputation.

Once again, in his primal rage against his father, Oedipus wrecks: he breaks things. In his deceptive public pronouncements, in his Trojan horse policy initiatives, most of all in his march to war in Iraq, George W. Bush has undermined the trust of the American people and the international community, and jeopardized the institutions that safeguard our security, economy, and environment. In doing so, he has proven willing to compromise the foundations of the present and the future while breaking deliberately from the past. His invasion of Iraq represents more than a denial of the particular values of his father, who despite his faults as president managed to stage his Mideast war without a precedent-shattering first-strike policy. The younger Bush's unilateral destruction of the relics of an ancient civilization resonates as an attack on history and tradition, on the laws of the father. On a deep level, the president who boasts to Bob Woodward that he doesn't have to answer to anybody is refusing to answer to history or tradition—religious, political, or familial. Thus, the twin bogeymen of bin Laden and Saddam's WMD can be absent from the State of the Union address he delivers after launching a war he justified by invoking both. And Bush has even gone beyond rewriting history to impede its being written altogether, blocking the commission that could find the facts behind the most tragic event of his presidency, sealing away the papers that would allow us to reconstruct his trail.

Bush's denial of history has extended to his own personal history as well. In normal mother-child relations there is a pattern of break and repair. But Bush has demonstrated a pattern of break and deny: smash something first, and then refuse to take responsibility for the breakage. He needs to break things, is unconsciously driven to do so. Breaking things means not only breaking historical links and causality, but also breaking the future of history by blocking access to presidential records. Overtly it is simply covering one's tracks; covertly it is an attack on the fertility of generative discourse. The individual who turns a blind eye to history, of course, will always remain unable to learn from it. Unfortunately, George W. Bush's position in the world is such that his failure to learn lessons affects others. On a family level, his efforts to maintain silence about the darker side of his personal history—for the benefit of his children, he said—was followed by his daughters' own arrest for offenses that duplicated his own; his children had been denied the useful spectacle of their father's mistakes to learn from.

Ultimately, though, it is on the global scale that Bush's mistakes—his historical perspective important among them—will affect us all. With a president who refuses to view history as anything but an enemy he cannot afford to acknowledge or engage, it's impossible not to wonder what painful lessons of history we may be doomed to repeat.

# NINE

## HE'S OUR MAN

*Perhaps in the flight of birds which Oliver had watched and won-
dered at in other days, the leader was not really a bold spirit trust-
ing to his own initiative and hypnotizing the flock to follow him
in his deliberate gyrations. Perhaps the leader was the blindest,
the most dependent of the swarm, pecked into taking wing before
the others, and then pressed and chased and driven by a thousand
hissing cries and fierce glances whipping him on. Perhaps these
majestic sweeps of his, and those sudden drops and turns which
seemed so joyously capricious, were really helpless effects, desperate escapes, in an induced somnambulism and a universal persecution. Well, this sort of servitude was envied by all the world; at
least it was a crowned slavery, and not intolerable. Why not
gladly be the creature of universal will, and taste in oneself the
quintessence of a general life: After all, there might be nothing to
choose between seeming to command and seeming to obey.*

—Santayana, *The Last Puritan*

*In the country of the blind the one-eyed man is king.*

—Erasmus

I F IT WEREN'T for the fact that he is president of the United States,
George W. Bush might be merely an interesting psychological case
study. Though one could certainly argue that the sum total of his

**163**

disabilities, delusions, and defense mechanisms doesn't immediately suggest an individual uniquely equipped to be the leader of the free world, the fact of the matter is that he is our president—and one whose popularity has sometimes risen quite high among the citizens he leads. Despite his failure to earn a majority—or even a plurality— of the votes cast in the 2000 election, Bush was sufficiently appealing to enough voters that the Supreme Court had to be called in to decide the very narrow margin of victory. Whatever the final tally, more than fifty million voters believed that George W. Bush possessed the qualities of leadership and integrity that they wanted to guide the nation into the twenty-first century.

Of course, many people ask now (as they did then): *What were they thinking?* Bush has presided over a great catastrophe, led the nation into two unfinished wars, divided its people more than ever, turned his back on education, the environment, and women, and created a huge federal deficit. And yet, when history writes its chapter on the presidency of George W. Bush, the question of his appeal may prove as vital as the questions surrounding his character. After all, America put Bush in the White House, or at least came close, and America will have to live with the rewards and repercussions of his presidency long after he has left office. The task of understanding President Bush's psychology is thus somewhat incomplete without attempting at least a partial understanding of the psychology behind his appeal to the voters who made him relevant.

The discipline of applied psychoanalysis is not without its limits, of course. Even in theory, no couch is big enough to fit all the voters who have supported Bush or elevated his approval ratings. A truly exhaustive exploration of Bush's popularity would also require the perspectives of history, sociology, political science, and other disciplines, which will no doubt be focusing their considerable resources on the issue of Bush's appeal for many years to come.

Nevertheless, the principles of applied psychoanalysis do manage to shed some worthwhile light on the matter. We have already touched on several ways that Bush actively solicits and sustains our support. Our discussion of the development of his affable personality, for example, noted various elements of his appeal, even as it exposed their psychologically self-serving roots. In considering the lasting impact of his drinking problem, we explored how the untreated alcoholic's family members can enable and perpetuate alcoholic behavior—in patterns that parallel our nation's response to the president. Our investigation of Bush's history of sadistic or outlaw behavior noted how such actions can appeal to the unfulfilled sadistic and defiant tendencies in all of us. And the frequently mentioned, ever-present effort to exert control—over impulse, anxiety, message, and more—can easily be detected in Bush's careful crafting of a public image designed to shape and preserve our affection for him.

Identifying what Bush does to win support doesn't explain why it works, however. The psychology of the follower plays as important a role in the process as that of the leader. To that end, all of the psychological constructs mentioned earlier, which have helped further an understanding of Bush's psyche, can also help to illuminate the mind of the body politic. Some are particularly relevant to a discussion of the dynamic that exists between a voter and the politician he supports and admires—particularly if that politician is George W. Bush. By exploring how several of those psychological mechanisms can influence and reinforce the allegiance Bush enjoys from his supporters, we can gain some valuable insight into why he is able to forge such a deep and durable connection with so many of us.

Central to Bush's appeal is the remarkable ease with which a wide variety of people identify with him. The dynamic of identifying with another individual originates in early childhood, when the infant identifies with the image of the "good mommy" into whom

he has projected his good qualities. By seeing his good self personified in his nurturing mother, he can see himself as good, and more
easily contend with the destructive parts of his personality without
having to resort to denial or projection. The same is true when identifying with a strong, moral, and loving father, the child can further
manage the unwanted parts of himself. This dynamic continues
throughout adulthood; we observe it in action whenever we feel
drawn to someone who demonstrates attributes we hope we have in
our own character.

The infant's ability to idealize is a prelude to identification, to in-
ternalizing the positive parent–child relationships. It has its roots in the
infant's efforts to protect the internal split by which he keeps positive
and negative feelings far apart. Splitting good and bad feelings is the
most primitive attempt to manage overwhelming anxiety. Idealization
keeps those opposite feelings even farther apart. When the relationship
between the child and his parents is troubled, idealization cannot progress to identification. In an older child, idealization is also a defense
against the dread of uncertainty, of unpredictability. The need to idealize evolves into a need to invest our faith in a figure of power and
goodness, who will protect us from the dread of uncertainty. What the
child actually dreads are any flaws in the mother that would invite attack by the child; thus he insists on her absolute goodness. Unpredictability gets projected into the world, which in turn becomes a
dangerous place, threatening his ideal protector.

At a deep level, George W. Bush seems to understand this process
instinctively. His behavior and policies continue to spread dread wher-
ever he goes, in the hope that *he* will be accepted as the idealized
hero, humanized by his forgivable linguistic gaffes. Bush encourages
this process with almost every statement he makes, stressing the danger of future 9/11-style attacks, fear-mongering over anthrax in his
State of the Union addresses. And the prominent placement of 9/11
footage (real and staged) in his campaign commercials makes it clear

that he seeks to represent himself only as the protector who can save us from future destruction—rather than the distracted and vengeful leader who failed to prevent the attacks and then took steps that might well inspire more such violence.

George W. Bush behaves like a modern version of the preachers during the witch-hunting days of Cotton Mather. Back then, one hung over the pits of hell by a slender thread; the only way to be safe was to listen to the preacher. Bush is doing something similar, playing into his childish understanding of a people's need for predictability. His constituents are like children who have just come into full awareness of their own aggression; their perceptions of their parents still involve a degree of uncertainty. This explains their attraction to religion, which affords them security against uncertainty. It also explains their need to believe in the messages of unreliable and potentially hypocritical voices. The believers really do believe, and are dominated by that need. We require such hypocrites as part of our need for magical thinking—even though we become enraged when we discover that they have tricked us. That is the process that has been set in motion by David Kay's report, with its conclusive message about the failure to discover WMD in Iraq. When a case of hypocrisy—such as Bush's dishonest claims about Iraq, which formed the pretense for going to war—is discovered, the people who once needed to believe the hypocritical claims suddenly feel betrayed, and often turn on the person they had once believed so uncritically.

Politics depends on voters who are willing to identify with candidates, and politicians encourage that process. Consider the spectacle of any successful political rally: thousands of people wear the name of their candidate on buttons, often worn where a nametag would normally go. When we identify ourselves as a given candidate's supporter, we become identified with the candidate. We project our values into the candidate, and derive reassurance from the candidate's ability to reflect those desirable aspects of ourselves back to us.

This sense of identification becomes even stronger when the candidate wins and validates our values—especially a candidate who invites identification as effectively as Bush. As Renana Brooks has pointed out, Bush personalizes both national problems and his proposed solutions by using the first-person singular pronoun in circumstances where previous presidents would have referred to "we" or to America. "I will not yield; I will not rest; I will not relent in waging this struggle," he says, and we understand that he is fighting our fight, and that our fight is his fight. Unconsciously we merge with our leader, become identified with him, become him. His strength becomes our strength in part because we want it to be so; he serves as a container for the magical power that we all wish we had, and we feel more powerful seeing him exhibit the strength we fantasize about having. Upon reflection, we may see that his speechwriters' pen is less mighty than his sword, but in the heat of his enthusiasm George W. Bush's conviction can be contagious—like the exuberance of a high-spirited child.

The success with which President Bush emanates positive energy is a key element of his charisma. He then deepens our existing bond of identification through his aforementioned regular evacuation of anxiety. At times Bush looks like a terrified little boy—particularly in televised addresses and press conferences, when his childlike anxiety emerges from behind the boyish bravado, exposing the insecurity that has haunted him since childhood. This makes possible another level of identification as we recognize our own insecurity in his. But that recognition is not entirely threatening, because Bush so explicitly exudes power—the walking penis, standing tall. Seeing that he can be vulnerable and strong at the same time, we're reassured that we can too.

Our awareness of Bush's fragility may also contribute to the enabling attitude of so many in the media, and therefore to his "popularity." The family with an alcoholic father not only needs their father to protect them, but needs their father not to collapse or fall apart—which they fear he might do if ugly reality breaks through his alcoholic haze. Watching the president's April 13, 2004, press conference, I felt an undeniable sense of compassion and concern—much the way I would if I found myself with a lost and frightened man in my consulting room.

I also recognized the kind of loving countertransference evident in Karen Hughes's description of one of her first meetings with Bush, when he came into her office at the Texas Republican Party headquarters in 1993. While looking at a photo of her son on her credenza, Bush asked, "You love him more than anything, don't you?" Hughes wrote that she was "somewhat taken aback by the sudden intimacy of the question from a relative stranger. . . . He went straight to the heart. 'He's more important than anything else in this world,' he said. 'He is,' I said nodding, feeling strangely tongue-tied, wondering if this man could read my mind or whether he was talking about his own children as much as mine."

It is a stunning vignette, though it seems just as likely that Bush had his own childhood yearnings for mother-love in mind, rather than those of his own children. Such stories have an immediate effect on the listener (as Hughes, loyal aide that she is, well knows): they make us want to take care of him. What is remarkable is that Bush— like a good used-car salesman—appears to have an acute ability to size up his customer and join him at the most fundamental emotional level: It's not impossible that Bush was simply using his charm to recruit Hughes to work for him. Whatever his own emotional dysfunctions may be, it seems likely that Bush may be able to size up the rest of us just as keenly.

What happens next is a subtle and powerful process. Without his having to ask us, we feel an impulse to take care of Bush—much as we need to take care of our vulnerable self. What's more, we feel that we are capable of doing so. Empowered by the strength he also projects, we feel ready to take the challenge of supporting him and making things better. Then, when he stands tall—in defiance of an enemy, or in the righteousness of his convictions—we feel able to stand tall beside him.

Many a successful politician has had such an empowering effect on his followers, but Bush is particularly well-suited to the task. His linguistic stumbles place into the foreground an element of imperfection that encourages our identification. We see him as one of us; he speaks the way we do, uses jokes and nicknames like people we know. He repeats simple sentences that any of us could remember and reiterate, and contrasts himself with intellectuals, who complicate matters with their elaborate, sophisticated flights of theory (and compound-complex syntax). His willingness as a candidate to own his ignorance of literature, of the world, even of the names of heads of state, made it easy for voters to identify. Bush's anti-intellectualism helps him present himself as a man who loves sports, TV, and God, and hates reading and long complex discussions—despite the fact that he graduated from Andover, Yale, and Harvard.

As his diplomas reveal, however, George W. Bush is by many standards especially ill suited to win our identification. His birth and background constitute a gulf of wealth, education, and connections that separate him from the vast majority of his followers. Yet his demeanor denies that gulf: he speaks like someone who is no smarter than the rest of us and rarely flaunts his wealth. This is one reason why his station in life appears not to invite the envy of the masses. Another is that his wealth and position are so far beyond almost any of us that they are too great even to envy. Because Clinton, for example, came from a modest background and accrued his political power through his intelligence and capabilities, he presented an image of what people not born to power wished they could become, thus inviting feelings of envy and competition. Bush's advantages, on the other hand, are all but unattainable: One can only be filled with wonder at his wealth and privilege, which remain abstract because he is so careful not to call attention to them. He seems more of a blunderer than a blue blood. He is different, yet still one of us; we tell ourselves that he is no better than we are, by any measure beyond the accident of his birth.

Ironically, some of the attributes that make Bush's supporters see him as accessible are in fact more accurately described as distancing mechanisms, as we've seen in our exploration of his affable personality and humanizing malapropisms. His supporters don't see them that way, in large part because they don't want to. While all presidents gather some measure of paternal transference—that is, we see them as father figures—Bush's perceived heroism, even in the face of evidence to the contrary, indicates that his supporters have been especially generous in the projection of their idealized notions of fatherhood. When a child is disappointed by his own father, Freud observed, he constructs the image of a perfectly caring and all-powerful parent who is loving and strong. It's safe to say that a large number of Bush voters were disappointed with Clinton as a father figure; a good number of them were also ultimately let down by Bush's own father, albeit for different reasons. Many of them may have been yearning for a candidate onto whom they could project their image of the perfect fantasy father, and Bush has more than met the task, promising that he will do whatever it takes to make America safe. For these voters, Bush's strength is thus the strength of the father who says his home is his castle, pledging protection for his obedient children.

The fact that Bush's own father is so fresh in the nation's memory adds another dimension to this. By defeating Gore (and, by extension, Clinton's legacy), and by winning the presidency on his first time out, Bush has triumphed over his father, who first had to settle for the vice presidency and then lost the White House to the Democrats. This is appealing to the oedipal yearnings in all of us. Bush's capture of Saddam Hussein further amplifies the victory: We can identify with the embattled, triumphant stance George W. Bush has taken against both his rival father and his father's rivals. Perhaps that's why so many of Bush's critics insist that he is being manipulated by his father's former associates: They are too resentful to admit that Bush has enjoyed the ancient, oedipal triumph that we are virtually hard-wired to identify with.

As we've seen, the oedipal struggle is fueled in part by a son's resentment over his dependency on his father. Dependency is a natural part of the father-son relationship; the ideal father is someone we can (and want to) depend on—that is, until we start resenting his power. In the long run, dependency doesn't breed popularity; it breeds feelings of helplessness and eventually resentment.

But helplessness can evolve into something resembling support, or at least the absence of dissent, among voters who remove themselves from the process after deciding that nothing they can do will make a difference. We see signs of this in the results of a poll published in March 2004: 59 percent of those polled felt we were "bogged down" in Iraq, yet almost an identical number said they approved of what Bush is doing. Somehow, though people know that Bush ignored repeated warnings of impending terrorist attacks, the majority feel that Bush is stronger than the war hero John Kerry on security. Such feelings of fear and need evoke childhood memories of dependence on our caregivers: Remembering our helplessness as children, we fall into the pattern once again. This feeling no doubt contributes to the advantage most incumbents enjoy when they run for reelection—and perhaps especially so with Bush, whose particular route to the White House in 2000 left many voters feeling powerless.

After the 2000 election, many voters who did not support Bush seemed to grow temporarily disillusioned with the entire electoral process. Their withdrawal, and relative silence—coupled with the desire for national unity after 9/11—contributed to a dampening of political opposition in America that many probably mistook for support. Not until Bush's designs on Iraq became public did this fragile "support" begin to dissipate. In the traditional oedipal structure, dependency and the resentment around helplessness don't become key issues until the child has become disillusioned with the father.

Until a child becomes disillusioned with his idealized parent, however, he is likely to remain in awe of the parent's power—even if only as a defense against the child's lingering feelings of helplessness. Bush's grandiose displays of omnipotence—from his symbolic gestures to the "shock and awe" reality of his new first-strike doctrine—appeal to our desire for the all-powerful father figure. And when we identify with the father's power, we can turn away from worries of our lack of our own. We collude in his flight to omnipotence, because the fantasy of his absolute protection is safer than the reality of our experience of vulnerability. Bush's power, in this model, becomes our power. If he doesn't need a permission slip from the United Nations, then we don't either. The members of the United Nations are suddenly made to seem like unreasonable parents or teachers who won't allow us—really, him—to have our way. As archetypal father figures, presidents are traditionally (and constitutionally) regarded as the ultimate upholders of the law. Yet this particular president sends the message that it is fine to break the law. He did it when he was younger, and he does it today, literally breaking treaties, or defying unwritten codes of foreign policy in matters of unprovoked war. As a rebel we can easily identify with, he gives us permission to swagger in ways that other father figures might not have allowed. As Ann Gerhart writes in her biography of Laura Bush, the president seems to revel in his daughters' misbehaviors and makes no effort to apologize for them. His strutting, swaggering behavior is infectious; it gives us license to feel as puffed up and powerful as he does.

Bush also shows us, by example, that we can assuage our narcissistic feelings of injury through fantasies of revenge. At the official day of mourning service three days after the 9/11 attacks, Bush introduced the notion that America deserved revenge and would seek it, "to answer these attacks and rid the world of evil." We all have primitive fantasies of taking revenge against people we feel have wronged us. Bush's rhetoric, and his subsequent actions, made it acceptable to pursue those fantasies and convert them into action and policy. His aggression toward the world sanctions that behavior, legitimizes it at a deep, unconscious level. It gives us all permission to be mean, to feel hatred and seek revenge within our own lives. What's more, his sadistic behavior demonstrates that we can not only take revenge, but also enjoy doing it. His pleasure in destruction appeals to our unconscious sadism, the satisfaction we all wish we could derive from cruelty. Our experience of omnipotence-by-association is more than just reassuring; it's deeply satisfying, in an almost forbidden way.

The power that Bush exhibits doesn't always inspire confidence, however; sometimes it instills fear. Bush's capacity for vindictiveness has sent the very clear message that crossing him can lead to reprisals. He's not afraid to use his power to keep people—and nations—in line. Fear may not breed love, but it can certainly breed loyalty, the essence of support, and silence—its functional equivalent. This begins with the media, whose silence and support serves to insulate him from the public. Members of the media know that Bush is ready and willing to cut off access—in effect, to deny them their livelihood—if their questions are too sharp, their commentary too critical; witness his treatment of veteran reporter Helen Thomas at press conferences after she openly challenged him. He continues to demonstrate his willingness to embarrass the press. His sharp sense of humor can both deflect criticism and stifle critics; like the sarcastic person at the office who appears to have the most friends, Bush is the kind of wit one allies with chiefly to avoid being caught in his line of fire.

When Bush's behavior isn't frightening, it's often because he himself appears frightened. We have noted his tendency to evacuate his own fear, spreading terror in the name of ending it. The world he lives in is a frightening place, and he wants us to know it. We fear the rest of the world in part because he encourages it (and in part because the rest of the world fears him, which makes for a scary set of circumstances). His exploitation of our fears, as in his anthrax parable in the 2003 State of the Union address, borders at times on the abusive; and like frightened children of an abusive parent, we cling to him for security, and hold him responsible for our safety.

The fear Bush spreads does more than enhance his image as a protector; it appeals to the conservatism in each of us. According to an extensive study conducted jointly by Stanford, UCLA Berkeley, and the University of Maryland, the fundamental difference between conservatives and liberals is a resistance to change that is based in fear. All of us on some level want to maintain the status quo, but the study found that conservatives exhibit a higher level of fear and pessimism about the future than do the more optimistic liberals. As George Will wrote in 1988, "Conservatives know the world is a dark and forbidding place where most new knowledge is false, most improvements for the worse." Bush's constant reminders that the threats to American security are ever present (and getting worse) only reinforce those fears and apprehensions.

On the surface, this idea—that Bush appeals to voters because he projects both the omnipotence we wish we had and the fears that have us in their grip—might seem self-contradictory. In psychological terms, however, these twin, conflicting projections are mutually supportive: Bush can evacuate his fear because he has positioned himself as powerful enough to vanquish the feared enemy. We feel more powerful precisely because we manage to survive in the face of such harmful forces.

The fact that such opposing forces can coexist within our relationship with President Bush is testament to the appeal of the primitive anxiety management tools on which Bush relies. We all want to deny our fears to some extent—otherwise they would be paralyzing. Any man who can recommend that the American public start shopping and traveling again in the immediate wake of 9/11 is as accomplished at denying fear as he is at cultivating it. In doing so, he sent a clear signal that compartmentalization is an effective and desirable way to manage anxiety. It appears to work for him, so it's logical and appealing to believe it will work for us as well.

Americans knew who George W. Bush was before 9/11, but the shock of those attacks invited, even forced, us to forget our concerns about his competence—to say nothing of what many considered his illegal seizure of the presidency. Before 9/11, we turned a blind eye to Bush's character, colluding with the press's whitewash of his presidency. Then, after 9/11, none of it seemed to matter anyway: regardless of what we knew or felt about George W. Bush, most of us looked for revenge to right the terrible devastation and loss inflicted upon us.

Today, we know who he is—and, by inference, who we are. We, too, are susceptible to bloodlust, and he is our ringleader.

You don't become a realist about others until you become a realist about yourself. We didn't see ourselves in the Bush administration until we recognized our own wishes to sidestep the law, to kill those who we feel wronged us—and to do it all without UN support, without an ounce of remorse or recrimination. And, by the same token, we will never be able to correct this course—to stop Bush and his administration's thirst for vengeance—until we recognize him for who he is. To do so, we must first engage in some self-examination; we must disabuse ourselves of the illusion that we are nothing but wholesome and compassionate. In truth, most of us have the same amount of bloodlust as the next guy.

Compartmentalization has its roots in the infant's original coping mechanism, the process of distinguishing (between the good breast and the bad, for example) that helps the baby develop an understanding of relationships and the world. This need to split runs deep in all of us, and its oversimplified way of viewing the world has an ancient appeal.

Learning to isolate and project our fears makes life easier—or at least makes it seem easier. Like children who insist on eating from divided plates that keep different kinds of foods from touching, we all want to be able to keep undesirable feelings from spilling over where they're not wanted. Bush's detachment can thus be seen as reassuring, because it suggests that he's learned to manage the very fears he encourages in us. He fans the flames, and then shows us how to turn them off; he sends young American men and women to die at war, then spends his time worrying about his own injured knee. President Bush has found a way to keep his peas out of his spaghetti—and his disengagement inspires us to behave the same way.

At the same time, Bush's consistently articulated worldview perpetuates and satisfies our need to create order by dividing the world into good guys and bad guys. This is as familiar as it is reassuring, for it recalls the way we all saw the world in infancy. As infants, of course, we don't know any better. As adults, we enjoy the illusion of clarity that comes with compartmentalization. They hate us because they hate our freedoms? Fine; now there's nothing more to think about. Having relieved our anxiety simply by settling for simple answers and limiting our discomfort, of course, we're left with little incentive to consider the true complexity of any given issue—reality be damned.

One result of this simplification is the dehumanization of anybody who is awarded "bad guy" status. George W. Bush demonstrates how indifference to the suffering of others can be rewarded by a reduction in inner conflict. He disregards the pain he inflicts on Iraqi citizens and American soldiers, and his apparent comfort and complacency makes it easier for us to do the same. Bush's remorselessness represents the triumph over guilt we would all on some level like to achieve. His denial of responsibility becomes our own—unless, of course, we are among those who are suffering. Bush's capacity for indifference begins to lose its appeal when voters see themselves as the objects of his neglect.

It's important to remember that Bush ran as "a uniter, not a divider." The distinction is a classic example of his polarized thinking; it also reveals his projection in full force. A statement like that should have aroused immediate suspicion that Bush had identified, split, and projected his divisive qualities, yet remained in their thrall. In retrospect, it's easy to see what he really was: a divider in uniter's clothing. What's less clear is whether that distinction was a conscious, cynical ploy, or merely an unconscious reflection of his own psychological landscape.

Ultimately, however, there was a chilling element of truth in his claim. Bush does invite us all to unite with him, beneath the umbrella of his worldview. He makes it a very appealing prospect, one that resonates on deep, elemental levels of our psyche. Those resonances describe the essence of his considerable appeal—as well as, more importantly, its durability. To identify with the Bush mind-set is to favor relieving one's anxiety over partaking in complex thought. We all want relief. But how many of us are denying our own suffering to attain the illusion of relief? And what are we willing to sacrifice to keep it?

# TEN

# I AM THE CHIEF

*I am a man more sinned against than sinning.*

—King Lear

THROUGHOUT MY TIME in medicine—from my years as a medical student to my career as a professor—the Psychiatry Case Conference has had a predictable format: The psychiatric resident presented a detailed history of a particular patient. During my residency days at Massachusetts Mental Health Center, one such subject was a man I'll call Mr. Matthews. After the ward staff presented its observations of how Mr. Matthews behaved in the hospital, the patient was interviewed by the clinical director, Dr. Elvin Semrad.

Dr. Semrad had a simple and direct interview style. He probed the patient, searching for the essential human being that Mr. Matthews had kept hidden from the world as well as from himself. He asked basic questions, such as "Tell me how you broke your heart," or "Tell me who loves you and whom you love." By the end of the case conference—and in those days we had five such conferences each week—the patient had opened himself up, and we were granted a closer look at both who he was and how he got to be that way. That look formed part of a summary assessment—the part of the case conference that was called the "psychodynamic formulation."

The formulation is the cornerstone of how psychiatric cases are conceptualized. As psychiatric specialists, we want to understand the patient's character and personality, the conflicts evidenced by his behavior. The psychodynamic formulation pulls together the various threads of the patient's history and behavior; it tries to make sense of the emotional information provided by interviews. On its basis, we refine our diagnosis and create a treatment plan. But Dr. Semrad always had a word of warning: The temptation to categorize and objectify any patient is dangerous. So when a resident asked, "Dr. Semrad, what is your diagnosis?" he would always reply, "My diagnosis of this patient is that he is Mr. Matthews." Psychodynamic formulations are continually modified during the course of treatment. Otherwise treatment would be static, and the living process of getting to know the patient would be defeated.

In that sense, this book is a work in progress, and I have proceeded with Dr. Semrad's cautionary tale in mind. For example, as this book was being completed, Bush's April 2004 press conference—and the disclosures from Bob Woodward's book a few days later—added support to many of the ideas presented herein, while also raising new questions. Why, for example, is Bush so comfortable disregarding his own place in history? (When asked "How is history likely to judge your Iraq war," Woodward reports, Bush "shrugged" and said, "History, we won't know. We'll all be dead.") What role do women play in his life? He appears to have asked his political aide, Karen Hughes, whether he should invade Iraq, but asked neither Powell nor Rumsfeld for a formal recommendation on the matter.)

More disturbing, how much is Bush's presidency guided by what psychology would characterize as "Armageddon thinking"? In April 2004, the *Washington Post* reports, "Bush told newspaper editors that Iran 'will be dealt with, starting through the United Nations,' if it does not stop developing nuclear weapons." Is Bush merely being cynical about the fallout from such a move, or is he speeding toward rapture?

In addition to having an evolving formulation, some of the steps within the traditional formulation model have not been relevant to my purposes: President Bush is not a patient, there is no chief complaint, and President Bush has not sought therapeutic consultation. There is no treatment history to review, as far as we know. President Bush's history of substance abuse, another standard element of any psychodynamic formulation, is certainly relevant, but has already been addressed at length; still, its origins and lasting impact can be detected in virtually every aspect of the president's mental health.

Even as formulations change over time, though, certain key components generally remain constant and relevant to a study such as this. In this case, they would include George W. Bush's personal, family, and medical histories, including any possible physical or neurological conditions that may affect his mental health. If I were making an actual psychodynamic formulation of President Bush, I would then link an assessment of the psychological conditions suggested by his symptoms with what I had been able to deduce from my own observations. As I described at the start, the evaluation of George W. Bush offered in these pages is subject to certain limits—but it is based on the same fundamental process, of drawing provisional but sound conclusions based on a combination of reported history and firsthand observation. Its goal, too, is identical: to understand who the subject is and how he got that way. And when the subject is president of the United States, even a provisional set of conclusions should be of interest to everyone affected by the decisions he makes.

Psychoanalysts know that many patients actually raise the essential questions they'll address in treatment in their very first remarks. When a patient starts therapy by presenting a dream, for example, the result can be an extraordinarily revealing window onto the fundamental problems the patient is facing. To understand these signals, however, the therapist must work to recognize the latent meaning of whatever the patient presents. In the consulting room, my fundamental goal is to evaluate both manifest content and latent content: that is, what the patient says and what he may mean by it. I do this in part by relying upon my countertransference, by which I mean my emotional reaction to the patient: observing behavior and body language, listening to associations in the manifest content, and looking for consistent themes—the veins of glue that hold the material together. While I try to identify a variety of defense mechanisms, I'm particularly attuned to examples of projection, in which the new patient attributes a personally undesirable quality to someone else.

At one initial interview, for example, a well-dressed, slightly overweight woman in her mid-forties—I'll call her Mrs. Ellis— arrived carrying a small paper bag from a gourmet grocery along with her purse. I instantly wondered to myself what was in the bag, and I started to feel hungry. She almost immediately started to cry through her smiles, talking about how rejected she felt by her husband. He was withholding, she said: sex, affection, praise, help with the children. Ten minutes into the session, a pattern seemed to be emerging: Mrs. Ellis was the driven, taciturn husband's unsupported wife, who felt she had to do everything on her own.

After a rush of sympathy for her situation, I noticed that I started to feel a bit cold toward her, and began to wonder if I could do anything to help her, even to reach her—an unfamiliar feeling, especially this early in a therapeutic relationship. Though I had expected to feel recruited to take her side against her unresponsive husband, I found that I was feeling unresponsive. As it turned out, Mrs. Ellis herself had grown up with a cold mother, who was preoccupied with other children along with her own depression, and who had counted on the young Mrs. Ellis to take care of her younger siblings. Later in treatment, it became clear that Mrs. Ellis was repeating her childhood pattern, being the good girl hoping for recognition from an overwhelmed mother. Though the husband she chose wasn't overwhelmed before they were married, ultimately she overwhelmed the quiet man, making him even quieter. Now, in our session, it gradually became clear that she was projecting her own coldness and resentment onto me. Unable to feel overtly resentful, she chose to kill with kindness instead. She was also hungry, and chose to feed herself rather than risk asking or taking something from her husband at home, or from me in the consulting room. All of these fundamental issues had been conveyed in the first ten minutes of our meeting: Defensively self-reliant, Mrs. Ellis even brought her own bag of food to our session, excluding me from her sphere while feeding her own feelings of resentful independence.

The same process can be applied to George W. Bush. Virtually any single speech from his first year of office—particularly those after the tragedy of 9/11—offers a meaningful digest of his character and his presidency. Take the following sequence, from his first speech to a joint session of Congress after 9/11:

> Why do they hate us? They hate our freedoms—our freedom of religion, our freedom of speech, our freedom to vote and assemble and disagree with each other. . . .
>
> Americans should not expect one battle but a lengthy campaign. . . .
>
> Every nation in every region now has a decision to make. Either you are with us, or you are with the terrorists. . . .

The latent meaning of these and other statements captures the fundamental elements of George W. Bush's character—elements that, in turn, have determined his policies.

Who is Bush really talking about when he says "they hate us?" Given what we know about the inattentiveness of his parents—who the young "Bushtail" understood to have rejected him—it's easy to see how this indifference could have been transposed in his mind into hatred, projecting his unrequited longing onto other targets. A second answer to the question is Bush himself, the man who hates the implications of freedom—among them autonomy and the potential questions it brings. Bush himself wants to be free to roam about his ranch; denying his inner desire for maternal or paternal attention, he insists instead on personal freedom with no interference whatsoever. As his unilateralist policies confirm, he hates controls; he takes action because he can. As he told Bob Woodward, for him the presidency means that he is no longer accountable to anyone for his actions—an interesting perspective for a man who reports to the entire nation.

Which leads to another question: Why does Bush hate us? Does he envy our freedom—our freedom from the burdens of the presidency, our freedom from having to prove something to his father every day, our freedom to lose control without fear of earthshaking repercussions? His contempt for the freedom to vote was evidenced by the Bush team's behavior in Florida during the 2000 election; his contempt for free speech is demonstrated by his practice of designating "free speech zones" in each city he visits—cordoned-off areas where protesters can gather, out of his line of vision, in order to express their alternative views. I fear that his deepest level of contempt is reserved for people who remind him of his parents—and of his own defects.

In that first post-9/11 speech, Bush also called for sacrifice—which, it later became clear, meant not just stocking up on duct tape, but sending our brave young troops off to fight his wars. And it also meant sacrificing a genuine political debate: If you're either with us or with the terrorists, the concepts of free speech and dissent have no meaning. As part of the never-ending sacrifice, he asked all Americans to prepare for a long "campaign"—which, it turns out, meant his own three-year campaign for re-election, peppered with wars and strident speeches and a nonstop fund-raising marathon. At the Washington Cathedral service days after the attacks, Bush even asked us to join him in mourning, quoting Scripture: "Blessed are those who mourn for they shall be comforted." Of course, as a boy Bush himself had been denied the formative experience of grieving, no doubt impeding his ability to mature; now he was calling upon the country to do with him—or for him?—what he had never done himself.

Though revealing and instructive, such initial insights are no substitute for a thorough psychodynamic formulation—which, in the case of George W. Bush, would turn on what is arguably the single characteristic that best defines his character: his inability to accept responsibility and make reparation for damage done.

To review the matter through the lens of chronology:

- Bush's mid-life decision to quit drinking, along with his spiritual rebirth, might have been a sign of newfound maturity. Instead, however, the evidence suggests that his conversion to Fundamentalist Christianity served primarily as an excuse to insulate himself from responsibility for the excesses of his youth. (As a recent episode of PBS's *Frontline* noted, Bush doesn't even attend church.) For George W., the experience of being "born again" has allowed him to bestow a kind of amnesty upon himself, absolving him of blame for any mistakes he made between his first and second births. Having decided, apparently on his own recognizance, to forgo what is regarded by the medical community as the one proven way of managing the disease of addiction, Bush has avoided the process of taking inventory and making amends that are central to the treatment of alcoholism. And the Fundamentalist strain of contemporary Christianity to which he subscribes has its own ways of absolving the individual of responsibility—removing the Bible reader's need to interpret the gospel in favor of a more rigid and literal understanding, for example, and characterizing all of humankind as sinners, which essentially lightens the burden of committing past or present sins.
- In his adult life, Bush's tendency to evade responsibility has affected virtually everything he does. His sadistic tendencies—some

quite explicit, others far more subtle—lead him to take pleasure in the pain his policies inflict on others, rather than taking responsibility for it. Throughout his career in private and public life, he has seen more than his share of failures, yet has been rescued time after time by his status as the privileged son of a powerful family. As a politician, he has shown a willingness to disregard law on a global, tragic scale—and an almost pathological aversion to owning up to his infractions. Though his discomfort with language is probably rooted deeply in his childhood, it has also allowed him to hide his mistakes and deceptions behind his haplessly inarticulate facade. And his conflicted compulsion to somehow emulate and yet vanquish his father has turned his life into a kind of permanent oedipal struggle, played out on the world stage for the highest of stakes.

Responsibility and reparation go hand in hand; if one is incapable of the former, one never feels the impulse to engage in the latter. Unfortunately, George W. Bush was raised under circumstances that facilitated—perhaps even encouraged—his early inclination to avoid the vital lessons of responsibility. As the Kleinian model shows, a breakdown in the early development of anxiety-management skills impedes a child's ability to accept his destructive capabilities—those aspects of self that drive one to commit acts for which one must later learn to take responsibility and make reparation. Such a child's limited view of himself eventually becomes a limited view of the world, characterized by a reliance on binary thinking that impedes his ability to recognize the humanity of others and accord them the empathy they deserve. The child also projects his understanding onto the world, attributing to others the unappealing aspects of himself that he is unequipped to integrate. What follows is a self-perpetuating cycle: An inability to perceive the humanity of others makes it easier to project negative attributes on them; once they are perceived as having negative attributes, it becomes even harder to feel sympathy for them; and so on.

Meanwhile, the habit of isolating and projecting negative attributes onto others enables a person like Bush to regard himself as exclusively good—a belief compounded in Bush's case by his born-again identification with God. Believing that one's actions are determined by God's wishes and commands leaves little room for admitting one's capacity for error, let alone harm. The man who feels he never injures anyone else—unless in a worthy, divinely ordained cause—has no reason to feel guilt, to consider making reparation. He repeats instead of repents, reprises instead of repairs.

Or he denies—denies wrongdoing, incessantly blaming others for the damage he has done; denies there is any damage to take responsibility for, declaring a war ended while the death toll still mounts; dismisses concerns about the future impact of his fiscal, social, and environmental initiatives. The pattern of reparation by denial is something Bush learned at a crucial moment in his childhood, when his grieving mother decided to put on a brave face so her seven-year-old son wouldn't have to worry about her. The move was no doubt motivated by a mother's love for her son, who was understandably frightened about all sorts of things—from concerns about the power of his own negative feelings toward his sister, to fears of getting leukemia himself, to guilt about being angry at his mother for being away so much during Robin's illness.

The death of Robin Bush was, no doubt, devastating to the Bush family. But the situation called for a response that acknowledged young George's pain and helped him process it, rather than one that swept all signs of pain under the rug. It was no more Mrs. Bush's job to suppress her grief on her son's behalf than it was for President Bush to tell America to drown their fears in shopping sprees after 9/11. Mrs. Bush may have felt good about letting George go out and play after Robin's death, but her decision may have done more to salve her own guilt than to help her son deal with his pain. Similarly, Bush's combination of denial, blame, and bravado following the attacks of 9/11 may have distracted him from his own shame and humiliation about having disregarded warning signs of the attack, far more than it answered the public's need for the reassurance and security that can only come from a thorough and candid accounting of how such a thing could have happened.

Reparation involves repairing damage, not just wishing it away. When I am late for an appointment, I apologize to the patient and then offer to make up the time at the end of the session if he can stay. On the surface, that offer alone might be considered sufficient reparation, but to my mind reparation is not just about giving the person their prearranged quantity of time. It is about listening to the experience the patient might have had while waiting for the door to open— was he angry? Embarrassed, jumping to the conclusion that he'd gotten the time wrong? Did he fear (or fantasize) that some harm had befallen me, or that I'd forgotten him, or that I preferred to be with some other, more interesting patient?

The offer to extend the session, in other words, is not merely about restoring the time lost because of my tardiness. That is only proper, since the patient pays for the time. The offer would also make me feel better about myself, giving me the satisfaction that comes with being fair and just; it might even make me feel stronger in relation to the weak—to the person one I've wronged. But it would not be fully reparative. Perhaps I could have simply been trying to convince myself that I'd never really done any damage—after all, in the end I'd given him his due. That is self-repair, a kind of fantasy of undoing what was done without really having to consider the other person's feelings or needs. It is only by giving the patient the chance to express his feelings—by acknowledging and sharing them, and perhaps expressing my own—that I can begin to offer genuine reparation.

Reparation, however, has not proven to be this president's strong suit. In the weeks, months, and now years after September 11, 2001, he has denied his grief and ours, redefining it almost immediately into a brittle, vengeful anger. He has projected his feelings of vindictiveness and shame onto a convenient enemy who happens to have threatened his own father. He has alternately dismissed our fears and encouraged them.

If there's one form of reparation the president is comfortable with, it is self-repair. He acts as if his choices have caused no harm, fully dismissing his behavior by denying its impact. "Everyone makes campaign pledges," he has said when asked to explain his broken promises to the voters. If I were to tell a patient that every doctor runs late, and then make up for the lost time without taking an interest in my patient's feelings, I would simply be making myself feel better. The person who inflicts harm also needs to be repaired—but until he, too, experiences responsibility, such repair is impossible.

Perhaps more than any element of his character, this incapacity for responsible reparation, along with its underlying causes and effects, has hampered Bush's ability to lead the nation. Unable to empathize with the suffering of others, he can neither address their pain nor stop himself from making it worse. Unable to accept responsibility for his actions, he can neither learn from his mistakes nor avoid repeating them. Unable to repair, he can only break and deny. A truly reparative president, one with genuine compassion, would seek to repair damage done to people who are less fortunate than he is, less fortunate than the majority of Americans. If Bush has any reparative fantasy goal for his presidency, it may be to repair the damage done to his family's reputation by Bill Clinton in 1992. But this is also a form of self-repair, not true reparation for any damage that he did himself. Or he may imagine that revenge *is* reparation—although, as we've seen in Iraq, the avenger's satisfactions are only temporary, and the damage left in its wake is considerable.

Genuine reparation must involve accepting that responsibility cannot be evaded simply by wishing or joking it away, or by destroying reminders of what one has or hasn't done, or by numbing one's awareness with alcohol or prayer. Unburdened by the standard laws of cause and effect, action and consequence, intent and responsibility, Bush seems bent on pursuing his personal psychological agenda—protecting his idealized self-image, managing his enormous anxiety, competing with his father and preserving his denial about it—at the expense of anyone who gets in his way. His view of the world allows him to deny the humanity of those who cross his path, whom he regards with a defensiveness that ranges from indifference to fear to contempt. The precise origins of this worldview may never be known to us though, as we've seen, the historical evidence offers plenty of clues. For the purposes of our formulation, however, tracing the evolution of this mindset over time has offered a coherent and credible theory that goes a long way toward explaining the psychological function it serves him— and toward helping us appreciate the scope of the psychic burden his position requires us all to share.

⟶

Any psychodynamic formulation involves a physical examination—more of a challenge to perform at a distance and without benefit of much detailed information. Nevertheless, President Bush's annual physicals are made public, and his medical history does suggest a few points of interest. The relationship between Bush's physical and psychological conditions is more important than has been the case with most presidents because of his history with alcohol. Two decades of heavy drinking can takes its toll on both the body and the brain; whatever lasting neurological impact Bush's alcohol addiction may have caused forms a necessary part of our understanding of his capabilities.

This is particularly important in the case of a self-proclaimed re-formed drinker, whose abstinence must be accepted only on his word as a matter of faith. Though no one likely wants to consider the prospect of this president's drinking in the White House, attention must be paid to an item from his summer physical that the press over-looked—the removal of a number of spider angiomas from his nose in August 2003. Spider angiomas are very small burst blood vessels—capillary bursts; while they can appear without any apparent cause, they are most often seen in two circumstances: pregnancy or chronic liver damage from excessive alcohol abuse. The report contained no mention of abnormal liver function, yet the angiomas remain a legit-imate source of concern.

The second important finding that may be relevant is Bush's low pulse rate of 35 to 45. On an athlete, such a low rate might normally be interpreted as an impressive sign of cardiac fitness. However, when viewed in conjunction with his detached demeanor, the slow heart rate begs further exploration, perhaps as an indicator of a suppressed level of arousal to various visual stimuli. Hypoarousal is typical of an-tisocial personalities; unable to perceive accurately the world around them; when challenged or attacked, such people tend to overreact in violent ways. They ignore facial and behavioral warning signs—and then exhibit rage reactions out of proportion to the particular insult. During most interactions, they remain dissociated, like the proverbial "sleeping dog"—a characteristic that certainly fits with both our the-ories of sadistic indifference and published reports of Bush's behavior in meetings. Learning disabilities can also inhibit the development of skills needed to recognize facial signals of anger or disgust that serve as warning signs to normal children, so any element of weakness on this front could be traced to something other than hypoarousal. Whether he was simply inattentive or impaired, it is clear that the president's record of missing warning signs—which in some cases may have led to tragic consequences—merits further investigation.

Yet another troubling possibility suggested by our limited knowledge of the president's physical condition concerns his history of trouble with impulse control. Bush may have a tighter rein on his temper than in the past—though Andrew Card still sees fit to guarantee Bush adequate play time to prevent his making decisions in impulsive anger. In a January 2004 interview, Card offered a revealing account of his regimen as the president's chief of staff. "My day starts very early. I get to the office between 5:30 and quarter of 6 in the morning, I greet the president when he shows up in the Oval Office. I say 'Good morning, Mr. President, can I have your homework?' And I kind of correct it. Or he corrects mine."

As Card revealed, one of the hardest parts of his job—scheduling the president's day—is made more difficult by the temperament of his charge. "There are only twenty-four hours in a day. The president has to have time to eat, sleep and be merry, or he'll make angry, grumpy decisions. So I have to make sure he has time to eat, sleep and be merry. But I also have to make sure he has the right time to do the right thing for the country, and that he gets the right information in time, rather than too late." Clearly, top officials of Bush's private staff know that he needs monitoring—a kind of therapeutic managing.

Bush is also well-known for his facial twitches and grimaces, even visibly fidgeting when attending funerals or sitting on stage waiting for another speaker. Bush touches people frequently, perhaps even excessively, and on the campaign trail would "bounce around" the plane—something written about by many reporters and captured on film by Alexandra Pelosi. He describes this pattern vividly in his 2000 campaign autobiography, *A Charge to Keep*: "Laura stays in her own space; I've always invaded other people's spaces, leaning into them, touching, hugging, getting close. . . . I am in perpetual motion. I provoke people, confront them in a teasing way. I pick at a problem." In recent months, David Letterman has made clips of Bush's jumpy, distracted behavior a regular comic feature of his show; after one such clip, he quipped: "I'm not sure who Bush is—Beavis or Butthead."

In the standard physical exam that serves as part of a proper psychodynamic formulation, such behavior would automatically raise the possibility of a neurological connection. Such impulsive discharges of energy can be seen as symptomatic of Tourette's syndrome; the line between a mild case of Tourette's and ADHD can often be a fine one, or the two may coexist. Most adults with Tourette's who present at clinics for treatment do so because of temper outbursts—the kind of event with which staffers like Card are evidently familiar. Another suggestive symptom, his characteristic nervous laughter—a habit noticed by many (including Bush impressionists) but rarely commented on by the president's serious observers—largely disappears when he gives speeches; this is a phenomenon well-documented in cases of people with Tourette's, whose neurochemistry temporarily shifts when they concentrate.

The prospect of the president having even a mild case of Tourette's is troubling. Of course, the symptoms of such a condition can be regulated with medication—a scenario that raises its own set of concerns. But what is troubling is the effort required to pay attention. No wonder Bush needs so much sleep. It is good that he gets it—good for him, and maybe even good for the nation, given the alternatives. Medication is numbing, and worrisome in its own right. *Washington Post's* Tom Shales has written about the herculean efforts Bush sometimes seems to be taking to manage his twitches when speaking on camera. Shales cited other correspondents with similar concerns as well: "Terry Moran of ABC News dared to say that the White House press corps had definitely seen Bush 'sharper' than he was last night. Tactfully and gingerly, Moran said Bush seemed to be 'trying to keep his mannerisms as cool as possible' as he fielded questions and spoke of ultimatums."

Shales himself was more direct. "Have ever a people been led more listlessly into war?" he asked. "Occasionally he would stare blankly into space during lengthy pauses between statements—pauses that once or twice threatened to be endless." As he observed, Bush's "statements did not come across as particularly cogent or consistent." Of course, given the distance at which the present assessment of the president's condition is being conducted, it's impossible to be certain of whether the culprit here is stage fright, or something more. But they certainly remind us that the public has an undeniable interest in whether such evaluations and measures have been taken, and to what end.

On the other hand, our relationship to President Bush does give us certain advantages. When assessing mood in such a case, one must note changes and shifts over time; such observation is impossible in one particular exam, but in the case of George W. Bush it is facilitated by the media's ongoing record of his public appearances. Consider Shales on Bush's State of the Union address in January 2004:

> George W. Bush had too many moments of cockiness last night. Often the words of the speech were written to sound lofty, but Bush had such a big Christmas-morning grin on his face that they came out sounding like taunts—taunts to the rest of the world or taunts to Democrats in the hall.

Shales concluded his review on a serious note:

> Though he's favored blue ties (sometimes baby blue) throughout his presidency, Bush wore a red necktie last night. Could this signify a change in terrorism alert status? Or maybe just the fact that Bush is now in full ramming mode, not merely a president but a politician again, up to his collar in the rigors of an election year? It was obviously the latter, and the fact that Bush appeared to be so happy, so elated, so giddily primed for another political slugfest was a little bit disheartening, and even a little bit scary.

The final component of the standard psychodynamic formulation is the psychiatric exam, which includes the assessment of intelligence.

This is impossible to do without proper testing, and there is more than one kind of intelligence to evaluate. In some respects—such as his ability to appeal to parts of the personality that exist in all of us—Bush displays an almost uncanny intelligence. At the same time, his intelligence is compromised by psychological deficiencies, perhaps most obviously by his persistent pattern of blaming others for his own errors—another shadow cast by the personal and family histories noted earlier, which ultimately impedes rigorous thinking. One wonders how his presidency would have been different if he were as disciplined a thinker as he is an exerciser.

Any assessment of Bush's intelligence would also have to note his remarkable lack of curiosity. His surprisingly narrow range of knowledge prior to preparing for the 2000 presidential campaign has been widely reported, as has his lack of interest in travel. As John Dean reports, before the 2000 election Bush himself conceded, "Nobody needs to tell me what to believe. But I *do* need somebody to tell me where Kosovo is." But Bush's blinkered, incurious view of the world has continued well into his presidency, with disastrous results.

Sadly for the victims of 9/11, Bush's incurious nature was probably responsible for his failure to register the August 6, 2001, briefing that explicitly mentioned hijacking airplanes. Bush has now gone on record repeatedly with his contention that he believes he "never saw any intelligence that indicated there was going to be an attack on America." He did, of course, see exactly that; what is astonishing is that they seem to have made no impression on him. "The fundamental question is, what was—was there any actionable intelligence," he said in an appearance a short time later. "And by that I mean, was there anything that the agency could tell me that would then cause me to have to do something to make a decision to protect America." Most Americans were under the impression that he'd made that decision on Inauguration Day.

He remains incurious, limited in almost every sphere of intellectual pursuit. As several local medical colleagues told me, when Bush attended a lecture on new advances in radiology at the National Institute of Health—his only visit in the first three years of his term—its attendees were eager to hear what Bush would say when he raised his hand for the postlecture question-and-answer session. His one question of the lecturer: "How old are you?"

From a practical perspective, Bush's almost willfully limited frame of reference does not bode well for a breadth of experiences and philosophies on which to draw when making decisions. When asked during his February 2004 appearance on *Meet the Press* whether he would testify before the 9/11 Committee, he smiled and answered "perhaps" while vigorously shaking his head *no*. Hanna Rosin wrote in the *Washington Post* that Bush is "someone who famously hates to be 'psychoanalyzed.'" From this perspective, one can hardly be encouraged to think that he has been any more curious in the development of his self-knowledge, a dispiriting assessment that has been borne out by our other observations.

A psychiatric examination would also look for signs of any thought disorders, by conducting a mental status exam to evaluate a patient's state of mind when he first arrived at the hospital admitting room. One of the drills we used during my residency was to ask the patient to interpret popular proverbs ("A rolling stone gathers no moss," "People in glass houses shouldn't throw stones," "A stitch in time saves nine") to determine whether or not he exhibited "concrete thinking"—that is, a limited capacity to think in abstract terms. One function served by this exercise is to reveal whether the patient personalizes them or not—if he appears to apply every such proverb to himself, it suggests that his thoughts are dominated by paranoid ideation. (My first admission was a college student whom I asked to give me a thumbnail sketch of what brought him to the hospital; he bit off a piece of his actual thumbnail and handed it to me. Another responded to the "glass house" proverb by saying "People in grass houses shouldn't get stoned." Once I asked a man to "wait here" while I made a phone call to the ward. As I stood up so did he and as I left the room he went and sat in my chair. "Waiting here" for him meant literally waiting in my chair.)

The public record offers much evidence of Bush's tendency toward concrete thinking:

> Families is where our nation finds hope, where wings take dream.
>
> —LaCrosse, Wisconsin, October 18, 2000

> We'll let our friends be the peacekeepers and the great country called America will be the pacemakers.
>
> —Houston, Texas, September 6, 2000

> The senator has got to understand if he's going to have—he can't have it both ways. He can't take the high horse and then claim the low road.
>
> —Florence, South Carolina, February 17, 2000

> We ought to make the pie higher.
>
> —South Carolina Republican Debate, Febuary 15, 2000

Bush seems especially uncomfortable with metaphor, unable to manage the interplay between the abstract image and its concrete meaning; as a result, his speech is often dotted with mixed, imperfect, or awkwardly clashing imagery.

Take a subtler example, from February 2003: "The doctrine of containment just doesn't hold any water, as far as I'm concerned." The mixed metaphor would seem comic if there were any evidence that Bush were making a joke. "Containment," which is after all a foundational concept in postwar American foreign policy, is meant to suggest blocking the spread of communism (or another enemy ideology) by surrounding it; by comparing the doctrine to a leaky vessel, Bush suggests that he's never actually grasped the image behind the term, that he is bound by a strictly concrete interpretation of the phrase.

Bush's spontaneous public statements also suggest that he listens to and uses words based on their sound, not on their meaning—a practice known in psychology as "clang association." This accounts for many of his famous malapropisms: commending American astronauts as "courageous spacial entrepreneurs," referring to the press as "the punditry," wondering whether his policies "resignate with the people," warning Saddam Hussein that he would be "persecuted as a war criminal" after the fall of Iraq. In his April 13 press conference, he spoke of "suiciders." He has a habit of reaching repeatedly for words that don't mean quite what he thinks they do—"commiserate" for "commensurate," "gracious" for "grateful." And even when he tries to joke about his mishandling of the English language, he gets it wrong: joking about his famous neologism "misunderestimated" at the Radio and Television Correspondents Association dinner in 2001, he said, "I've coined new words, like, misunderstanding and Hispanically."

Bush's concrete thinking, his tendency to repeat the same phrases whenever he speaks in public, and his predilection for "clang association" would alert most preliminary examiners to the possibility of a mild thought disorder. A person with disordered thinking—someone who hears a reference to the long "reign" of Queen Elizabeth II and envisions a drenching "rain" shower instead—will have an unusually difficult time absorbing and processing the information necessary to make well-informed decisions. Thus, it's no surprise that every entity that George W. Bush has directed has gone sour under his stewardship: Even the state of Texas became more polluted and less well-educated than before he was governor.

The concept of disordered thought is important here: Bush often seems to confuse cause and effect, or dismiss the role of causation as downright irrelevant. Thus, he assumes that the Iraqi people will greet American servicemen as liberators, because that's what they *should* do—after all, we are freeing them from a despot, aren't we? When interviewed by Tim Russert, Bush insisted that he wasn't going to change his position about tax cuts, regardless of his experience. He declares that the problem with Vietnam was that it was a political war and that we should learn from our mistakes about having politicians run military operations. And yet by all accounts his decision to invade Iraq was made largely against the military's recommendations. His lying and backpedaling may also point to thought disorder: disinclined to do the work of thinking things through, he shows the disordered person's habit of relying on magical solutions.

The psychiatric exam is where we look for paranoid ideation as well. Paranoia is a loaded term that one hesitates to use lightly or without precision. Melanie Klein writes of paranoia in the infant to describe the result of his splitting and projecting his destructive, undesirable aspects of self; his world is thus filled with persecutors he has essentially created through his own projections. Klein uses the term to describe a person's state of mind, rather than as a diagnosis. President Bush's continued habit of seeing the world as peopled with threats, however, is so consistent and unmistakable that it can safely be described as paranoid. His strict insistence on absolute loyalty—as Paul O'Neill, among others, have described—suggests how deeply his paranoid suspicions run: he experiences any disloyalty or disagreement as attack. And the disengagement that Bush so frequently exhibits is the typical escape for the paranoid individual. A remarkably isolated man for someone so ostensibly gregarious—in Washington, the Bushes are known for entertaining guests far less often than their predecessors— Bush retreats into solitude and routine. Cutting down underbrush on the ranch, mixed with exercise and prayer, suggests the isolation of an individual unable to trust other people, a condition he masks with the glad-handing charm he uses to keep others at a distance.

We also see evidence of paranoia in the tenacious grip that Bush exerts on mistaken ideas, even after they have been proven false. Freud identified the maintenance of a "protective delusion" as a powerful defense against paranoid thoughts and fears. The individual seizes and holds on to an idea that he repeats, his belief in it gaining strength with repetition, despite evidence to the contrary. By tenaciously holding on to a fixed idea, he turns it into a shield. As Bush repeats epigrammatic phrases or idiosyncratic ideas—"Free nations are peaceful nations. Free nations don't attack each other. Free nations don't develop weapons of mass destruction," he said in October 2003—he fashions them into a kind of psychological cloak that protects him from the prospect of an uncertain future. After a while, the repeated phrase becomes a form of emotional armor, used to block out loss or attack.

---

The combination of paranoia and protective delusion leads inexorably to the crux of the formulation: the summary analysis of Bush's psychic state. A careful consideration of the evidence suggests that behind Bush's affable exterior operates a powerful but obscure delusional system that drives his behavior. The most precise psychiatric term to describe his pathology is most frequently used to identify a particular condition exhibited by schizophrenics that, as we'll see, has broader applications as well: megalomania.

The psychological concept of megalomania refers as much to a mental attitude as to actual behavioral manifestations. A megalomanic sees himself as the center of the world, the one figure who has all the answers. He tolerates no disagreement, and sees external reality as either threatening or nonexistent. This view stems from a need to triumph over insecurity and fear, to deny and annihilate internal fantasies of persecution and fears of being attacked. It is a condition easier to detect in psychotic patients, but it can lurk beneath the surface of the most ordinary person. And all of us, as we've noted earlier, have grandiose fantasies at one point or another in our lives.

Freud calls megalomania a protective delusion of power and greatness that serves as a defense against fear, against paranoid anxieties. In response to fears of persecution, the megalomanic individual develops a false sense of invulnerability—a belief that the self is not only great, but all-knowing. He magically replaces hope for the future with an omnipotent sense of knowing the future. He knows what the right way is—to him, it is that simple. This characteristic is what makes Bush different from other presidents, all of whom had significant lust for power. This is about omnipotent magical grandiosity that attacks all thought. He celebrates his ignorance, which helps him to preserve his omnipotent sense of self.

The roots of this kind of thinking are often apparent in the behavior of children. A little girl cousin of mine was once in a hotel lobby where President Reagan was staying. He saw her, picked her up for the cameras, and then put her down. Her mother said, "Do you know who that was?" The little girl answered, "Yes, but how did he know who I was?" In a child, such confusion is charming. In an adult, it qualifies as an extreme form of self-love, and potentially a delusional worldview.

Specifically, megalomania has its roots in the child's delusions of omnipotence. There is a part of every child, dating from infancy, when he understands the world as revolving around him. In normal cases, these childhood tendencies are socialized out as the baby realizes the limits of its power. Yet if the baby fails to develop the ability to recognize his capacity to hurt others willfully—and to feel compassion, or the need to repair, as a result—these fantasies can go underground and persist into adult life. The unconscious ideas associated with megalomania take root as a powerful psychotic core of the personality; unless they are detected and addressed, they will influence both thought and action throughout the individual's adult life.

Since the relationship between mother and infant plays such an important role in the baby's development of compassion, it should come as no surprise that the mother can play an equally big role in the development of megalomania. The child naturally idealizes his mother, into whose image he has projected his good self. If the mother does not return that love—because she is depressed, perhaps, or distracted, or frustrated by an overactive baby—the child, who already overvalues her, reflects that overvaluing back onto himself.

At the same time, this breakdown in the nurturing process impedes the child's growing ability to integrate the destructive fantasies we all have. He sees himself as both omnipotent and vulnerable, threatening and threatened. This pair of self-images—one inferior, one defensively overvalued—coexists with these violent fantasies, which serve only to increase the child's need to see himself in grandiose, omnipotent terms. The child may repress his violent fantasies, but only temporarily; they are never properly processed or integrated, and they linger in the unconscious as unfulfilled wishes, ready to be reactivated when the fears of persecution finally become too strong.

The characteristics of George W. Bush's personality we've already studied overlap meaningfully with this description of the megalomanic state. The troubles in Bush's early childhood might have made a megalomaniac solution an attractive way to adapt—to cope with, and even triumph over, his circumstances. Both megalomania and mania exhibit three overtly similar defensive characteristics: control, contempt, and triumph. Simple mania involves love and the need to deny dependency or loss of a loved person; megalomania involves hate and a need to triumph over paranoid fears. A manic person wants to repair the damage he's caused, once he recognizes it. He feels guilt. The megalomaniac is indifferent to any damage he caused, because he had a reason for his actions; he is without guilt or compassion, and incapable of even thinking about making reparation. The greater the powers of the persecutors—who hide in holes everywhere, and pose limitless, unknowable dangers to our nation—the greater the power the megalomanic personality must feel in order to face the challenge.

He makes himself exalted: *They hate us,* he says over and over, *because we are the greatest nation on earth.* And when reality threatens to intrude on the megalomanic's worldview, he isolates himself from the world in order to nurture his delusion without distraction or risk of exposure.

Freud writes that "observation of normal adults shows that their former megalomania has been damped down and . . . effaced." In normal development pride leads to self-respect, which supports the socialization of megalomanic tendencies. But in the case of the undernurtured and uncontained child, pride cannot shift to self-respect; instead it becomes arrogance, a defensive over-valuation of the self-developed to protect against the pain of maternal rejection. And with arrogance come indifference, contempt, and an unshakable paranoid fear that the hostility of an antagonistic world will be directed against the self. Just as important, with arrogance comes an inner alliance and deep idealization of the destructive parts of the self. Megalomaniacs love to break things: it makes them feel all-powerful.

The defining characteristic of adult megalomania is the need—driven by a terrifying fear of internal persecution—to pinpoint and then annihilate all persecutors perceived as outside threats. The desire to be triumphantly free from anxiety fuels this drive—and yet it can never succeed, because people who suffer from such internal anxiety can never be fully free. In a normal individual, anxiety—and self-knowledge—serve as vital sources of information about one's persecutors, in the way that recurring eyestrain can alert us to the need for a new prescription in our glasses. But the megalomanic personality misinterprets such information, and generally attempts to evade anxiety through the numbing strategies we've described. The refusal to process such information usually leads the megalomanic individual to dehumanize the "enemy"; he becomes incapable of empathy, unable to take responsibility or make reparation for the destruction his fantasies compel him to commit.

For more than fifty years, members of the Bush family have held high public office—senator, governor, vice president, president. With such power at their disposal, who needs megalomania? As George W. Bush's history of personal deprivation suggests, there's a very good chance that he does. The Bush family's dynastic aura, coupled with his self-perceived profound limitations—his sense of academic and athletic inferiority, his inability to protect his mother from her depression—fuel his need for a megalomaniac solution.

Growing up, socialization required the young Bush to downplay and deny his arrogance; he appeared humble both to conceal his actual wealth and power, and to defend against the threat they would pose to an individual who felt inferior and incapable of living up to expectations. But his arrogance came out in attitudes we have already seen—in his mocking, his sadism, his disregard for the law. His arrogance remains evident today, in his refusal to take seriously any objections posed by others; he prefers investigating others to investigating himself. On some level, of course, we all do the same thing—just as our common childhood megalomania has a way of reappearing from time to time, in trace form, in adulthood. It is only when the individual lacks more sophisticated mechanisms to manage his anxieties and self-image that megalomania threatens to take over, fueling an overactive tendency to imagine the threats posed by the world, and an almost magical self-regard of his abilities to triumph over them.

George W. Bush's ability to assume, and maintain, an affable, humble everyman exterior has helped him to hide his megalomanic tendencies, particularly from his supporters. But closer inspection has revealed both the shape of his delusions, and the vigor with which he believes in them. Seen in this light, his quasi-divine sense of calling to the presidency, and to defeat Saddam Hussein, offer classic examples of the megalomanic overvaluation of the self. As his close friend Don Evans—and now cabinet member—has said, "Bush knows that we're all here to serve a calling greater than self. That's what he's committed his life to do. He understands that he is the one person in the country, in this case really the one person in the world, who has a responsibility to protect and defend freedom." The omnipotent braggadocio Bush has demonstrated in his appearance on the USS *Abraham Lincoln* (among many other instances) has an interesting relationship with the expressions of humility he has shown elsewhere—as when he affects the personality of an ordinary, common man, rather than a man born to wealth and power. In the Bush megalomanic model, such humility functions as a cover for internal feelings of superiority—which compensate in turn for an overtly incomprehensible sense of shame. William A. White wrote that the megalomaniac has an "egotism that brooks no contradiction." This preening grandiosity, he said, is "too often the expression of an over-compensation for grave defects of character." The "Mission Accomplished" banner may seem intended to rally the troops and the voters, but in the end its grand indulgence in magical thinking—in the fantasy that a dangerous mission only just begun had already ended successfully—is about Bush himself, about his desperate need to triumph over his internal sense of inferiority and inadequacy.

Bush's impulsive behavior also provides telling glimpses of the destructive fantasies that drive him still. When he blurted out "Fuck Saddam, we're taking him out"—back when the war in Iraq was still an unrealized fantasy—his words were merely a symptom of his omnipotent delusions. Once he had rallied an army, and concocted an excuse, to fuck his imagined persecutor, however, he was able to send Americans to their deaths to support his magical thinking. And when the false pretenses for his exercise in omnipotence began to be exposed, he proved incapable of claiming responsibility or making reparations to the American people he deceived; instead, he allowed the blame to fall upon others—on the vague but telling concept of "false intelligence," a tragically apt if misplaced description of the real culprit—for having led him to do so.

When Bush succeeds in defeating his self-constructed enemies, his megalomanic satisfaction is apparent in the glee with which he responds to the news. Just before his sober four-minute speech on March 20, 2003, announcing the commencement of America's bombing of Iraq, Bush was captured on an internal White House TV monitor pumping his fist, exclaiming "Feels good." In December 2003, the delight he took in Saddam's capture was apparent in both his gloating demeanor and his dime-novel rhetoric: "Good riddance," he crowed. "The world is better off without you, Mr. Saddam Hussein. I find it very interesting that when the heat got on, you dug yourself a hole and you crawled in it."

Longtime Bush observers are familiar with such behavior, dating back to Bush's days in Texas as the nation's leading executioner. His smug smiles had little to do with the individual convicts he put to death. They were moments of celebration—and relief—at the prospect of annihilating yet another recipient of his internal hostility, which he had no psychic choice but to project. Criminals make easy targets for megalomanic projection, in part because their dehumanization is generally socially acceptable. So it is that the "compassionate conservative" and avowed Christian can refuse ever to commute a sentence: these were not humans he was executing, but manifestations of his own desperately projected destructiveness, whose deaths served to reaffirm the awesome power he had accrued for himself.

In the final analysis, of course, Bush doesn't hear their pleas because he can't afford to. The megalomanic's delusions of omnipotence and feared persecution are evenly matched; it is a delicate balance, always at risk of tipping into vulnerability. (As President-Elect Bush quipped during his first visit with congressional leaders in December 2000: "If this were a dictatorship, it'd be a heck of a lot easier—just so long as I'm the dictator.") The idea of reining in one's destruction is anathema to the megalomanic individual: The threat of defeat is ever present, a constant distraction, so dire that in the throes of his destruction Bush feels able to ask for the nation's prayers, to appeal to others for help shoring up his fragile belief system.

The tragedy of 9/11 came as an attack on Bush's tenuous equilibrium, undermining the sense of omnipotence on which he depended, and igniting memories of the days of humiliation and inadequacy he had constructed his entire identity to deny. Thanks, however, to the circumstances of his recent election—a series of events that could only have bolstered his faith in magical solutions (even as they ate away at voters' faith in the electoral system), Bush soon remembered his conviction that he is the most powerful man in the world, and expanded his overvaluing of self to encompass the entire nation. "I want to thank all my citizens for coming," he told a 2002 South Dakota audience, allowing a startling glimpse of his megalomanic projection to slip out: The citizenry is his, *L'etat c'est moi*. As Freud wrote, "The *grande nation* can not face the idea that it can be defeated in war. *Ergo* it was not defeated; the victory does not count. It provides an example of mass paranoia and invents the delusion of betrayal." To Bush, the attack on his nation was an attack on himself, and consequently must be avenged.

⟵✦⟶

Mounting evidence continues to eradicate any doubt that the vengeance visited on Saddam in the name of 9/11 and WMD had little to do with either. We've seen the oedipal origins of Bush's aggression; the megalomania model sheds even more light. The megalomaniac loves his delusion the way he loves himself, hence Bush's indifference to any evidence contradicting his assertions. In fact, words are irrelevant to the megalomaniac; triumph is everything. His delusion may be full of internal contradictions, but these are easily dismissible—as along as there is an evil-doer over whom to triumph.

Freud writes of the "characteristic indefiniteness concerning the evil-doers," who are of course less relevant for the evil they do than for what they represent to the megalomanic individual. The vagueness about so much of Bush's war on terror—from the ambiguity of its scope, to the empty language of his pronouncements, to the dissembling and denial about Saddam's WMD—suggests how thoroughly Bush's megalomanic motivations have shaped this tragic, destructive endeavor. Even before 9/11, Bush's thinking was already running this way: "We don't know who they are," he said of international terrorists during the 2000 campaign, "but we know they're there," offering a startling, prescient glimpse of the megalomanic mind-set that would soon take charge of the U.S. military.

The megalomanic personality's blurring of reality is ultimately self-serving. To preserve both his fantasies of persecution and his overvalued sense of self, Bush is often forced to distort reality by misinterpreting what others say and do, which allows him to fit his already limited experience and input into his preconceived notion of the world. He clings to his misinterpretations the way a baby clings to his mother's breast (not for nothing is this phenomenon often referred to as "nursing a grudge"). Bush's strictly enforced premium on loyalty speaks to this tendency as well: he insists that the people surrounding him fulfill his fixed ideas of them, in part because he is incapable of adapting those ideas to reflect reality.

Of course, the ultimate hope to which Bush clings is the notion that in his omnipotence his solutions will be magically successful; his worldview is defined by a desperate need that those solutions succeed, so grave are the alternatives his paranoid imagination suggests. No wonder he listens to no one, allows no criticism or dissent. And no wonder he raises the stakes so quickly, morphing in less than three years from an advocate of a "humble" foreign policy (as he vowed during the 2000 campaign) to the commander of a first-strike policy. The megalomanic must keep ahead of the "grave and gathering threat" that is fixed in his imagination, the fear of reprisal dictated by the uncon-scious Law of Talion that he fears he will one day fail to outrun.

In the end, what Bush is driven to avoid at all costs is the pain of self-recognition. In recent years, fiscal conservatives have begun to question Bush's comfort with unprecedented deficit spending. What they fail to recognize is that his need to diminish future progress is an unconscious attack on his own parents; his need to destroy their cre-ative power is far greater than any need to adhere to a conservative philosophy of fiscal responsibility. He wants to do what he wants to do—and nobody can stop him. The megalomanic hates anybody else having power—it is always a potential threat to his own.

Yet Bush is tremendously invested in the illusion of his inner goodness, which he can maintain only by externalizing his consider-able capacity for destruction. By capturing the man who threatened to kill his father, he both saved his father's honor and conjured a persua-sive counterpoint to his own negative feelings toward Bush the father. In the end, George W. would go down in history not as the enemy of his father, but as the enemy of his father's enemy. Terrified of losing this image of himself, he must eliminate any threat to his fantasy of well-being. Even being the most powerful man on earth doesn't re-lieve him from pain and panic, so he is forced to annihilate any recog-nition of himself as impotent or as a failure, by defining and then extinguishing external persecutors.

In his own mind, the megalomanic person can never lose. His bat-tles are less about political beliefs than about securing triumph. By pre-serving his delusions, he becomes the great destroyer, ready to take a wrecking ball to the world, even though what he is actually attacking are the pain and suffering of real life. As his delusions persist and grow, he needs an audience and a stage of ever-growing proportions on which to vanquish his foes.

For George W. Bush, tragically, all the world's a stage.

# EPILOGUE

*next to of course god america i*
*love you land of the pilgrims' and so forth.*

—ee cummings, *next to of course god America i*

*This Republic was founded in part because of the arrogance of a king who expected his subjects to do as they were told, without question, without hesitation. Our forefathers overthrew that tyrant and adopted a system of government where dissent is not only important, but it is also mandatory. Questioning flawed leadership is a requirement of this government. Failing to question, failing to speak out, is failing the legacy of the Founding Fathers.*

—U.S. Senator Robert Byrd, April 7, 2004

**W**hat to do? That is the question ultimately raised by this inquiry. An analyst might frame the question in terms of treatment: If George W. Bush were actually a patient, what approach would be appropriate? There are, of course, diagnostic tests that might shed more objective light on his condition: tests for paranoia and megalomania, for cognitive capacity and learning styles, for ADHD, for alcoholism. But that still leaves open the question of prognosis. The analyst treating President Bush would foresee that his prognosis would depend on whether or not he accepted treatment, and how that treatment was administered.

But the implications of George W. Bush's psychology extend far beyond the president himself. More important than his personal struggle is what we might consider the prognosis for America—a question that looms large as the time approaches to decide whether he should remain in office.

For the readers of this book—particularly the American voter—the purpose of trying to understand President Bush is not to reduce him, but to enrich our way of knowing him. Of course, Bush is not a patient; he is our leader. But he is also our employee—he works for all of us. I began this project with the hope that it would help us to understand him with empathy, while at the same time offering an argument that he is not fit to work as our president. As fellow human beings, we should extend to George W. Bush our concern. As conscientious Americans, however, it would be irresponsible for us to allow him to continue in a position for which he is so ill-suited, and in which he has done so much harm to the interests of his employer—the American people. Like any compassionate manager, we must recognize that our employee is incompetent and that we have an obligation to provide him with resources to address his problems—and a dignified exit strategy from the workplace.

Is there any likelihood that Bush might somehow *become* fit for office? Not without treatment—by all accounts an unlikely prospect. The presidency is an extraordinarily effective defense system for someone of Bush's mind-set. There he is protected by the cloak of his own manias and projections; after tentatively conquering his addiction, investing supreme faith in a rigid regimen religion and exercise, he has found the perfect perch from which to indulge his tendencies toward sadism and paranoia while hiding behind his charismatic personality. As long as that arrangement prevails, it's nearly impossible to imagine him becoming anxious enough to be confronted about who he is and what he's done.

Yet in his April 13, 2004, press conference, there were finally signs that Bush's facade might be breaking down. In the face of the most forthright questioning of his presidency, his defenses could only carry him so far; soon he began to ramble, stringing together phrases the way a patient who has lost his sense of identity empties his wallet and displays all his cards and pictures in an attempt to reclaim his sense of self. Looking at times like a lost boy who was in over his head, Bush seemed unable to understand either the questions or the consequences of his actions.

Ironically, it was when he was most paralyzed by anxiety—telling a reporter "you just put me on the spot here and maybe I'm not quick"—that Bush appeared to be most honest about himself. He said what he felt at the moment: He was paralyzed, and he admitted it. It may not have been the best forum for his honesty to reveal itself—we don't want a president to show the world that he is paralyzed by fear—but in a therapy group, Bush's admission would have been a major breakthrough.

It seems unlikely, in any event, that he feels the need for help. His behavior is what psychoanalysts call egosyntonic, meaning that his actions—the lies he tells and the harm he inflicts on others—don't appear to cause him much conscious anxiety. For example, people who have ADD are often capable of believing the lies they tell, because they're actually cognitively impaired; it is as if they don't know they are lying. Unconsciously, of course, Bush's anxieties are more pronounced—particularly the dread of retribution that haunts him, which he manages by increasing his vigilance and ours.

I have never been successful treating anyone who came to see me because somebody else said he should. The person must be aware of his own need for treatment, as well as be willing to seek help; Bush is neither. He reminds me of a patient in the hospital who insisted that he was dead. The resident argued with him until he was at wit's end. Finally, the doctor said, "Dead men don't bleed, do they?" The patient said, "That is true." The resident then suggested they both stick their fingers with needles and see what happened. They did, and they bled. The patient then said, "Doc, I was wrong—dead men *do* bleed." With his persistence in clinging to disproved theories of all stripes, it's easy to imagine George W. reacting the same way.

Separating a patient from his delusional system is always difficult, and even more so when he has not been separated from the setting where he has indulged his delusions for so long. A proper treatment for George W. Bush, thus, would involve leaving the presidency. Short of that, however, there are some other approaches that could help.

The first stage of treatment would be to begin to compromise his defenses by making him anxious. In this approach, the patient is discouraged from resorting to his customary means of controlling his anxiety. I once had a patient who would retreat into grandiose fantasies whenever he became anxious. His retreat involved compulsively and greedily overeating; the indulgence made him feel all-powerful. The first step in his treatment was to monitor his food strictly for a week; once his anxieties had increased to the point where he could no longer suppress them easily, he was able to confront—and work on—his inner pain.

People obviously have many methods of numbing anxiety, the most familiar being alcohol. Bush now numbs himself through exercise, prayer, and sleep—activities that can be just as compulsive as overeating. A doctor treating Bush wouldn't be right to stop him from sleeping altogether, but depriving him of his routine—or limiting his trips to Crawford—might prove constructive. Having removed these anxiety suppressors, the doctor would create a therapeutic setting powerful enough to help the patient face himself—a requirement for treating a person with character pathology as strong as Bush's. This is similar to the intervention model used to treat alcoholics and addicts. There's some evidence to suggest that Bush would respond to intervention—as he did on February 13, 2004, when he bowed to mounting media pressure and released four hundred pages of vague National Guard material for the press to sift through. Though the truest intervention would be separating him from the powers of his office, even the threat of losing the election might be intimidating enough to force even this recalcitrant president to reexamine his beliefs. (Remember, for the president of the United States, delusion and reality must be hard to differentiate: He thinks he is the most powerful person in the world, in part, because he actually is.)

Once a proper therapeutic atmosphere had been created, Bush's treatment would require him to reclaim his projections, healing the split worldview he learned in infancy. The therapist would then be freer to empathize with the lost boy inside the man. Unfortunately, his projections do have some material support in reality, and among the general public: Saddam really *is* a bad person, who killed more of his own people than the U.S. invasion did. The paranoid needs to be quarantined to the point where his projections have no easy places to rest. Of course, this is easier said than done: As another psychoanalytic pioneer, Carl Jung, once wrote, there would be no more war only if people were willing to come to terms with the opposites within their own natures. Obviously, that hasn't happened yet.

The more pathological the patient, the more severe is his resistance. The madman always creates wiggle room, always finds a hook on which to hang his projections, his tenacity bolstered by his fear of imminent collapse. And Bush has certainly demonstrated his tenacity time and again. His history is one of a determined person who gets his way—he loves a good fight (or a dirty one). He is so effective that the diagnosis of megalomania merits some qualification; after all, most megalomaniacs are in hospitals and not in the White House. And his mode of retreat—a combination of prayer, exercise, and sleep—is qualitatively different from the delusional state into which most megalomaniacs retreat.

Nevertheless, though he is strong in so many ways, Bush is at his core a fragile man. That much is apparent in his frightened eyes, in the staged theatrics of his appearances; spontaneity itself is unsafe for him. A cause for concern as long as he is in office, Bush's fragility can also be seen as a reason for hope—a hope, albeit a small one, that if he is one day stripped of his coping mechanisms in a therapeutic setting, he could finally open himself to healing. (Still, another outcome is far more likely—that he would escalate his attacks as a protection against collapse. To some critics, that is what he seemed to do immediately after his shaky press conference, when he antagonized the Arab world by reenforcing his support of Israeli prime minister Sharon.)

As we have noted, some of Bush's fragility may be neurological, so Bush's treatment would require that other underlying conditions also be addressed. The tests for dyslexia, thought disorder, ADHD, Tourette's, and alcohol-related brain damage would help by suggesting effective ways to combat those roadblocks to clear and effective thinking. A Rorschach projective test could help determine his level of paranoia and assess how concrete or symbolic his thinking capabilities are. These tests are reliable and instructive, and would be considered a standard element of any comprehensive psychodynamic examination of a patient presenting the symptoms we see in Bush. Their findings would provide essential guidance on how he could be treated for maximum effectiveness.

And yet, even if he presented himself as a willing patient, treating George W. Bush would be a difficult prospect. In *The Price of Loyalty,* Ron Suskind describes an exchange that underscores the potential problem. At one point in the book, O'Neill and Bush get momentarily lost in a tunnel leading into the Treasury building, an incident that puts them in a chatty, almost playful frame of mind. Upon emerging from the tunnel—an environment eerily reminiscent of the cave-like spaces Bush is fond of evoking in his references to Saddam and Osama—O'Neill proceeded to present Bush with his argument against massive deficit spending. Suddenly, Suskind writes, "the conviviality had burned off. Bush looked at him with the flat, inexpressive stare to which O'Neill had become accustomed. 'I won't negotiate with myself,' Bush finally said. . . . O'Neill's mind raced. . . . But he just nodded. The President made it clear that this was not about analysis. It was about tactics." It was also about binary thinking, and the limitations it imposes on him. He may seem decisive, but his behavior represents the fall-back position of someone trying to manage the anxiety of not being able to think clearly.

Another discouraging moment occurred during Diane Sawyer's interview with Bush after the capture of Saddam, just after he dismissed her questions about weapons of mass destruction by asking, "what's the difference?" Not only did he deny her the opportunity to answer his question, he responded to her queries about the possibilities that the public had been misled with a stunning impenetrability, staying on message as he refused to internalize any aspect of the inquiry. "Diane, you can keep asking the question," he finally said. "I'm telling you—I made the right decision for America." Such stubbornness, of course, could prove problematic—even fatal—to the prospect of successful treatment.

The beginning of treatment, then, would be the first step of what would likely be a long and difficult journey. His ability to think is already seriously compromised. There is no way to ask Bush "how he broke his heart," the classic psychodynamic query, when he does not consider his heart to be broken—when his heart is surrounded by a lifetime of undisturbed defenses, from exercise to God to the authority of holding the highest office in the land.

Without treatment, however, it's unlikely that Bush will change—at least not for the better. As he told Tim Russert flatly, "I'm not going to change. . . . I won't change my philosophy or point of view." Unfortunately, recognizing a need for treatment is itself a kind of change—and treatment cannot begin without a patient who wants it. Once commenced, there is no limit to the vicissitudes that treatment can take. But you have to get the person through the door, a threshold Bush is unlikely to cross if he doesn't feel a need to come in the first place.

In the end, then, there are two prognoses in this situation—one for President Bush, and the other for the nation at large. Having seen the depth and range of Bush's psychological flaws, it should now be easier to observe President Bush's actions and policies with an appreciation of the conditions that underlie his behavior. Just two days after the revelation that U.S. troops have been torturing Iraqi prisoners, for example, in early May 2004 Bush felt able to board a campaign bus tour to the Midwest. In trying to understand this ill-timed trip—which the president explained by saying that he wanted to "get out of Washington," that "peace and freedom depend on this election"—the enlightened voter might ask, is this the behavior of a man who fully grasps his priorities? Or the latest evasion of responsibility by a megalomanic personality who sees himself as an Exception?

Though we are not a nation of psychoanalysts, it is useful to know that psychoanalysts are required to be analyzed before they begin to work with patients, and to continue their own personal analysis for as long as necessary. As my old mentor Dr. Semrad said, "Psychotherapy is the case of a big mess taking care of a bigger mess." Being in treatment enables us both to see what we have in common with our patients—and it often is a lot—and how we differ from them.

The same is true for American voters, as we assess our upcoming decision about President Bush's future. This isn't to say that we all need treatment in order to monitor and assess our president, but we must consider the ways in which we are enablers, akin to the children of alcoholics. As we've noted earlier, Bush's popularity relies on the interplay between his appeal and our tendency to respond and relate to his qualities.

Throughout his life, George W. Bush has taken many detours from the path to self-knowledge. As we re-examine the president's popularity in this election year, it's worth asking whether we have also allowed ourselves to be led similarly astray. We are all human, and we benefit from recognizing traits in others that we ourselves share.

Many of us rely to varying degrees on our own models of projection, of anxiety management, of distraction and disguise. All are worthy of exploration. But as we re-evaluate President Bush, the most important mechanism to understand may be *denial*. As we've seen, George W. Bush has spent his life in strenuous denial of his many sources of anxiety. From the 2000 campaign through the first few years of his term, it seems that much of America—the media included—have relied just as desperately on denial.

The presidency may be the only job that could make George W. Bush feel safe; as president he is in control of everything and surrounded by people who will protect him. Yet his position is comparable to that of many CEOs and other corporate executives—functioning megalomanics who are driven to satisfy their grandiose needs though a string of business risks that eventually lead to failure (as, indeed, Bush himself learned in his early business career). Such failures can, sometimes, shatter an individual's denial, and lead the individual to undertake a more realistic self-assessment.

For the moment, though, George W. Bush still inhabits a uniquely favored position of power, and the enterprise he is poised to add to his history of failures is the future of our nation. Our collective denial helped put him in that position. And unless we overcome that denial, it will keep him there.

Our sole treatment option—for his benefit and for ours—is to remove President Bush from office. It is up to all of us—Congress, the media, and voters—to do so, before it is too late.

# SOURCE NOTES

## INTRODUCTION: CURIOUS ABOUT GEORGE

xi  "at-a-distance leader personality assessment . . .": Jerrold M. Post, "Leader Personality Assessments in Support of Government Policy," in Post, ed., *The Psychological Assessment of Political Leaders* (Ann Arbor: University of Michigan Press, 2003), p. 39.

xi  "At the time of his confirmation hearings . . . Accentuated by some of the recent intelligence 'surprises,' . . .": Ibid., p. 61.

xii  "to understand shaping events . . .": Post, "Assessing Leaders at a Distance: The Political Personality Profile," Ibid., p. 70

xii  "the leader who cannot adapt . . .": Ibid., p. 77.

## ONE: THE FIRST FAMILY

2  "as different from Rye, New York . . .": Barbara Bush, *Barbara Bush: A Memoir* (New York: Scribner, 1994), p. 34.

3  "I had moments where I was jealous of attractive young women out in a man's world . . .": Pamela Kilian, *Barbara Bush: Matriarch of a Dynasty* (New York: Thomas Dunne Books/St. Martin's Press, 2002), pp. 40–41.

4  "the one who instills fear . . .": Bill Minutaglio, *First Son: George W. Bush and the Bush Family Dynasty* (New York: Crown, 1999), p. 49.

4  "bust them up and slap them around . . .": Ibid.

4  "heaven-sent message . . .": Barbara Bush, interviewed by Jamie Gangel on *Dateline NBC,* October 19, 2003.

5        "My mother never cooked . . . .": Ron Suskind, *The Price of Loyalty* (New York: Simon & Schuster, 2004), p. 189.

5        "you can criticize me, but don't . . .": Barbara Bush, interviewed by Larry King, *Larry King Live, CNN,* October 22, 2003.

5        "Well, now, that's behind us . . .": George W. Bush, *A Charge to Keep* (New York: William Morrow, 1999), p. 4.

5        "would determine who [among her circle of friends]. . . She was sort of the leader bully. . . .": Kilian, *Barbara Bush: Matriarch of a Dynasty,* pp. 16–17.

6        "did most of the scolding . . .": Barbara Bush, *Barbara Bush: A Memoir,* p. 11.

6        "humiliating incident . . . outrageous . . .": Ibid., p. 6.

6        "striking beauty . . . remember that mother cooked . . .": Ibid., p. 10.

6        "things like how to cook, clean and wash clothes . . . should be able to pick [them] up reading . . .": Ibid., p. 26.

6        "like a second mother . . .": Ibid., p. 14.

7        "the biggest pain in the world . . .": Ibid., p. 10.

7        "always raised [her] hand . . . being the last girl chosen . . . by far the prettiest . . . humiliated . . .": Ibid., p. 15.

7        "was an inadvertent one . . . when my ship comes in . . . ship had come in—she just didn't know it . . . .": Ibid., p. 10.

13       "There are no shades of gray . . .": Mark Crispin Miller, *The Bush Dyslexicon* (New York: W. W. Norton, updated paperback edition, 2002), p. 337.

15       "not long after Robin's death . . . usually insouciant . . . Throughout the night . . . was watching, unsure what was happening . . .": Minutaglio, *First Son,* pp. 46–47.

16       "apparent incapacity for any show of sorrow . . . If this were a psychobiography. . . .": Miller, *The Bush Dyslexicon,* p. 322.

17       "all in all, it's been a fabulous year . . .": Ibid., p. 348.

17       "surrogate parents . . . My father doesn't have . . . could see that Bush felt . . .": Minutaglio, *First Son,* p. 117.

17       "to express the intimacy . . .": Ibid., p. 337.

## TWO: AFFABILITY AND DISABILITY

20    "The best way to describe . . .": "President Bush, Ambassador Bremer Discuss Progress in Iraq," October 27, 2003, www.whitehouse.gov.

20    "There is no doubt in my mind . . .": Eric Alterman and Mark Green, *The Book on Bush* (New York: Viking Press, 2004), pp. 7–8.

20    "I am confident we have not . . .": Ibid., p. 176.

21    "We're both clowns . . .": Minutaglio, *First Son,* p. 46.

21    "I was too much of a burden . . .": Barbara Bush, *Barbara Bush: A Memoir,* p. 50.

22    "Bushtail . . .": George Lardner Jr. and Lois Romano, "Tragedy Created Bush Mother-Son Bond," *Washington Post,* July 26, 1999.

25    "never anguishes over decisions . . .": Kenneth T. Walsh, "A Case of Confidence," *U.S. News and World Report,* November 17, 2003.

26    "advisors have admitted that the staff . . .": Alterman and Green, *The Book on Bush,* p. 3.

26    "major-league asshole . . .": Miller, *The Bush Dyslexicon,* p. 51n.

26    "The line between effervescence . . . like a blowfish . . .": Frank Bruni, *Ambling into History* (New York: HarperCollins, 2002), p. 19.

26    "stay in [Bush's] hotel room until late . . . wanted everyone to know that nothing [of the kind] was happening . . .": Stephen Mansfield, *The Faith of George W. Bush* (New York: Jeremy P. Tarcher, 2003), p. 79.

27    "I had dabbled in many things . . . had a taste of many different jobs . . . .": George W. Bush, *A Charge to Keep,* pp. 59–60.

27    "hunters . . . farmers . . .": Page: 6 *Attention Deficit Disorder: A Different Perception,* p. 14.

28    "tighten[ing] the net . . . smoking Al Qaeda out of their caves . . . on the run . . .": White House Press Conference, October 11, 2001, www.whitehouse.gov.

28    "smoke these al Qaeda types out . . .": White House Press Conference, March 6, 2003, www.whitehouse.gov.

28    "When I was a kid . . .": Miller, *The Bush Dyslexicon,* p. 338.

28    "tone it down . . .": Bob Woodward, *Bush at War* (New York: Simon & Schuster, 2002), pp. 100–101.

28    "Others are mirror readers . . . 'filament' for 'firmament' . . .": Edward M. Hallowell and John J. Ratey, *Driven to Distraction* (New York: Pantheon, 1994), p. 164.

28    "gets his news from people . . .": Interview with Diane Sawyer, *ABC News,* December 16, 2003.

29    "I glance at the headlines . . . I rarely read the stories . . .": Washington, D.C., September 21, 2003, in Jacob Weisberg, "The Complete Bushisms," www.slate.com.

29    "not real serious, studious . . .": Minutaglio, *First Son,* p. 86.

29    "Their home lacked an encyclopedia . . .": "Mommy Dearest: Barbara's Bad Parenting" by Marjorie Perloff, October 5, 1992, in the *New Republic.*

29    "I never interviewed her . . .": Frank Bruni, "The 2000 Campaign: Reporter's Notebook; Bush's Tune Is the Same Even as the Pitch Varies," *New York Times,* September 16, 2000.

29    "a 119 number for dyslexics . . .": Bush made the joke in a 1998 speech to the D.C. Alfalfa Club. *Washington Post,* February 2, 1998.

30    "seeing the cows . . . talk to me . . .": Craig Unger, *House of Bush, House of Saud* (New York: Scribner, 2004), p. 237.

32    "In an attempt to dress up his language . . . competitive boarding school . . .": Minutaglio, *First Son,* pp. 63–64.

33    "He rose to a certain prominence . . . he just never seemed very warm . . . He just didn't let people get to know him . . .": Ibid., pp. 62–63.

35    "willing to wear a cross . . .": Peter Schweizer and Rochelle Schweizer, *The Bushes: Portrait of a Dynasty* (New York: Doubleday, 2004), p. 531.

## THREE: MESSAGE IN THE BOTTLE

38    "to go *mano a mano* right here . . .": Minutaglio, *First Son,* p. 6.

38    "I don't think I was clinically an alcoholic . . .": "In His Own Words: I Made Mistakes," *Washington Post,* July 25, 1999.

38    "I had a drinking problem. Right now I should be in a bar, not the Oval Office . . .": David Frum, *The Right Man* (New York: Random House, 2003), p. 283.

39    "characterized by . . . impaired control over drinking . . .": ASAM definition, *Journal of the American Medical Association* 268(8), (1992): 1012–1015.

40    "Bush has said publicly that he quit drinking without the help of AA or any substance abuse program . . .": Cary Tennis, "My Name Is George, and I'm an Alcoholic," July 26, 2001, www.salon.com.

40    "There is only one reason . . .": Frum, *The Right Man,* p. 283.

43    "42 percent of his first seven months as president . . .": Mike Allen, "A White House on the Range: Bush Retreats to Ranch for 'Working Vacation'," *Washington Post,* August 7, 2001.

44    "America did the right thing in Iraq . . .": "Bush, CIA Defend Iraq War," Reuters, February 6, 2004.

49    "The president may have been . . .": Tom Shales, *Washington Post,* March 7, 2003.

49    "a chance to allow the inspectors . . . Hussein had, in fact . . ." Dana Priest and Dana Milbank, "Bush defends change, quality of intelligence," *Washington Post,* July 15, 2003.

49    "no doubt in my mind . . .": Alterman and Green, *The Book on Bush,* pp. 7–8, 176.

50    "their level of drinking constitutes a problem . . .": "Study: Heavy Social Drinkers Show Brain Damage," Reuters, April 15, 2004, www.cnn.com.

## FOUR: IN GOD I TRUST

55    "was possessed of a deep spiritual nature . . .": Mansfield, *The Faith of George W. Bush,* pp. 6–7.

55    "'righteous . . . the Commandments Man . . .": Ibid., p. 9.

56    "Midland was hurting . . .": Ibid, p. 61.

56    "Would you rather live with Jesus . . . take control of [Bush's] life . . . make [his] home in heaven . . .": Ibid, p. 65.

56    "Unless a man is born again he shall not see the kingdom of God . . .": Ibid., p. 67.

57    "a mustard seed in my soul . . .": George W. Bush, *A Charge to Keep,* p. 136.

57    "George has been born again . . . .": Mansfield, *The Faith of George W. Bush,* p. 69.

58    "sensation of reward we experience . . . .": Medical News Archive, "What Do We Want? Rewards! When Do We Want 'Em? Now!" Neil Osterwill, reviewed by Dr. Jacqueline Brooks, May 25, 2001.

58    "certain people have genetic abnormalities in their reward systems' that can 'lead not only to potential problems with addictive behaviors but with impulsivity in general' . . .": Ibid., citing the work of David Cummings, M.D.

58    "endorphins have proven to be just as addicting . . .": Robert Ornstein and David Sobel, *The Healing Brain* (New York: Simon & Schuster, 1987), p. 93.

59    "It doesn't do any good . . . .": Minutaglio, *First Son,* p. 320.

60    "overseas experience was pretty much . . .": Nicholas D. Kristof, "The 2000 Campaign: The Decision; For Bush, His Toughest Call Was the Choice to Run at All," *New York Times,* October 29, 2000.

61    "we can substitute concurrence . . . .": Ron Britton, *Belief and Imagination* (New York: Routledge Press, 1998), p. 2.

63    "pervasive sense of unreality": Britton, *Belief and Imagination,* p. 59.

64    "He just decides, *This sentence is worthless . . .":* "Interview with Darrell Hammond," *Reliable Sources,* November 30, 2003, www.cnn.com.

65    "Bush seemed jangled . . .": Timothy Noah, "How Bush Blew His Press Conference," July 30, 2003, www.slate.com.

65    "vague and sometimes nearly incoherent . . .": "Sidestepping on Iraq," *New York Times,* July 31, 2003.

65    "And so we're making progress . . .": "President Bush Discusses Top Priorities for the U.S.," July 30, 2003, www.whitehouse.gov.

67 "was not awakened to be told . . .": Mike Sandalow, "All's Calm for the Hands-Off, Decisive Commander in Chief: Confident Bush Not Losing Any Sleep over War," *San Francisco Chronicle,* March 23, 2003.

68 "a president 'who had no trouble' . . .": Harold Meyerson, *Washington Post,* April 7, 2004.

68 "he wished he were Robin . . .": Minutaglio, *First Son,* p. 45.

69 "Mr. President, the Director of the CIA . . .": Interview with President Bush, *Meet the Press,* February 8, 2004.

71 "Given the rambling non-answers . . .": "Sidestepping on Iraq"[Editorial], *New York Times,* July 31, 2003.

71 "I feel like God wants me to run . . .": Mansfield, *The Faith of George W. Bush,* p. 109.

72 "I always laugh when people say. . .": Peter Schweizer and Rochelle Schweizer, *The Bushes: Portrait of a Dynasty,* p. 465.

72 "God told me to strike at al Qaida . . .": Arnon Regular, " 'Road map is a life saver for us,' PM Abbas tells Hamas," www. Haaretz.com.

72 "He's in the White House because . . . .": "And He's Head of Intelligence?" *Newsweek,* October 27, 2003.

73 "It was, of course, picked up and politicized . . .": Mansfield, *The Faith of George W. Bush,* p. 95.

74 "crusade . . .": Miller, *The Bush Dyslexicon,* pp. 332–333.

74 "They hate progress and freedom . . .": Ibid., p. 341.

76 "Heck, I don't know . . .": Tim Russert interview with President Bush, *Meet the Press,* February 8, 2004.

## FIVE: OUTLAW

77 "every individual is virtually an enemy of civilization . . .": Sigmund Freud, "The Future of an Illusion," *The Standard Edition of the Complete Psychological Works of Sigmund Freud,* Vol. 21 (London: Hogarth Press, 1927) p. 6.

78 "more international treaties in the first year . . .": Mansfield, *The Faith of George W. Bush,* p. 123.

78    "they suggest a pack of devils . . . .": Roger Money-Kyrle, *Man's Picture of His World* (New York: International University Press, 1961), p. 127.

78    "an unconscious sense of guilt . . .": Freud, "Criminals from a Sense of Guilt," *The Standard Edition of the Complete Psychological Works of Sigmund Freud,* Vol. 14 (London: Hogarth Press, 1916) p. 332; of three essays called "Some Character Types met with in Psychoanalytic Work," *The Standard Edition of the Complete Psychological Works of Sigmund Freud,* pp. 311–336.

78    "the Exceptions . . .": Ibid. "The Exceptions" 1916, p. 311.

79    "His mother is descended from President Franklin Pierce . . .": Kevin Phillips, *American Dynasty* (New York: Viking, 2004), p. 19.

79    "Four generations of building . . . .": Ibid., p. ix.

79    "clandestine arms deals . . . .": Ibid., p. x.

80    "George W. Bush reportedly sold fake ID cards . . .": Robert Kahn, "Coyote Speaks," Courthouse News, March 21, 2000, http://www.courthousenews.com/editorials/kahn/coyote23.htm.

80    "arrested for disorderly conduct in New Haven . . . detained and questioned by Princeton police . . .": Minutaglio, *First Son,* p. 34.

80    "burning pledges with a hot branding iron . . . 'only a cigarette burn' . . .": Ibid.

81    "Once ensconced in their offices . . .": John Dean, *Worse than Watergate* (New York: Little, Brown, 2004), p. xv.

81    "With little notice . . .": Ibid., p. 121.

81    "It is difficult to trust . . .": Ibid., p. 197.

82    "the culture of secrecy . . .": Phillips, *American Dynasty,* p. xi.

83    "The interesting thing about being the president . . .": Woodward, *Bush at War,* p. 146.

85    "I did eat with my family . . .": Hoaq Levins, "President Bush Ad Makes Fun of His Mother," *Ad Age,* September 22, 2003.

87    "enemies of freedom . . . aggressive tyrant [who] possessed terrible weapons . . .": White House address, September 7, 2003.

90    "So constant is [Bush's] fibbing . . .": Corn, *The Lies of George W. Bush,* p. 1.

90    "honest-man routine . . .": Ibid., p. 12.

90    "a candidate who rises to power . . . .": Ibid., p. 7.

90    "I have been very candid . . . .": Ibid., p. 29.

91    "exonerated in correspondence from the SEC . . .": Molly Ivins and Lou Dubose, *Bushwhacked* (New York: Random House, 2003), p. 14.

92    "there are pledges all the time . . .": Corn, *The Lies of George W. Bush*, p. 15.

92    "So what's the difference? . . .": Interview with Diane Sawyer, *ABC News*, December 16, 2003.

92    "we have a responsibility to respect the law . . . the court cloaked its ruling in legalistic language . . .": Corn, *The Lies of George W. Bush*, pp. 60–61.

92    "We must uncover every detail . . .": Ibid., p. 145.

92    "I take personal responsibility . . .": Ibid., p. 295.

93    "International law? I better call my lawyer! . . .": White House press release, December 11, 2003.

93    "became independently wealthy . . . .": Corn, *The Lies of George W. Bush*, p. 193n.

93    "Why should we hear about body bags . . .": Diane Sawyer, *ABC News*, March 18, 2003.

94    "We were buying political influence . . .": Dean, *Worse than Watergate*, p. 28.

95    "dismissed as merely one of many contributors . . .": Joe Conason, *Big Lies* (New York: Thomas Dunne Books/St. Martin's Press, 2002), p. 150.

96    "the provider with the prop turkey": Mike Allen, *Washington Post*, December 4, 2003.

98    "there was nobody in our government . . .": White House Press Conference, April 13, 2003, www.whitehouse.gov.

98    "Islamic terrorists might attempt to kill President Bush . . .": "Italy Tells of Threat at Genoa Summit," *Los Angeles Times*, September 27, 2001.

98    "the war on terror goes on . . .": White House Press Conference, July 30, 2003.

99    "This conflict was begun on the timing . . .": Ibid., p. 6.

99    "It is the calling of our time . . .": George W. Bush et al., *We Will Prevail* (Continuum Publishing Group, 2003), p. 78.

## SIX: THE SMIRK

101    "Bush inserted firecrackers . . .": Shireen Parsons, *Roanoke Times*, January 23, 2004, p. B9.

101    "smirking over the executions of death row inmates . . .": Alan Berlow, "The Texas Clemency Memos," *Atlantic Monthly*, July/August 2003.

101    "master of low expectations . . .": Corn, *The Lies of George W. Bush*, p. 313.

102    "Guess what? The three men . . .": Miller, *The Bush Dyslexicon*, p. 52.

102    "I'd rather have them . . .": Fort Meade, Maryland, June 4, 2002, from Weisberg, "The Complete Bushisms," www.salon.com.

104    "Melanie Klein expanded on Freud's ideas . . .": Klein wrote about this internal infantile confusion throughout her career, beginning with her 1932 book *The Psychoanalysis of Children*.

105    "branding each initiate . . .": Miller, *The Bush Dyslexicon*, p. 55.

106    "plays even rougher with its enemies . . .": Dean, *Worse than Watergate*, p. 169.

107    "I thought they played dirty at the Nixon White House . . .": Ibid., p. 171.

107    "a $15 billion humanitarian pledge . . .": Ivins and Dubose, *Bushwhacked*, p. 289.

107    "providing low income heating assistance . . .": Ibid., p. 181.

107    "Bush's assault on the meat inspection system . . .": Ibid., p. 141.

107    "I don't understand how poor people think . . .": Elizabeth Bumiller, "Bush's 'Compassion Agenda: A liability in '04?'" *New York Times*, August 23, 2003.

108    "commitment [to] provide excellent health care . . .": Associated Press, "Bush has knees examined, visits with wounded troops," *USA Today*, December 18, 2003.

108 "hundreds of sick and wounded . . .": Mark Benjamin, "Sick, wounded U.S. troops held in squalor," UPI, October 17, 2003.

108 "Talk is cheap—and getting cheaper . . . Taken piecemeal, all these corner-cutting moves . . . But even flesh wounds . . .": *Army Times,* July 2, 2003.

109 "I try to go for longer runs . . .": Bob Wischnia and Paul Carrozza, "20 Questions for President George W. Bush: A Running Conversation," *Runner's World,* October 2002.

110 "My New Year's resolution this year is to work . . . It's going to be a year in which . . .": Press pool interview, January 2, 2004.

110 "let the terrorists achieve the objective . . .": White House Press Conference, October 11, 2001, www.whitehouse.gov.

111 "He spent the day before the strikes . . .": Bruni, *Ambling into History,* p. 262.

111 "I remember campaigning in Chicago . . .": William Rivers Pitt, *The Greatest Sedition is Silence* (Sterling, Virginia: Pluto Press, 2003), p. 45.

111 " 'Please,' Bush whimpers . . .": Al Franken, "Irrational Affairs: Is Bush Dumb?" *Rolling Stone,* October 11, 2000, citing Tucker Carlson, *Talk* magazine, September 1999.

112 "one bite of the apple . . .": Berlow, "The Texas Clemency Memos," *Atlantic Monthly,* July/August 2003.

112 "Imagine those nineteen hijackers . . . All told, more than three thousand . . .": State of the Union address, January 28, 2003.

113 "killing people without any . . .": Peter Singer, *The President of Good and Evil* (New York: Dutton, 2004), p. 84.

114 "Fuck Saddam, we're taking him out . . .": Michael Elliot and James Carney, *Time,* March 24, 2003.

117 "omnipotently hijack human righteousness . . .": Eric Brenman, "Cruelty and Narrowmindedness," in E. B. Spellius, ed., *Melanie Klein Today* (London: Karnac Books, 1989), p. 257.

117 "I made the right decision for America . . .": Diane Sawyer, *ABC News,* December 16, 2003.

117 "tried to kill my dad . . .": Mansfield, *The Faith of George W. Bush,* p. 146.

## SEVEN: TWISTED TONGUES

122 "there needs to be a wholesale effort . . . .": presidential debate, October 11, 2000; in Miller, *The Bush Dyslexicon,* p. 232.

122 "I will have a foreign-handed foreign policy . . .": Redwood, California, September 27, 2000; in Miller, *The Bush Dyslexicon,* p. 200.

122 "I am a person who recognized . . .": William Goldschlag, New York *Daily News,* September 20, 2000, p. 5.

122 "Security is the essential roadblock . . . .": Washington, D.C., July 25, 2003, from Weisberg, "The Complete Bushisms," www.slate.com.

122 "There is no doubt in my mind . . . .": South Bend, Indiana, September 5, 2002, from Ibid.

122 "These are Jebby's kids": www.abcnews.com, August 1988.

124 "I do know that mothers and dads . . . .": *Good Morning America,* May 11, 1999.

125 "I kind of like ducking questions . . . ": Dan Froomkin, "Ramblin' Man," www.washingtonpost.com, April 22, 2004.

126 "with the flailing of a nervous, befuddled student . . . marvel of free-floating pronouns . . . 'When I was coming up . . .' ": Bruni, *Ambling into History,* p. 44.

128 "Fifty percent of the American people . . .": Interview with Diane Sawyer, *ABC News,* December 17, 2003.

129 "The next most reticent president . . .": *New Yorker,* January 19, 2004, p. 60.

129 "They hate our freedoms . . .": George W. Bush et al., *We Will Prevail,* p. 14.

129 "This nation is very reluctant . . .": White House Press Conference, October 28, 2003, www.whitehouse.gov.

129 "there are some who would like to rewrite history . . . .": James Carville, *Had Enough?* (New York: Simon & Schuster, 2003), p. 182.

130 "even though it didn't start operations . . .": Unger, *House of Bush, House of Saud,* p. 166.

130 "is notable in that . . .": Dean, *Worse than Watergate,* p. 26.

131   "will say almost anything to get elected . . .": Corn, *The Lies of George W. Bush,* p. 38.

132   "the usurpation of the domain of reality . . .": W. R. Bion, p. 128 0IUP.

132   "The public education system in America . . .": "Remarks by the President at Simon for Governor Luncheon," Santa Clara, California, May 1, 2002, www.whitehouse.gov.

133   "good works [that] deserve our praise . . .": Alterman and Green, *The Book on Bush,* p. 172.

133   "a face for radio . . .": Romenesko, "White House Reporters See the Many Sides of Bush at Press Conference," *Los Angeles Times,* October 29, 2003, at http://www.poynter.org/dg.lts/id.45/aid.52979/column.htm.

133   "that you and your administration . . . The guy memorizes four words . . .": "President Bush Meets with French President Chirac," May 26, 2002, www.whitehouse.gov.

134   "Off the record . . .": Bruni, *Ambling into History,* p. 115.

135   "the lump in the bed next to me . . .": "Remarks by the President at Bush-Cheney 2004 Reception," June 27, 2003, www.whitehouse.gov.

135   "As I recall, the facts are these . . .": Miller, *The Bush Dyslexicon,* p. 256.

135   "My fellow citizens . . .": "President Bush Addresses the Nation," March 19, 2003, www.whitehouse.gov.

136   "Events during the past two years . . .": "President Bush Addresses United Nations General Assembly," September 23, 2003, www.whitehouse.gov.

136   "Clear Skies Initiative . . .": Jack Huberman, *The Bush-Hater's Handbook* (New York: Nation Books, 2004), p. 12.

136–137   "Healthy Forests Initiative . . .": Ibid., p. 166.

137   "He has no trouble speaking off the cuff . . . When he struts and thumps his chest . . .": Murray Whyte, *Toronto Star,* November 28, 2002.

137   "mastery of emotional language . . .*empty language . . . negative framework* . . .": Renana Brooks, *Nation,* June 30, 2003.

138    "We recognize that the starting point . . .": "President Bush, Egyptian President Mubarak Meet with Reporters," April 12, 2004, www.whitehouse.gov.

138    "God loves you, and I love you . . .": from Weisberg, "The Complete Bushisms," March 3, 2004, www.slate.com.

## EIGHT: OEDIPUS WRECKS

141    "I want to be a fighter pilot because my father was, . . .": Minutaglio, *First Son,* p. 120.

142    "barely hidden pressure for [George W.] to emulate [his] father . . . family and friends said . . . . 'Dad was shy,' . . . I never had a sense . . . We never had . . .": Ibid., p. 101.

142    "Pussy . . .": Jake Tapper, "Prodigal Son," April 9, 1999, www.salon.com.

144    "Even when we were growing up . . . Mom was always the one . . .": Minutaglio, *First Son,* p. 57.

149    "He is the wrong father to appeal to . . .": Bob Woodward, *Plan of Attack* (New York: Simon & Schuster, 2004), p. 421.

150    "described homosexuality as a 'deathstyle' . . .": Alterman and Green, *The Book on Bush,* pp. 153–154.

151    "sit down and decide for everyone else . . . .": Hanna Rosin, "The Seeds of a Philosophy," *Washington Post,* July 23, 2000.

151    "away from the snobs . . . intellectual arrogance . . .": Minutaglio, *First Son,* p. 85.

152    "so guilty they had been given . . .": Ibid.

152    "I don't remember any kind of heaviness . . .": Ibid., p. 117.

152    "I had fun at Yale . . .": Rosin, "The Seeds of a Philosophy," *Washington Post,* July 23, 2000.

152    "trick questions . . .": *Harper's.*

152    "I just wanted to let you know . . . .": Minutaglio, *First Son,* p. 148.

153    "littered with Bush baseball cards . . .": Ibid., p. 251.

154 "the display turkey in his photo op . . .": Mike Allen, *Washington Post,* December 4, 2003.

154 "In fact, as Dean points out . . .": Dean, *Worse than Watergate,* p. 83.

154 "not in the loop . . .": Corn, *The Lies of George W. Bush,* p. 4.

155 "There is plenty that the Bushes . . .": Ann Gerhart, *The Perfect Wife* (New York: Simon & Schuster, 2004), p. 136.

156 "behind her mother's Neiman Marcus dress bag . . .": Ibid., p. 135.

156 "I may have been a candidate for Governor . . .": George W. Bush, *A Charge to Keep,* p. 87.

156 "The next day, he went on vacation to Florida . . . As he boarded the plane. . . .": Gerhart, *The Perfect Wife,* p. 146.

157–158 "wash over with anger . . . publicly [admitted] something that he had never admitted before . . .": Minutaglio, *First Son,* p. 229.

158 "The strategy was to make him . . .": Ibid., p. 8.

158 "hurled his glasses across the room . . .": J. H. Hatfield, *Fortunate Son* (New York: Soft Skull Press, 2002, 2003 CK), p 155.

160 "blind man in a room full of deaf people . . .": Suskind, *The Price of Loyalty,* p. 149.

## NINE: HE'S OUR MAN

168 "I will not yield; I will not rest; . . .": "Address to a Joint Session of Congress and the American People," September 20, 2001, www. whitehouse.gov.

169 "You love him more than anything, don't you? . . .": Karen Hughes, *Ten Minutes from Normal* (New York: Viking Press, 2004), pp. 5–6.

172 "59 percent of those polled felt we were 'bogged down' . . .": Richard Morin and Claudia Deane, "Support for Bush Declines as Casualties Mount in Iraq," *Washington Post,* July 12, 2003.

174 "to answer these attacks and rid the world of evil . . .": "Our Unity Is a Kinship of Grief," *Washington Post,* September 15, 2001.

175 "Conservatives know the world . . .": George Will, quoted in J. Jost, et al., "Political Conservatism as Motivated by Social Cognition," *Psychological Bulletin of the American Psychological Association,* 2002, p. 21.

178 "a uniter, not a divider . . .": Miller, *The Bush Dyslexicon,* p. 122.

## TEN: I AM THE CHIEF

180 "History, we won't know . . .": Woodward, *Plan of Attack,* p. 443.

180 "Bush told newspaper editors . . .": Mike Allen, "Iran 'Will Be Dealt With,' Bush Says," *Washington Post,* April 22, 2004.

183 "Why do they hate us? . . . Americans should not expect one battle . . . Every nation in every region . . .": George W. Bush et al., *We Will Prevail,* pp. 14–15.

184 "Blessed are those who mourn for they shall be comforted . . .": Ibid., p. 4.

185 "Bush doesn't even attend church": "The Jesus Factor," *Frontline,* PBS, April 29, 2004.

191 "Bush's low pulse rate of 35 to 45 . . .": "Bush Gets High Grade After Checkup," United Press International, August 3, 2003.

192 "My day starts very early . . . There are only twenty-four hours . . .": Dan Froomkin, "Managing the President," January 22, 2004, www.washingtonpost.com.

192 "Laura stays in her own space . . .": George W. Bush, *A Charge to Keep,* p. 81.

193 "Terry Moran of ABC News dared to say . . . Have ever a people been led . . . Occasionally he would stare . . . statements did not come across as . . .": Tom Shales, "Bush's Wake-Up Call Was a Snooze Alarm," *Washington Post,* March 7, 2003.

194 "George W. Bush had too many moments of cockiness . . . . Though he's favored blue ties . . . .": Tom Shales, "State of the Union: Long on Long, Short on Lofty," *Washington Post,* January 21, 2004.

195  "Nobody needs to tell me . . .": Dean, *Worse than Watergate,* p. 105.

196  "perhaps . . .": Tim Russert interview with President Bush, *Meet the Press,* February 8, 2004.

196  "someone who famously hates . . .": Rosin, "The Seeds of a Philosophy," *Washington Post,* July 23, 2000.

197  "Families is where our nation . . . We'll let our friends be . . . The senator has got to understand . . . We ought to make the pie higher . . .": Weisberg, "The Complete Bushisms," www.slate.com.

197  "The doctrine of containment just doesn't . . .": "Bush, Blair: Time running out for Saddam," January 31, 2003, www.cnn.com.

198  "courageous spacial entrepreneurs . . . the punditry . . . resignate with the people . . . persecuted as a war criminal . . . 'commiserate' for 'commensurate' . . . 'gracious' for 'grateful.' . . . I've coined new words . . .": from Weisberg, "The Complete Bushisms," www.slate.com.

200  "Free nations are peaceful nations . . .": from Ibid.

204  "Bush knows that we're all here . . .": Judy Keen, "Strain of Iraq War Showing on Bush," *USA Today,* April 2, 2003.

205  "egotism that brooks no contradiction . . . too often the expression of an over-compensation . . .": William A. White, M.D., *Mechanisms of Character Formation* (New York: Macmillan & Co., 1926), p. 90.

206  "Feels good . . .": Martin Merzer, Ron Hutcheson and Drew Brown, "War Begins in Iraq with Strikes Aimed at 'Leadership Targets'," Knight-Ridder Newspapers, March 20, 2003.

206  "Good riddance . . . The world is better off . . . .": White House Press Conference, December 15, 2003, www.whitehouse.gov.

206  "If this were a dictatorship . . .": "Transition of Power: President-Elect Bush Meets with Congressional Leaders on Capitol Hill," December 18, 2000, www.cnn.com.

207  "I want to thank all my citizens . . .": Weisberg, "The Complete Bushisms," www.slate.com.

207  "The *grande nation* can not face the idea . . .": Freud, *The Standard Edition of the Complete Psychological Works of Sigmund Freud,* Vol. 1 (London: Hogarth Press), p. 210.

208    "characteristic indefiniteness concerning the evil-doers . . .": Sigmund Freud, "Extracts from the Fleiss Papers; Letter 57," from *The Standard Edition of the Works of Sigmund Freud, Vol. I* (London: Hogarth Press), p. 244.

208    "We don't know who they are . . .": Bruni, *Ambling into History,* p. 44.

## EPILOGUE

213    "you just put me on the spot here . . .": White House Press Conference, April 13, 2004, www.whitehouse.gov.

216    "the conviviality had burned off. . . .": Suskind, *The Price of Loyalty,* p. 117.

217    "Diane, you can keep asking . . . .": Interview with Diane Sawyer, *ABC News,* December 16, 2003.

217    "I'm not going to change . . .": *Meet the Press,* February 8, 2004.

218    "get out of Washington": Mike Allen, "President Gets Back on the Bus," *Washington Post,* May 4, 2004.

# ACKNOWLEDGMENTS

THERE ARE MANY people to whom I am grateful. This book started with a paper I gave at a professional meeting of psychoanalysts and writers in Washington, D.C., after Dr. Lindsay Clarkson had agreed to my request that my talk link psychoanalysis and politics. It had already become clear to me that after more than thirty years of psychoanalytic practice I could no longer leave my professional expertise in the consulting room whenever I wanted to express my social or political concerns. As I was writing my paper, political consultant Sam Popkin contacted me to say that literary agent Sandy Dijkstra was looking for a psychoanalyst to write about President George W. Bush. It was out of a series of intense conversations with Sandy that the idea for *Bush on the Couch* was born. Sandy thought of the title.

With the energetic help of my agent Jonathon Lazear, Cal Morgan of ReganBooks agreed to edit this psychoanalytic-political study. Cal is a person whose judicious intelligence is matched only by his indefatigability and warm disposition. *Bush on the Couch* is a much better book because of his work. I had already been encouraged by literary editor Andrea Schulz. Numerous professional colleagues and friends helped along the way. Eventually I organized a group loosely known as "The Bush League," made up largely of psychiatrists and therapists, who read and challenged my ideas. I am immensely grateful for the political help and medical insights of Dr. Louis Borgenicht, as well as Bob and Ray, and J. Plant, who found numerous references to enrich the project. I also thank Steve, who shared his own literary experiences; Harvey, who says that truth is the best defense; Nancy and Carole, who offered thoughts about Bush and women's rights; Shauna Miller Wertheim for her whose thoughtful consistency and humor; Kleinian colleagues and friends Drs. Alberto and Nydia Pieczanski, who generously offered their invaluable insights and helpful clarifications to some of my theoretical approaches; colleague Hannah Fox, who stayed up all night reading the manuscript; Michele Kearney; Tom Goodbody; Mary Joyce Carlson; and Walter Romanek.

I also want to thank the intellectually rigorous Gerald Stern, who suggested approaching this like a detective story; historian Gar Alperowitz, who helped with my initial proposal; Sharon Alperowitz, who helped keep me on track; Britt Harter, who gave me the chapter title "Oedipus Wrecks"; Yelena Kalinsky, who never stopped her questions; cousin Dr. Teddy Rothschild; Mike Kazin; Karen Scheinman; longtime (at least thirty years) close friends and colleagues Drs. Dan Auerbach, Tom Goldman, Sam Goodman, Fred Meisel, Marty Stein, and Jerry Zupnick. There are others, especially the seriously ironic Keith Byers; Jeff Fox; Yaz Boyum; Sabrina Cassagnol; Bob Kaplan and Marilyn Black; Jesse Kornbluth; Aviva Kempner; Casey Kennedy; Carlos Campbell; John and Kay Spilker; Janet David; Marjorie Swett; Judy Epstein; Joseph Ganz; Janet Zalman; Jaime O'Neill; Cindy Goldman; my much loved brother-in-law Steve Dickman, and my smart and delightful niece Nyssa. Thanks also to Dr. Robert King, who said that the book's subtitle should read "Being President means never having to say you're sorry"; to Tony Perram and his family—especially Elise; and to my spiritual cousin Fred Ciccone. Friends of my children also were helpful at times, especially Sophia and Anya Ciccone, Rachel Tailer, Gabe Winer, Emily Witt, and Modele Oyewole.

I consulted many colleagues, books, and journals over the years that influenced me, and which, though not listed in the Source

Notes, remain sources nonetheless. Among the most influential are Hiatt Williams, the late Roger Shapiro, Barry Richards, the late Norman Tamarkin, Anne Kilcoyne, Franco Fornari's *The Psychoanalysis of War,* Philip Slater's *Microcosm,* C. Fred Alford's *Melanie Klein and Critical Social Theory,* Hannah Segal, Elizabeth Spelius, Lloyd deMause, Robert Hinshelwood, Michael Feldman, Robert Lifton, Erich Fromm, John Steiner, Leston Havens, William Rivers Pitt, *The Five Books of Moses* translated by Everett Fox, and the King James *Bible.*

Members of my psychotherapy seminars graciously endured my absence while I worked on the book, for which I am grateful. They include Fran Rosenfeld, Jaedene Levy, Maxine Penn, Denise Schauer, Linda Dickson, Linda Schwartz, Allen DuMont, Helen Krackow, Cary Gallaudet, Connie Kagel, Pat Slatt, Kim Sarasohn, Janet Black, Anne Harcourt, Connie Lucke, Ellen Rosensweig, Andrea Feldman, Marge Rosen, Eileen Hunter, Judy Brandzell, Ann Curtin-Knight, Ruth and Wes Rapaport, Kathy Sinclair, Sheila Hill, Rachel Kaplan, Ann Devaney, and Kris MacGaffin.

I was told to expect surprises when writing a book—lots of them. One of the best was meeting someone who not only offered many good ideas and much encouragement, but who also did the hard work of going over almost every word. I am deeply grateful for the help of Chip Yost.

Thanks to Nancy Kerr, who good-naturedly and professionally became my research assistant—she was thorough, thoughtful, and careful. Suzanne Rosenberg was active from the beginning: Both matchmaker and gadfly, she helped me find writer Tom Spain, and helped shape my thoughts about what a psychoanalyst can offer us that social critics or political/economic analysts cannot. Linda Stern and Steve Scheinman gave and give me consistent and selfless support, not to mention generously lending their ears.

The clinical depth of this book owes a great deal to my patients—current and former—who have deeply enriched my life and thinking over the past thirty-five years.

Tom Spain provided not just fine organizational skills, but also an eloquent and graceful writing style. This book is in essence the product of our rich collaboration. Tom is brilliant as well as experienced and kind—and I feel lucky to have worked with him. And *Bush on the Couch* would never have happened without the steady vote of confidence backed by the keen intelligence and hard work of Heather Perram.

My incisive sister Ellen helped keep this endeavor moving forward. She regularly contributed intelligent encouragement. I am deeply grateful to Micheline Klagsbrun Frank, who helped me to live outside the box, to not be dominated by what others might think. And, finally, my children—Joey, Abe, and Ginevra—from whom I have taken time to write this book. I am thankful to my sons for being such supportive, loving, funny young men with big hearts and deep souls. Their sardonic irreverence has helped me keep my perspective. My loving daughter Ginevra read and listened to me read parts of this book. Her enthusiasm and rich support are infectious, and her confidence in me and in this endeavor means the world.

# INDEX

## A

Abraham, Karl, 104
Allen, Mike, 43
Alterman, Eric, *The Book on Bush,* 26, 150
*Ambling into History* (Bruni), 26, 126, 134
*American Dynasty* (Phillips), 79
Americorps funding, 133
Arbusto partnership, 130
Arrested psychological development, 12–14
Attention Deficit Hyperactivity Disorder (ADHD), 24–25
Auletta, Ken, 129
Axis of Evil, 74

## B

Beidler, June, 5
bin Laden, Osama, 27–28, 64, 130
Bion, Wilfred, 131–132, 155
Blessitt, Athur, 56
*Book on Bush, The* (Alterman and Green), 26, 150
Boykin, William, 72
Britton, Ron, 61–63
Brooks, Renana, 137, 138, 168

Bruni, Frank, *Ambling into History,* 26, 126, 134
Bumiller, Elizabeth, 107–108
Bush, Barbara (daughter), 155–157
Bush, Barbara (mother), 93–94, 187
    childhood, 5–7
    cooking, 4–5, 85
    as enforcer, 4
    loyalty, 5
    as mother, 2–3, 5, 187
    overeating, 6–7
*Bush Dyslexicon, The* (Miller), 16–17, 137, 138
Bush, George H. W. (father), 141
    early years, 2
    fatherhood, 17–18
    racism, 122
    relationship with G. W., 38, 141–161
Bush, George W.:
    ADHD, 24, 121–139
    affability, 19
    alcohol abuse, 37–51
    Americorps funding, 133
    antics, 21–22, 80–105
    Arbusto partnership, 130
    arrested psychological development, 12–14
    Axis of Evil, 74

Bush, George W. *(Continued)*
  breaking and repairing, 34–35
  character, 183–184
  *Charge to Keep, A* (Bush), 27, 55
  childhood behavior, 2–4, 14, 101
  communicator, 20
  concrete thinking, evidence of,
    197–198
  dehumanization, 35–36
  dyslexia, 28–30
  as exception, 78–79, 92, 94
  fake ID cards, 80
  fragility, 168–169
  fraternity antics, 80–105
  Freudian slips, 121–122
  as governor, 26, 73, 102
  grandiosity, 35, 109
  humor, 134–135, 174
  impulsiveness, 26–27
  intelligence, 194–196
  language problems, 30–32,
    121–139, 197
  laws, living outside, 77–100
  learning disabilities, 121–139,
    191
  megalomania, 200–206
  National Guard, 91
  oedipal complex, 141–161,
    171–172
  omnipotent thinking, 82–88, 97
  physical examination, 190–193
  popularity, 163–178
  pretzel incident, 4
  psychodynamic formulation,
    179–209
  relationship with father, 38,
    141–161
  and religion, 53–76
  reparation, 187–190
  sadistic behavior, 101–119
  school experience, 32–33
  shame, 35
  sibling's death, 2, 14
  smirk, 101–119
  sorrow, reaction to, 16–17
Bush, Jeb, 1, 144
  birth, 3
  children, 122
Bush, Jenna, 155–157
Bush, Laura, 66, 85–86, 135, 173,
  192
Bush, Marvin, 41
Bush, Neil, 29
Bush, Prescott, 55, 79–80
Bush, Robin, 2–3, 14–16, 68,
  187
Bushtail, 22, 183
*Bushwacked* (Ivins and Dubose),
  107
*Bush at War, Plan of Attack*
  (Woodward), 28, 83, 91, 115,
  149, 180

## C

Card, Andrew, 192
Carlson, Tucker, 111
Carville, James, *Had Enough?,*
  129
*Charge to Keep, A* (Bush, George
  W.), 27, 55
Cheney, Dick, 87, 150
Clang association, 197
Corn, David, *The Lies of George
  W. Bush,* 89–90, 92, 93
Crawford, Texas, 43, 95, 137, 155,
  160

**D**

Dean, John, *Worse Than Watergate,* 81, 87, 89, 94, 106, 130, 145, 154
Dry drunks, 40–41
Dubose, Mark, *Bushwacked,* 107
Dyslexia, 28–30

**E**

Ellis, John, 72
Endorphins, 57–58
Enforcer, Barbara Bush as the, 4
Exceptions, 78–79, 92, 94

**F**

*Faith of George W. Bush, The* (Mansfield), 26, 55, 56, 71, 78
Fenichel, Otto, 117
Fink, David, 142
Franken, Al, *Lies and the Lying Liars Who Tell Them,* 89, 90
"free speech zones," 184
Freud, Sigmund, 53
   on exceptions, 78–79
   on megalomania, 200–203
   on oedipal complex traits, 145–146
   on sadism, 103–104
Frum, David, 38, 40

**G**

Gerhart, Ann, 155, 156, 173
Green, Mark, *The Book on Bush,* 26, 150
Graham, Billy, 40, 55, 57

**H**

*Had Enough?* (Carville), 129
Hammond, Darrell, 64
Harken Energy, 92, 94, 151
*House of Bush* (Unger), 130
Hubble telescope funding, 133
Hughes, Karen, 169, 180
Hussein, Saddam, 20, 44, 69, 87, 89, 95, 98, 101, 112, 113–116, 146, 198
Hypoarousal, 191

**I**

Idealization, 165–166
Ivins, Molly, *Bushwacked,* 90, 107

**J**

Johnson, Clay, 17
Jones, Don, 57

**K**

Kay, David, 167
Kennedy, Edward, 106

"Kenny Who?" defense (KWD), 96

Killian, Pauline, *Matriarch of a Dynasty,* 3, 5

King, Larry, 5

Klein, Melanie, 37, 75
  and Freud, 53–54
  model of infant development, 12, 22–23
  nurturing, 7–11
  oedipal theories, 104–105, 144
  on paranoia, 199
  theories of, 7–9


**L**

Language, problems with, 30–32

Lay, Kenneth, 95, 96

Learning disabilities, 191

Leno, Jay, 41

Letterman, David, 192

*Lies of George W. Bush, The* (Corn), 89–90, 92, 93

*Lies and the Lying Liars Who Tell Them* (Franken), 89, 90

Likerman, Meira, 24


**M**

Mansfield, Stephen, *The Faith of George W. Bush,* 26, 55, 56, 71, 78

*Matriarch of a Dynasty* (Killian), 3, 5

Meyerson, Harold, 68

Miller, Mark Crispin, *The Bush Dyslexicon,* 16–17, 137, 138

Minutaglio, Bill, 15, 17, 142, 144, 153, 157–158

Money-Kyrle, Roger, 78

Moran, Terry, 193


**N**

Noah, Timothy, 65

Nurturing, theories on, 7–11


**O**

O'Neill, Paul, 35, 160, 216


**P**

Paranoid ideation, 199–200

Pelosi, Alexandra, *Travels with George* [film], 128, 192

Phillips, Karen, *American Dynasty,* 79

Pickering, Charles, 106

Pierce, Franklin, 79

Pierce, Pauline Robinson, 3, 6

*Price of Loyalty, The* (Suskind), 5, 35

Psychobabble, 1


**R**

Reparation, 187–190

Responsibility One, 91

Rice, Condoleezza, 81–82, 98, 155

Robison, James, 71

Roden, Randall, 15
Rosin, Hanna, 196
Russert, Tim, 69–70, 76, 132,
    198, 217

# S

Sawyer, Diane, 28, 92, 93, 117,
    124, 128, 132, 217
Schoolfield family, 6
Schweizer, Peter and Rochelle, 72
Securities and Exchange
    Commission (SEC), 91
Shales, Tom, 49, 193–194
Sheehy, Gail, 29
Singer, Peter, 113
Skull and Bones, 34, 82, 141
Suskind, Ron, *The Price of
    Loyalty,* 5, 216
Symington, Jean, 60

# T

Talion, Law of, 77–100
Thomas, Clarence, 94, 150
Thomas, Helen, 174

Tourette's syndrome, 193
*Travels with George* [film]
    (Pelosi), 128, 192
Tucker, Karla Faye, 74, 111

# U

Unger, Craig, *House of Bush,* 130
*U.S. News and World Report,* 25
*USS Abraham Lincoln,* 68, 86,
    146, 204

# W

Walker, George Herbert, 79–80
Wallis, Jim, 107
White, William A., 205
Will, George, 175
Williams, Meg Harris, 97–98
Woodward, Bob, *Bush at War,
    Plan of Attack,* 28, 83, 91,
    115, 149, 180, 184
*Worse Than Watergate* (Dean), 81,
    87, 89, 94, 106, 130, 145,
    154